A Fitting Death for

BILLY THE KID

A Fitting Death for
BILLY
THE KID

by *Ramon F. Adams*

UNIVERSITY OF OKLAHOMA PRESS : NORMAN

Library of Congress Catalog Card Number: 60–5112

Dedicated

with warm good wishes to two good friends and outstanding collectors of Western Americana, Jeff C. Dykes and Martin E. Ismert, both of whom entertained me in their homes and went to every inconvenience to dig out books for me to examine for another work.

Contents

Illustrations

A Fitting Death for

BILLY THE KID

Prologue

For those who have made a serious study of Billy the Kid's life, this prologue is unnecessary. But there are many persons interested in this young outlaw who have not had the opportunity to dig into the records and have possibly read only such books as the reprints of Pat Garrett's *The Authentic Life of Billy the Kid,* Walter Noble Burns's *The Saga of Billy the Kid,* or the books by Charlie Siringo.

It is not my purpose to write a biography of this lawless character, but to make some attempt at correcting accounts that have already been written about him under the guise of fact. Perhaps too much has been written about him in the past, and certainly the many legends centered around him have been handed down as fact far too long.

In order that the reader may more fully understand my attempt to correct this false history, it might be well to prepare the way by touching the high spots of some of the incidents upon which the many legends have been founded. It is my purpose in this book to point out and correct the various legends which have been repeated for more than seventy-five years. Surely it is time we learned the truth.

The Kid is supposed to have been born in New York City, November 23, 1859, but no records have ever been found to substantiate this date. It is based solely upon Ash Upson's questionable authority. Billy's father is said to have died when the Kid was three, and it is a fact that his mother married again in Santa Fe, New Mexico, on March 1, 1873, although most writers have her marrying in Colorado. She was married to William H. Antrim in the First Presbyterian Church, Rev. D. F. McFarland performing the ceremony, with her two sons, Joe and Henry McCarty, as witnesses. Henry later assumed the name William H. Bonney.

The Kid's mother died in Silver City, New Mexico, of consumption on the sixteenth of September, 1874. Shortly afterward Billy got into trouble—for the first time—by stealing some clothing from a pair of Chinamen and was placed in jail, from which he soon escaped. He fled to Arizona, where he killed his first man, E. P. Cahill. It was then that he assumed the name William H. (after his stepfather) Bonney, the source of this surname unknown.

After fleeing from Arizona, he went to Mesilla, New Mexico, but was soon accused of horse stealing and fled to Lincoln County, where he joined Jesse Evans. Rustlers were stealing cattle from John Chisum and selling them to Jim Dolan, of the L. G. Murphy firm, for a fraction of their value. Billy went to work for this outfit, but soon had a quarrel with Billy Morton, the foreman.

Shortly afterward he met J. H. Tunstall, an English rancher and merchant associated with Alexander McSween. Although their stations in life were far apart, they became fast friends. By associating himself with the McSween-Tunstall combination, Billy naturally became the enemy of the Murphy-Dolan faction, and the rest of his life was shaped by the enmity between the two.

When his friend Tunstall was murdered by a posse of Dolan's men, including Morton, Baker, Roberts, and about a dozen others, he became very bitter. He was with a posse which hunted these killers down, and Morton and Baker were killed while trying to escape.

Tunstall, with Dick Brewer, John Middleton, Bob Widenmann, and the Kid, had been apprehensive when they left the ranch to drive a band of horses exempt from the attachment orders of Murphy's court. But after driving until five-thirty in the afternoon without trouble, they relaxed their tension. The Kid and Middleton were some hundred or so yards to the rear hunting turkeys and Brewer and Widenmann were off the trail some distance ahead, leaving Tunstall all alone. Morton's posse surrounded Tunstall, who offered no resistance and was in the act of handing over his gun, butt first, when he was shot in the back of the head by Tom Hill, his valuable horse also being killed. This was the spark which exploded the Lincoln County War into action.

The Kid and Fred Waite were seized and held under arrest by Sheriff Brady, a Murphy tool, and so could not attend Tunstall's funeral, despite the many accounts to the contrary. Sheriff Brady made no effort to arrest the men who had murdered Tunstall in spite of the fact that Justice Wilson had signed warrants for their arrest.

Following his release, the Kid, with five companions, was sent into Lincoln by Dick Brewer to protect the women of the McSween party. As they came into town, they saw Sheriff Brady, George Hindman, Billy Matthews, Jack Long, and George Peppin coming up the street. The latter were going to the courthouse to post a notice about the opening of court, but the Kid thought they were after him and his friends. Therefore the Kid's party hid behind a plank gate just east of the rear of Tunstall's store, and as Brady and his men walked down the middle of the street, the gang opened fire, killing Brady and wounding Hindman, who shortly died from his wounds. The others escaped.

Shortly after this incident, the Kid was joined by a newcomer from Uvalde, Texas, a youth named Tom O'Folliard—a name often misspelled in contemporary and later accounts. From this time on, he was the Kid's constant companion.

Another high light of the Kid's life was the killing of Buckshot Roberts at Blazer's Mill. Charlie Bowdre gave Roberts his mortal wound, though the Kid was accused of the deed. Before Roberts died, he in turn killed Dick Brewer the leader of the McSween faction, and from this time the leadership seemed to fall naturally upon the Kid's shoulders.

The feud reached its climax with the battle of the McSween home. There were several days of desultory firing, during which Sheriff Peppin wrote a note to Colonel Dudley, commander at Fort Stanton, asking for help. Although the McSween forces were scattered, some being at the Ellis House, some at the Montano House and elsewhere, the Murphy faction concentrated their attack on the McSween home, for McSween was the man they most wanted. Tunstall was dead. Chisum had fled. McSween was the only one left with the money to finance the fight.

On the morning of the third day, Colonel Dudley, with a company of soldiers and two cannon, arrived in Lincoln and pitched camp near the McSween home, threatening to blow the house apart if a shot was fired. During the entire conflict he showed decided favoritism toward the Murphy crowd, and when Mrs. McSween went to him repeatedly with pleas to stop the fight, he became progressively insulting. He looked on as Murphy's men set fire to the McSween home, a fire which burned from room to room until only one room was left. It was then that the Kid and his men made a break for freedom. During this break McSween was killed by Beckwith, who, in turn, was killed by the Kid. When that battle was over, five men lay dead—McSween, Bob Beckwith, Harvey Morris, Vicente Romero, and Francisco Zamora. There was no carnival-like celebration afterward, as some writers claim.

The next high light in the Kid's career was the killing of Bernstein, a clerk at the Mescalero reservation, the true account of which is given later in this book. By now Billy was a hunted man, and Pat Garrett was elected sheriff especially to get him. Although he and the Kid had gambled, danced, and stolen cattle together, they were now avowed enemies.

Governor Axtell, of New Mexico, who definitely favored the Murphy crowd and the Santa Fe Ring, was removed from office by the federal government, and General Lew Wallace was sent to take his place. Wallace held some secret meetings with the Kid at Squire Wilson's home and promised the Kid "exemption from prosecution" if he would come in and testify against the murderers of Chapman, Mrs. McSween's lawyer, but the Kid was afraid of treachery.

Chisum had failed to pay the men who fought his war, and the Kid began to hate him for this. He did not, as legend has it, kill one of Chisum's men for every five dollars owed him, but he did make an effort to collect the debt in stolen cattle.

The killing of Carlyle at the Greathouse and Kuck's stage station is another milestone in the Kid's life. Many writers assert positively that Carlyle was killed by the Kid, but there is no proof, since many others were shooting from both sides. Pat Garrett and his posse had surrounded an abandoned stone hut at Stinking Springs in which the Kid and his friends were holed up during a severe snowstorm. It was here that Charlie Bowdre was killed. The tempting smell of cooking food prompted the hungry, half-frozen men inside to surrender. The prisoners were taken to the Wilcox ranch, from which they were transported to Las Vegas in a wagon. After being held there in jail for the night, they were put on the train for Santa Fe. It was at this time that a mob gathered and threatened to take Dave Rudabaugh because he had murdered a native jailer there earlier.

From Santa Fe the Kid was taken to Mesilla to be tried for the killing of Buckshot Roberts, but Judge Leonard had this indictment quashed. Then the Kid was tried for the killing of Sheriff Brady, found guilty, and sentenced to hang. That old legend of the Kid's impudent reply to the Judge's sentence is strictly a myth and is entirely out of character.

The Kid was taken 150 miles to Lincoln, guarded by Bob Olinger, Kinney, an outlaw, and Matthews, the Kid's bitter enemy. He was placed in irons and held upstairs in the old Murphy store, now serving as a courthouse and jail.

Many varying tales have been told about how the Kid got a gun when he made his escape from his Lincoln jail. As near as we can get the truth through the thorough research of such historians as Maurice Garland Fulton and others, it seems that Sam Corbett had hidden a revolver, wrapped in newspaper, in the jail's outdoor privy. He then slipped the Kid a note about the gun, which he secured when Bell, one of his guards, escorted him to the outhouse. On coming out, he covered Bell, disarmed him, and marched him back upstairs. Upon reaching a hall not far from the top landing, Bell made a break for the stairs, but was shot by the Kid when he was halfway down. It is said that the Kid's shot missed Bell but hit the left-hand wall and ricocheted into Bell's right side, and he tumbled down the stairs a dead man.

Hobbling back inside the room (he was still in irons), the Kid grabbed a double-barreled shotgun belonging to Olinger, his other guard, who was absent, and hurried to a window. He saw Olinger returning to investigate the shot. When he got beneath the window, the Kid said, "Hello, Bob," and as Olinger looked up, he filled him with buckshot.

Godfrey Gauss, the jail cook, was next commanded to throw up a file, but the best he could do was a prospector's pick, with which Billy pried loose the rivets on one leg iron. Then, securing a horse, he made his escape without any interference from the onlookers across the street.

Some weeks later Garrett, with his deputies Poe and McKinney, came into Fort Sumner searching for the Kid. On the night of July 14, 1881, they went to Pete Maxwell's to seek information. While Poe and McKinney waited outside, Garrett went in to talk with Maxwell, who had gone to bed. While he was there, the Kid came in, seeking a piece of meat for the meal his girl friend was preparing for him. As he approached barefooted, with a butcher knife in his hand and a gun in his pants' waist, he spied the deputies and inquired who they were. Going inside, he asked Maxwell about them. Seeing a figure sitting near the head of Maxwell's bed in the dim light, he jumped back and again asked who was there. Garrett recognized the voice and shot twice, the first shot killing the Kid, the second missing.

This, in brief, is the story of the Kid's life, as nearly accurate as I can reconstruct it from many years of research.

A Fitting Death for Billy the Kid

Ash Upson, in ghosting Pat Garrett's book about the Kid, stated that the Kid was born William H. Bonney, Jr., in New York City, November 23, 1859. We now know that the name "Bonney" as a family name is false, and the chances are that the place and date of his birth are also incorrect. But it seems we are stuck with the latter since no one has been able to find any record in the vital statistics or other documentary evidence. Therefore, since biographers have been unable to find such evidence, we have accepted Upson's statements. It does seem strange, however, that he chose for the Kid's birth date the same month and day as his own, for Upson, too, was born on November 23, of an earlier year (1828). Yet if it was a guess on his part, he must have hit close to the correct year, for if the Kid really was twenty-one when he was killed, July 14, 1881, he would have been in his twenty-first year, lacking a little over four months of being twenty-two.

The early dime novels about the Kid were mostly sensational fiction, but they were the first and only ones to call him by his true name of McCarty. Their authors evidently had seen the early newspaper accounts or had read the exchanges in the eastern papers which called the Kid by his real name, Henry McCarty. For several years the New Mexico newspapers did report the Kid's activities under the name Henry McCarty, Henry Antrim, or Kid Antrim. For this reason it seems very strange that Upson should have called him "Bonney" even in recounting his birth. Upson, a newspaperman himself, who, moreover, had boarded with Mrs. Antrim, surely had read the newspapers or had heard the Kid called by these other names.

His statement that the "Bonney" family moved to Coffeyville, Kansas, in 1862, is indeed a poor piece of reporting, because the first house was not built there until 1869, when James A. Coffey hauled a load of lumber and built his home on the site. The town was not incorporated until 1872. Furthermore, while most other writers follow Upson in stating that the Kid's mother married Antrim in Colorado, I will prove that she was married in Santa Fe, New Mexico.

All that folderol about the Kid's killing a blacksmith who insulted his mother, his various escapades in Mexico, and his rescue of wagon trains is the result of the vivid imagination of a writer who had to create a background for a super Robin Hood. In truth, the Kid lived a normal boyhood until his middle teens, when he became wayward. I do not find any record of his committing any murders in Grant County in his youth, as claimed by Upson, although, he did become a petty thief. Sheriff Whitehall, the first man to arrest the Kid, liked him and put him in jail for theft in the hope that a real scare might wake him up to the responsibilities of good citizenship. There was a notice of his arrest in the *Grant County Herald,* as follows: "Henry McCarty, who was arrested on Thursday and committed to the jail to await the action of the Grand Jury upon the charge of stealing clothes from Charley Sun and Sam Chung, celestials, sans cues, sans joss sticks, escaped from prison yesterday through the chimney. It's believed that Henry was simply the tool of 'Sombrero Jack,' who done the stealing whilst Henry done the hiding. Jack has skinned out." Perhaps ungrammatical, but it gives some record of the Kid's boyhood activities.

When the Kid escaped, he kept running until he reached Arizona, and here he got into real trouble. He stopped at Fort Grant, Pima County, Arizona, which joined Grant County, New Mexico, on the west. Here, on August 17, 1877, he killed a blacksmith, who some say took pleasure in bullying the Kid on account of his youth. In the September 1, 1877, issue of the *Grant County Herald,* there appeared the following statement, copied from the *Tucson Citizen:* "Henry Antrim shot F. P. Cahill near Camp Grant on the 17th inst., and the latter died on the 18th. Cahill made a statement before death to the effect that he had some trouble with Antrim during which the shooting was done. . . . The coroner's jury found that the shooting 'was criminal and unjustifiable, and that Henry Antrim, alias Kid, is guilty thereof.' "

Gus Gildea, associate of various gunmen of his day, with whom I corresponded for several years while he lived in Pearce, Arizona, said that Cahill, whom everyone called "Windy" because he was such a blow-hard, was continually trying to humiliate the Kid. On the day that he was killed, he had the Kid down on the floor of George Adkins' saloon and was slapping his face. The Kid pleaded with the husky blacksmith to let him up, but Cahill just laughed at him, so "the Kid shot him off."

We find, as we read the many books on Billy the Kid, that there are a number of different versions of his killing a man at Fort Union. Some identify the victim as a Negro soldier who cheated at cards, some a Negro blacksmith, and some a white blacksmith who, while shoeing the Kid's horse, hit the horse with a hammer, for which act the Kid shot him. These stories seem to be a confusion of the Cahill killing.

After the Kid returned to New Mexico and got into the Lincoln County trouble, many writers declare that he was absent when his new-found friend Tunstall was killed, although the Kid was on the trail with Tunstall when this war-starting tragedy took place. Many different causes of the Lincoln County War have been detailed, but you will learn that the fight was not between Chisum and the small cattlemen, nor between cattlemen and sheepmen, as has been often claimed.

I also hope to prove to you who killed Tunstall, and why he was killed, how he was avenged, and who really killed Buckshot Roberts.

Most of the accounts of the deaths of Brady and Hindman contain discrepancies, as does the story of the battle and the burning of the McSween home. Practically every writer, even to the present day, insists on having Mrs. McSween play her piano while her home burned, but this is not true.

I hope to give you the truth on the killing of Bernstein, for whose death the Kid was unjustly blamed, and his own version of the killing of Carlyle. Many misstatements have also been made regarding the mob at Las Vegas, and as many versions of the Kid's escape from the Lincoln courthouse have been told as there are writers who wrote about it. I hope to point out the errors of all these happenings as we go, as well as the many misspelled names, which reminds me that practically every writer spells Olinger's name with two *l*s as "Ollinger." I find that the family records, the Lincoln County records of his application for appointment as deputy sheriff of Doña Ana County, on April 15, 1881, and the transcript of the inquest on his death, April 29, 1881, just fourteen days later, all spell the name with one *l*.

All accounts of the Kid's escape at Lincoln are guesswork, many authors proclaiming that Garrett's version should be accepted, but it, too, is hearsay. Neither Garrett nor Upson was there, Garrett being forty-one miles away at White Oaks, some say buying lumber for the Kid's gallows, though Garrett himself says he was on tax business.

Likewise, many versions of the Kid's death have been told, some preposterous, some more logical.

Concerning this controversy, W. A. Keleher, in an article entitled "In 'Re' Billy the Kid," published in volume IV of the *New Mexico Folklore Record* (1948–49), wrote: "William H. Bonney, twenty-one years old, was shot and killed by Sheriff Pat Garrett, of Lincoln County, at Fort Sumner, New Mexico, on July 14, 1881. From the moment of the shooting to this very day, a period of almost seventy years [1949], the story of the shooting of 'Billy the Kid' has provided a background for controversy and dispute without parallel in the history of the Southwest. No western state has at its disposal the story of the career of an outlaw which can be compared to that of 'Billy the Kid.' Small wonder that attendants at the State Museum in Santa Fe are weary and discouraged explaining to tourists that they have no 'Billy the Kid' exhibit, that they know very little about him. The actual count shows that nine out of ten tourists in Santa Fe ask for 'Billy the Kid' picture postcards to send back home as proof that they have been in the cowboy country of the West.

"What explanation can be offered for the continued, intense, ever increasing interest in the life and career of William H. Bonney? The answer is that the story of Bonney's life and death holds everything that a dramatist requires to catch and hold what is known as 'audience attention.' There is the element of mystery. What about the Kid's birth? Was he really born in New York, on November 23, 1859 . . . , or was it some other person bearing the same name? Is there any foundation for the belief that the Kid was really a Texan? If it is true that he was born in New York City and moved west with his mother, first to Coffeyville, Kansas, and then to Santa Fe, and later to Silver City, how, where, and when did he learn to ride and shoot? Is there any evidence at all tending to prove the Kid killed twenty-one people, 'not including Indians,' before he reached his twenty-first birthday? Or would it be a more accurate statement to say he killed seven men, and that he killed all of them under circumstances that might be justified under the code of the killer of his day? Was Pat Garrett justified in killing the Kid in the parlor [?] of Pete Maxwell's residence at Fort Sumner that summer night in July, so long ago, without having given him even the slightest chance to know that his life was in jeopardy? Did the Kid, at the time he was killed, have a butcher knife in his hand, and was he on his way to the kitchen to slice off a chunk of meat from the hindquarter of a beef, because he was hungry, or did he have a .41 double action Colts revolver in a holster under his arm, prepared to shoot Pat Garrett or any other officer at an instant's warning? These, and many other questions like them, will be debated from now on out. No doubt but that William H. Bonney has been in his grave at Fort Sumner almost seventy years, although there is always some old timer willing to rise up and volunteer information generally on the anniversary of the Kid's death, that he is either the Kid, or that he had seen him a few years ago in New Mexico, Texas, or Mexico."

Mr. Keleher ends his article with this paragraph: "The 'Billy the Kid' story today is part fact, part legend, part myth. The word 'saga,' chosen by Burns as the title for his book, perhaps best expresses the mystery, allure, the suspense, the ever present and recurring interest in a young man who made his home for some years in New Mexico. There are two schools of thought concerning him: One school holds that he was a courageous, dashing, hero-like youngster, victimized and murdered in cold blood. The other school argues that he was a thief, a cattle rustler, a coward, an assassin, a cold-blooded murderer."

Some historians and biographers are still trying to winnow the wheat from the chaff, and if this work convinces anyone that most of the history of Billy the Kid has been recorded in the careless writing of unthinking—let us not say historians, but rather chroniclers—I feel that the effort has not been wasted. I hope that it at least, will prepare the ground for a more able historian of future years.

1. Billy the Kid, Man and Myth

IN HIS SPLENDID BOOK *Pardner of the Wind,* Jack Thorp has a chapter on Billy the Kid in which he says, "He is not history any more, but legend, romanticized out of all likeness to the gun-totin', rambunctious, carefree cowboy kid that all his friends and enemies knew, and he has become a sort of super-hero. It is hard, maybe impossible, to separate the truth about him from falsehood, the fact from fiction." And in another place he writes, "The most curious thing about Billy is not what he actually was in the flesh, but the steps by which his reputation grew so that he is now transformed into the kind of person the thrill-hungry public imagines him to be."

No doubt I will be criticized for taking the glamour from a folk-hero, for denying people the right to satisfy appetites greedy for thrills and blood. But the tall tales written about our western outlaws have been allowed to run unbridled too long. What about the historians and biographers of future generations? The real historian wants the truth. Too many historians are of the rockingchair variety, too willing to take someone else's word for what has happened in the past. When we see these so-called historians, through the second and third generation, repeating legends which originated in the mind of some dime novelist and recording them as fact, it fills a lover of truth with resentment. It is not pleasant for him to see truth smothered by legend until that truth is no longer believable.

"As some of us see it," wrote the late Maurice Garland Fulton, one of New Mexico's reliable historians, "the real importance of William Bonney, alias William Antrim, has little to do with the young man himself. His true significance lies in the legendary figure into which the American people have chosen to make him."

Because a statement has been handed down unchallenged year after year does not make it a historical fact. When it was born of falsehood, age does not purify it. Many readers prefer romance to cold facts. Knowing this, far too many writers cater to their tastes, perhaps adding their own embellishments through the years. After all, few of them are historians at heart. They want to be read and remembered as having written books that were "best sellers." Some, following tradition, have lied about the Kid unknowingly; others have lied about him simply to satisfy the appetite they know awaits such tales or to create romantic and dramatic situations.

The cowboy has always been glamorous to the average American reader; otherwise, he would never have become such a popular subject. A shooting and hunted cowboy is even more glamorous. The public seizes any gun-smoking legend in its never ending search for a hero. The more dramatic and romantic the tales told, the more they take the subject to their hearts. As time passes, increasing the mists and shadows, the more glamorous he becomes, and when the facts are distorted enough to make him fit the role they want him to have, they seize him as their individual hero.

There is no doubt but that the Kid had a certain fascination for women and that he had a degree of courage. These facts have made the legends more glamorous. Yet, if we would be honest enough to see and believe the ways in which he committed his murders, it would cool our ardor. I hope to point these things out to you as we go along.

One of the principal appeals to the average reader in Billy the Kid literature is his youth and the fact that he had killed "twenty-one men, not counting Indians," a man for every year of his young but brief life. Almost every writer on the subject repeats this statement, even today. The dime novelists who created the legend were wise in the use of the tools of their trade. They created many situations to give dramatic suspense and glamour, such as the Kid's being killed when on the way to see his sweetheart, or Mrs. McSween's theatrical gesture of playing her piano while her home burned. Neither incident really happened, yet practically every writer on the life of the Kid has repeated them in some form or another. Statements concerning these incidents will be pointed out as we progress.

In Pat Garrett's book, *The Authentic Life of Billy, the Kid,* it its told that the Kid, before he was eighteen, had killed the man who insulted his mother, three Indians on the Chiricahua Apache Indian reservation, a Negro blacksmith at Fort Union, two monte dealers in Old Mexico (one at Sonora and one at Chihuahua City), about fourteen Mescalero Apache Indians (to save an emigrant train), and an uncounted number of Apaches in the Guadalupe Mountains. But what the Kid did in the first eighteen years of his life, and until he came back to Lincoln County to work and take part in the Lincoln County War, is mostly a matter of conjecture. These killings, during the years of his wanderings in Arizona and Old Mexico, are beyond proof or investigation. They happened mostly in the imagination of Ash Upson, who wrote the book in Garrett's name.

Maurice G. Fulton, in his introduction to the revised edition of Garrett's book, said: "One of the perennial questions in connection with the Kid is, how many men did he kill? On this point there will in all likelihood be continued disagreement, but it is safe to find in the traditional total of 'twenty-one, not counting Mexicans and Indians,' the exaggeration usual in the holocausts of Western gun-men. If such a total ever came from the Kid's own lips, it must have been born in some moment of thrasonical brag, a quality of which he was not perhaps entirely free."

In an article entitled "Billy the Kid in Life and Books," appearing in the *New Mexico Folklore Record* (Vol. IV), Mr. Fulton comments further: ". . . there are three writers most responsible for the conception of this young man which this generation feeds upon. At the head of the line is the Pecos Valley's Ash Upson to whose inventive and somewhat wanton imagination we are indebted for the details of his boyhood in Silver City as set forth in the *Authentic Life of Billy, the Kid.*"

This "first" killing, of the man who insulted his mother in Silver City, never happened. The Kid is supposed to have killed this man, not at the time he insulted his mother, but when he and two other ruffians jumped on Ed Moulton, who had come to the Kid's rescue at the time the blacksmith had made the insulting remarks. Moulton's son-in-law wrote in later years that "Billie never did kill anyone in Silver City. That story is all false. The story of him killing a man over Ed Moulton is positively not true." Furthermore, all other old-timers who lived in Silver City denied that he had ever killed a man in Grant County. His troubles in Silver City started after the death of his mother.

Neither have any of the Kid's early killings been proved, nor do there seem to have been any witnesses. Let us examine the murders (for such they were) that he is supposed to have committed after he became a participant in the Lincoln County War. According to the only records we have, there were eleven. Let us examine these separately to see how many can conclusively be credited to the Kid.

To begin with, there was the killing of Billy Morton and Frank Baker, almost the first blood shed in the Lincoln County War. A posse headed by these two had killed J. H. Tunstall, the Kid's employer and friend. The McSween faction then appointed Dick Brewer to arrest them, and the Kid was a member of his posse. Upson gives the Kid credit for killing these two men, but the exact truth of this affair will never be known. Although the Kid had sworn to kill every man who had anything to do with the murder of his friend, there were eleven men in Brewer's posse, all shooting; and when the bodies were examined, it was found that Morton and Baker had both been shot eleven times. Upson himself saw Baker's body, yet he did not report that it had received so many bullets. It would certainly be hard to believe that only the Kid's bullets were the fatal ones. We can neither deny nor affirm that these two can be claimed solely as his victims. What we do know is that they were unarmed and trying to escape after their arrest when they were shot, and that it therefore took no courage to shoot them down.

Another killing credited to the Kid is that of Sheriff Brady and his deputy Hindman, shot down on the streets of Lincoln. Various counts—from three to twelve—have been given of the number of men in the ambush behind a plank gate from which Brady and Hindman were waylaid. Most accounts have the assassins hiding behind an adobe wall, but actual witnesses claimed they were behind a gate which could not be seen from the street until one had passed the Tunstall store. All we know for certain is that the Kid was one of them and that he was credited with the killing. In spite of the fact that Brady was shot sixteen times, the grand jury indicted the Kid alone for the sheriff's death, and he was tried, found guilty, and sentenced to be hanged for the killing.

Garrett, or Upson, did not know who killed whom and makes no positive statement about it, yet he contrives to leave the impression that it was the Kid's work. Nor will we ever know the truth of this matter, though Garrett later told Governor Otero that he "doubted if the Kid even fired at Brady" because Billy Matthews, a member of the sheriff's party, was the man the Kid hated most and really wanted to kill. There is no way to prove that any of Billy's bullets were effective. It could be that he shot at Matthews while Brady and Hindman were killed by others. Billy himself later said that he shot at Matthews and missed. The one sure fact is that here again there was a butchery from ambushed protection, which adds nothing heroic to the Kid's stature. Yet it was not justice to charge him alone with this murder. But the powerful "Santa Fe Ring" was at the helm and wanted the Kid out of the way. Governor Wallace failed to keep his promise of exemption from prosecution, and even the judge's charge to the jury was biased in that it declared that if the Kid was even present at the time of the shooting, he was "as guilty as if he'd fired the fatal shot." The Kid was convicted on circumstantial evidence. The shooting had been done through holes from behind a gate by an undetermined number of men.

Another killing charged to the Kid is that of Buckshot Roberts at Blazer's Mill, April 4, 1878. Again Upson wrote without verification, and credits the Kid with giving Buckshot the mortal wound. According to George Coe, who was a member of the party at the time, the shot that killed

Roberts came from Charlie Bowdre's gun early in the conflict. "Bowdre had the drop on Roberts," he wrote, "as the latter had to raise his gun from his lap. With his refusal to throw up his hands they fired simultaneously. Bowdre's bullet struck Roberts right through the middle, the Roberts' ball glanced off Bowdre's cartridge belt and with my usual luck, I got there just in time to stop the bullet with my right hand."

Once more we find one man trying to defend himself against a crowd and fail to see anything heroic in the Kid's behavior. Garrett's book says the Kid was acquitted of this killing by the federal court, but the records of the United States District Court show that the indictment was quashed. It has been said that he was charged with this killing in order to get a United States charge against him, but his attorney proved that Blazer's Mill was not on the Indian reservation, hence the murder was not a federal offense.

Another of the victims credited to the Kid's account was Bob Beckwith, the killing of whom caused Bob Olinger's hatred of the Kid to soar. No one has really denied that the Kid killed Beckwith, though there was a general battle going on at the time. Here the killed might have become the killer just as easily, and there was no shooting of an unarmed man, nor a killing from ambush, yet the element of surprise—if he did the killing—favored the Kid as he stepped to the door of the burning house and saw Beckwith before Beckwith spied him.

The coroner's jury found Beckwith's death due to rifle shots fired by Harvey Morris, Francisco Zamora, Vicente Romero, and A. A. McSween; but they made a mistake, for Morris had been killed earlier and McSween never carried a gun at any time. Many accounts say that during

the battle McSween shouted out his name and declared
he wanted to surrender, but Beckwith shot him. On the
other hand, the testimony in the proceedings of the Court
of Inquiry in the case of Colonel Dudley, in the National
Archives, contain the statement that McSween, when
asked to surrender, replied, "I shall never surrender." During this time both McSween and Beckwith were killed,
and there is really no record of who killed whom.

Another killing nearly all writers credit to Billy was that
of Morris J. Bernstein, a bookkeeper at the Mescalero Indian Agency. Of this event Upson says, "On the 5th day of
August, 1878, they [the Kid's gang] rode up in full sight
of the agency and were coolly appropriating some horses,
when the book-keeper, named Bernstein, mounted a horse
and said he would go stop them. He was warned of his
danger by persons who knew the Kid and his gang, but,
unheeding, he rode boldly up and commanded them to
desist. The only reply was from the Kid's Winchester, and
poor Bernstein answered for his temerity with his life."
Siringo, and many others after him said that the Kid's excuse for this killing was that "he didn't like a Jew nohow."

Billy was tried for this crime and found not guilty.
George Coe, a member of the party at the time declared
that they were not on a horse-stealing expedition, as Garrett claimed, but were trying to learn where the body of
their former leader, Dick Brewer, had been buried after
he had been killed by Buckshot Roberts.

"Up to that time," he writes, "we had never learned what
had happened to the body of our captain, Dick Brewer, or
the details of what had taken place after his death.

"One day the Kid said to me: 'George, we must go over
there and see what they did with poor old Dick. You need
a change from your hand-nursing [he had lost a finger and

thumb when Roberts' bullet had glanced off Bowdre's cartridge belt] so we'll just make you "captain of the guard.'"

"There were only three or four of us left in camp at that time, and Billy realized that this was not a sufficient number to break in on a suspecting community. He went down and rounded up six or eight Mexicans, who, with Hendry Brown, Billy and myself, made up the party.

"We pulled out for the Indian Agency. About a mile from our destination, the road ran up the hill through thick timber. There was a spring of clear water on the opposite side of the open canyon. I insisted that we ride over to get a drink and dampen the cloth on my wounded hand. The Mexicans did not seem inclined to go, so I told them to remain where they were while the Kid, Hendry Brown and I went to the spring. Billy jumped off his horse, and was in the act of taking a drink, Hendry and I were still mounted, when we heard a fusillade of shots from our Mexicans. It sounded as though a battle was in progress. The noise frightened Billy's bronc, and, jerking loose, he ran toward the Agency. Billy jumped up behind me, and we started at a dead run back to our crowd. Suddenly from the deep timber the shooting began again. Bullets whizzed by us like hailstones. We lay flat against the side of our horse, and fairly flew until we reached the Mexicans.

" 'What's all the shooting about?' I yelled.

" 'Five men rode up to the top of the bank,' they answered excitedly. 'We told them to halt, but instead they whirled their horses around and began shooting at us. We fired in return and killed one of the five.'

"... We had no idea whom our Mexicans had killed, but after investigation we learned that it was Bernstein, a clerk at the Indian Agency. It is a matter of record that the Kid was accused of this killing, tried for the offense and ac-

25

quitted. Several writers have attributed this murder to him as one of the most blood-curdling crimes of his career. Since I was present at the time, I can testify that he had nothing whatever to do with it, which was no doubt a disappointment to the Kid. He has a sufficient list of target victims to his credit without saddling him with this one."

In further substantiation that the Kid did not kill Bernstein, the *Las Vegas Gazette* of September 14, 1878, related that "Bernstein had been killed by a shot from the gun of Atanacio Martinez under justified circumstances."

The *Mesilla Independent* reported: "It is positively asserted that Bernstein was killed by a Mexican who was with a party bound from San Patricio to Tularosa to assist in recovering a lot of stolen stock in the possession of Frank Wheeler and others at San Nicholas. When the Mexicans reached the water alongside of the road of the Agency, they stopped to water their horses. Bernstein saw them and probably supposing them to be a party of the Regulators, attacked them with a party of Indians; he rode upon one Mexican and fired two shots at him; the man took shelter behind a tree. Bernstein still advancing rode close to the tree and fired again at the man who returned the fire and killed Bernstein.

"The Mexican says he acted strictly in self-defense and will at any time deliver himself up for trial. His name is Atanacio Martinez."

Strange to say, Martínez was never indicted, but warrants were issued for William Bonney, George Coe, Fred Waite, and Hendry Brown. That the government canceled all these indictments except the one against the Kid shows how much his enemies were trying to get rid of him and that he was being blamed for every crime in the Territory.

On the other hand, the killing of Joe Grant in a Lincoln

saloon can be attributed to none other than the Kid. No doubt Grant was looking for trouble and needed killing, but the manner in which Billy killed him was like shooting fish in a barrel. It added nothing to his glamour, though it did speak loudly of his prowess and warn all who knew him that he was a dangerous man to fool with.

The Kid had heard of Grant's boast that he would kill him. Then one day when he entered Bob Hargrove's saloon, he found Grant drunk and toying with a gun, one of those fancy pearl-handled ones, and admiringly asked to see it. (Some say that Grant had taken the gun from the holster of Finan Chisum.) The Kid intended to remove a shell or two, but when he found that there were only three shells in it, he merely twirled the cylinder so that the trigger would have to be snapped a couple of times before the hammer would fall upon a loaded chamber. Not long after the Kid handed back the gun Grant thought he had caught the Kid off guard. But the falling of the hammer on an empty chamber was his death knell. A killer had been outsmarted.

Another killing for which the Kid received credit was that of Jimmy Carlyle. If the Kid really did kill him, it would be another tally for shooting an unarmed man in the back. Held as hostage and tormented with threats until he became panicky, Carlyle tried to escape by jumping through a window, and this was the act which brought his death. Once more there is no absolute proof that the Kid's bullets were the fatal ones. There were others shooting, too. Even Garrett admits that Carlyle's death came from a *volley* fired from within the house by unseen men as Carlyle crashed through the window.

Emerson Hough, in an *Everybody's Magazine* (September, 1901) article, wrote: "Late in the afternoon, when everyone was cold and hungry and well-nigh exhausted in the besieging line, Carlyle attempted an escape. He sprang through a window and ran as hard as he could for cover. What hope had he before the steady muzzles which covered him as he ran? Hardly a shot fired after him missed him, and he fell dead in the sand in the shallow wheel tracks of the trail." There is nothing here to indicate that Carlyle was killed by the Kid, but Burns states positively that the Kid "sent a bullet through him."

The Kid himself claimed that Carlyle was a victim of his own posse and that when he jumped through the window, they thought he was the Kid. To tell his side of the story, he wrote a letter to Governor Lew Wallace from Fort Sumner, dated December 12, 1880:

"I noticed in the *Las Vegas Gazette* a piece which stated that Billy the Kid, the name by which I am known in the country, was the Captain of a Band of Outlaws who hold Forth at the Portales. There is no such organization in existence. So the gentleman must have drawn very heavily on his Imagination. My business at White Oaks the time I was waylaid and my horse killed was to see Judge Leonard who has my case in hand. He had written me to come up, that he thought he could get everything straightened up.

"I did not find him at the Oaks & should have gone to Lincoln if I had met with no accident. After mine and Billie Wilson's horses were killed we both made our way to a Station, forty miles from the Oaks kept by Mr. Greathouse. When I got up the next morning the house was surrounded by an outfit led by one Carlyle, who came into the house and demanded a surrender. I asked for their papers and they had none. So I concluded it amounted to nothing more than a mob and told Carlyle that he would have to stay in the house and lead the way out that night. Soon after a note was brought in stating that if Carlyle did not come out inside five minutes they would kill the Station keeper [Greathouse] who had left the house and was with them. In a short time a shot was fired on the outside and Carlyle thinking Greathouse was killed jumped through the window, breaking the sash as he went and was killed by his own Party they think[ing] it was me trying to make my escape. The Party then withdrew . . . ."

This letter was hidden for many years in the private papers of Governor Wallace and did not come to light until all his papers were given to the Indiana Historical Library.

The next and last killings attributed to the Kid were those of Bell and Olinger, and there are as many versions of these killings as there are persons who wrote about them. I shall try to give the various versions as we proceed. There were no actual witnesses of the manner in which Bell was killed, and we can take our choice. Here again, however, we do know that there was nothing brave or heroic about these killings. They were the acts of a desperate man. The nerviest action was the chance taken in securing Bell's gun, and according to those who claim the Kid used his handcuffs to hit Bell over the head, this did not take an undue amount of courage. He killed Olinger when that individual, unexpectedly called by name from above, looked up to spot the caller.

Thus, the fable of the Kid's killing a man for every year of his life is exploded. We can only count for sure Cahill, Beckwith, Grant, Carlyle, Bell, and Olinger, making six all together. Take away Carlyle and Beckwith, since absolute proof that they were killed by bullets from the Kid's gun is lacking, and the total is still smaller. It is perhaps true that some of his bullets could have been found in the bodies of Morton, Baker, Brady, and Hindman, but others were also shooting and there is no way of knowing whose bullets were the fatal ones. Roberts and Bernstein we know definitely he did not kill. Of the nine "possibles" three—Morton, Baker, and Carlyle—were shot while unarmed; two, Brady and Hindman, were shot from ambush; one, Grant, was killed after the Kid had tampered with his gun to make sure his first attempt to shoot would fail. Only three, Beckwith, Bell, and Olinger, might be considered to have been met on fairly equal terms, and even this would be an exaggeration.

Many of the accounts of the Kid have led readers to believe that he was a young, smiling, misunderstood boy whom all the women loved and his friends admired. If this be true, it may be cruel of me to disillusion them; yet after all is said and done, an ounce of truth is worth more than a pound of legend. It will be my task in the following chapters to try to convince my readers, in spite of the reams of false history masquerading as fact, how legendary the accounts of his life have become.

2. Dime Novelists, Creators of a Legend

THE FIRST WRITINGS about Billy the Kid, aside from a few newspaper reports, were dime novels. At this time the Kid's activities in New Mexico were creating a sensation in the East, and writers in that section of the country have always seized upon happenings in the wild West for their sensational fiction. Several of these novels were published just before and immediately after the Kid was killed.

The *Police Gazette* had long exploited the western outlaw in fictitious and sensational stories. Perhaps one of the first stories dealing with the Kid was *Billy LeRoy, the Colorado Bandit; or, the King of American Highwaymen,* published by the *Police Gazette* in 1881, before the Kid met his end at Pete Maxwell's. There may have been no real attempt on the part of the writer to make this a story of the Kid's life, as in the early eighties there actually was an outlaw, Arthur Pond, who went by the alias "Billy LeRoy." Yet the author of this tale used some names belonging to men in the Kid's gang, such as Dave Rudabaugh and Tom O'Phallier [*sic*], as well as many incidents in the Lincoln County War. If the "hero" was, in fact, the Kid, the very title is false not only in his name but also in the statement that the Kid was a highwayman. He could never be accused of this particular crime.

The story contains nothing but the vivid imaginings of a hack writer, with just enough half-truths to make it confusing. Its author makes his hero an actor doing female impersonations, though he was a professional killer. He relates that he was born in Indianapolis, Indiana, "of poor but honest parents," and lays the scene of his activities in Colorado instead of New Mexico. He joins the noted desperadoes Tom O'Phallier and Dave Rudabaugh and is taken to their cave for an initiation into the gang.

Many incidents in the Lincoln County War are touched upon in a careless sort of way, as, for example, the Kid's being in the burning house in Lincoln: "On one occasion he was hotly pursued and was obliged to take refuge in a house in Lincoln, which was surrounded by sixty colored soldiers. To the demand to surrender he only laughed and shot down a soldier to show that he was game. The house was set on fire, when the Kid, after loading his Winchester rifle, leaped from the burning building and made a dash for liberty." In this story the Kid kills Chisum's cowboys to cancel a debt he claimed Chisum owed him. Here perhaps is the start of this fable, which so many other writers have since used. Indeed, the influence of these trashy dime novels upon subsequent authors has been significant.

This particular author invented a brother, Sam, who joined the Kid. (In one place he calls him Arthur.) The whole bloodthirsty account ends in *Del Norte, Colorado*, where a mob breaks into the jail and hangs the culprits. Possibly Richard K. Fox, the publisher of these barroom and barbershop classics, and his writers were running out of material, and hence were creating imaginary characters and incidents to keep the presses rolling. The recipe for these novels seemed to be to take a few half-truths, stir in a portion of wild imagination, and scramble the whole, garnishing with a few names of real people.

Just a little over a month after the Kid was killed, Frank

Tousey published a "dime novel" by John Woodruff Lewis, written under the pseudonym of Don Jernado and entitled *The True Life of Billy the Kid.* It is characteristic of these early novels that the words "true" and "authentic" are used in their titles and subtitles. And this is one reason gullible people took them to be fact.

Since *The True Life* was published on August 29, 1881, it was on the stands almost immediately after the Kid's death. It is utterly incorrect in all details. The Kid's true name is given as William McCarthy and he is said to have been born in the state of New York in 1859 or 1860: "some have located his birthplace as the City of New York, but this is doubtless a mistake." In addition, the Kid is given a brother and a sister. The story tells that Billy was a very small boy when his family emigrated to New Mexico, where the lad's father "died when he was thirteen years of age, and his mother married a man named Henry Antum[*sic*]." It is at once apparent that the author is confused about names. They should have been Henry McCarty and William Antrim.

The Kid met up with Tom O'Fallaher [*sic*], and together they started their crime wave by burglarizing a store. The Kid was caught and put in jail, but the jailer's wife and daughter helped him to escape. He seems to have had a way with women from the start. Billy's first killing, according to this writer, was of a rival for the hand of a Mexican beauty. The unsuspecting rival was shot in the head as he stooped to get a drink of water from a stream.

The Lincoln County War "started because of the determination of old John Chisum, the great cattle king, and his partner, Alex McSwain [*sic*], to establish a monopoly in the cattle-grazing business." To forestall their herds' being "swept away" by these two ruthless men, the smaller ranchers joined Murphy and Dolan, and the war was on. A fantastic tale is told about the killing of Morton and Baker, after which the Kid organized a gang which began "robbing stagecoaches, stealing cattle, murdering and plundering indiscriminately."

This writer no doubt originated the legend about Mrs. McSween's playing the piano while her home burned. "Mrs. McSwain [sic]," he writes, "opened the piano, and as coolly as though she was entertaining an evening party, seated herself before it. Her jeweled fingers ran over the keys and sent forth soul-stirring notes. High above the roar of battle, crash of bullets and cries of combatants, rose the sweet clear voice, in soul-stirring songs. The sound of that beautiful voice and sweet-toned piano, in such cheering strains seemed to make demons of the outlaws." Furthermore, when the besiegers got the range of the piano from its sound and began sending bullets into it, the brave Mrs. McSween was not disturbed until the keyboard was practically shattered. One would think that any writer with only a mite of common sense should know that such fiction would strain the credulity even of the most naïve reader. No person, no matter how brave, would be so foolish as to play a piano while bullets were shattering its keyboard.

This writer has Bell, the Kid's jailer, walking him a block to jail when the Kid hit him over the head with his handcuffs, stunning him sufficiently to allow the Kid to grab the officer's gun and shoot him. When Olinger (whom he calls a deputy United States marshal) heard the shot, he came running around the corner and was shot with a shotgun the Kid had taken from Bell. All these early tales are filled with half-truths, and it seems strange that their authors could not just as easily have told the whole truth.

It seems that a Mexican named Riaz told Garrett (whom

the writer makes a deputy sheriff instead of a sheriff) where he could find the Kid. It was the Kid's custom to stop at Pete Maxwell's house after visiting his sweetheart near by, but he never went to Maxwell's until around midnight and always left before daylight in order to escape detection. The story reads: "A short time before midnight Garrett went to Maxwell's house and found the door open, but the building deserted. He went in and concealed himself in the dark corner, *behind*[1] Maxwell's bed. Here he waited with breathless anxiety, resting upon one knee, *his rifle cocked.*" When the Kid came in after midnight, "crack" went Garrett's *rifle* and the Kid was no more. This happened on the fourteenth day of *August,* 1881. We know definitely that the Kid was shot with a six-gun, not a rifle, and in July, not August.

About a month later there appeared another novel, entitled *The Life of Billy the Kid, a Juvenile Outlaw,* by John W. Morrison, one of "Morrison's Sensational Series." This writer gives the Kid's "true" name as Michael McCarthy, and says that the first man he killed was Tom Moore. This killing took place in New York City on September 9, 1879, after which the Kid fled the city. (This would have been a year after Tunstall was killed, and the Kid would have lacked two months of being twenty years old.) Then on his way West he robbed a cattle drover and the U. S. mail and committed other crimes near Chicago. After being captured, he made his escape dressed as a girl—an idea no doubt taken from the Billy LeRoy novel of the *Police Gazette,* which was on the stands at the time and makes the Kid a female impersonator doing the very same things. He made his way to Leadville, Colorado, where he started holding up stagecoaches—more of the Billy LeRoy legend.

[1] Italics mine—to indicate misstatements.

If Billy's parents left New York for Kansas when he was three, he would have been a little young to become a killer while still in New York.

In reading these early "penny dreadfuls," one can see how they influenced writers who followed. When the Kid, as most of them record, got to New Mexico and fell out with Chisum because he did not pay his debt, he rode up to four of his cowboys, shot down three of them, and sent the fourth to tell him he would allow five dollars' credit for each cowboy killed until the debt was paid. This story was repeated for years by later writers, but Billy was never that bloodthirsty. All the rest of this novel—the Kid's escape when he killed Bell and Olinger, his own death at the hands of Pat Garrett—are just garbled figments of a vivid imagination.

Billy the Kid's death had created quite a news item in the East, and novels about him were rolling off the presses with astounding frequency while the news was hot. During the same month that the above item appeared (September, 1881), another hit the stands. Not to be outdone by the New York publishers, the westerners got into the act, this one being published in Denver, Colorado, as "Western Border Series No. 1," and written by Edmund Fable, Jr., under the title *Billy the Kid, the New Mexican Outlaw*.

Here is a most amazing distortion of facts. Although this author, like all the rest, states in his subtitle that his account is a "true and impartial" history, there is scarcely a sentence from beginning to end which contains a grain of truth. The preface is dated July 15, 1881, the day after the Kid was killed, though the book does not seem to have been published until the following month. In this preface the author writes: "Whatever merit this volume may possess, attaches, in the estimation of its author, altogether to the *accuracy* of the incidents narrated and the *correctness* of the details connected with the career of 'Billy the Kid.' There has been no necessity to draw upon a vivid imagination to enhance its interest, for without any of the blazonry of humbug or the embroidery of fiction, the true history of 'Billy the Kid' eclipses any border romance, and dims by comparison the tales woven from the realms of fiction." A most brazen misstatement of fact if I ever read one. The authors of these blood and thunder stories loved to try to make it appear that their writings were factual—perhaps their readers really wanted to know the truth about such much-discussed subjects.

In the very first paragraph of his book, this author says that "the very mention of his [the Kid's] name in New Mexico struck terror to the stoutest hearts and made brave men quail as they thought of some unlucky chance that might throw them in the way of this terror of the New Mexico Territory."

He goes on to tell that after the death of the Kid's father, his mother married Thomas Antrim [*sic*], "a well-to-do mechanic," *while still living in New York*. While the Kid was growing up in New York City, his wild imaginings of the wild West and his desire to live in it were so strong that he ran away from home and "started out for the undulating plains and the rising, overshadowing mountains." According to his account, the kids of New York, "who had learned to love him for his daring and prowess," gave him the name of Billy the Kid. All these, of course, are preposterous statements.

The Kid makes his way slowly until he lands in Colorado, but soon continues until he reaches New Mexico. Here he immediately becomes an efficient cowboy, though he probably had never seen a horse in his New York boyhood—or should we say babyhood? When the roundup is over, he goes to Silver City with his earnings in his pocket. On the very first night there he is attracted to a saloon by its music and gaiety, and here one of the "syrens" of the joint charms him with her wiles and drugs his drink before she relieves him of his money. At closing time he is thrown out by the bartender, and finding his money gone, he makes his way to a store where a robbery happens to be in progress. The two robbers get away, but the proprietor nabs the Kid as an accomplice and takes him to jail.

"Lying within the shadow of his cell," writes Mr. Fable, "the Kid gave himself up to thought. Reviewing the experience through which he had passed since his arrival in Silver City, he grew despondent and melancholy.

"It was the turning point of his career," the writer continues. "The influences which were to guide his future course for good or for evil were at work, and what wonder was it, when finding honest effort resulting so disastrously he should determine upon a course as wicked as that which had been wrongfully mapped out for him?

"'I have tried to do right,' thought he [of course the author knew his hero's innermost thoughts], 'since I came to this country I have molested no man, and see where I am? Robbed of all my hard earnings, passing my time in this dingy prison, why should I strive any longer for that which in this country seems impossible? I'm done with it. After this I'll hold my own with the best of them. I'll begin right now by getting out of this damnable hole!'" And so starts the Kid's amazing criminal career, the author putting words into his mouth just as amazing—for an uneducated cowboy.

After escaping jail by going up a chimney, he crawls into a wagon and falls asleep. When he awakes he is on his way to a ranch on the "Río Dorsa" (?). Here he is given a job as a helper to the blacksmith, who is a bully and abusive. When he starts to hit the Kid with a hammer, the young helper shoots and kills him. While making his escape on a horse, the Kid does some more "thinking," such as, "If they take me . . . they will have to shoot quicker than I can and I don't think I've forgot all I *learned in the Bowery in New York on that subject.*" Children back in those days must have been born with a gun in their hand.

The Kid gets a job with *Tontsill* [*sic*], and his new boss has the Kid and two others accompany him on a mission to try to recover some of his cattle stolen the Sunday before. They meet the Dolan-Riley party with "twenty-two" men and there is a "battle" in which Tunstall is killed. Following this, two of the Dolan-Riley party are killed and one more of Tunstall's men, though the author does not name this victim. He makes Chisom [*sic*] a cow thief with whom the Kid operated, and although William Morton and Frank Baker were the men said to have helped kill Tunstall, Mr. Fable has them members of Chisum's gang; and after the gang has stolen a herd of cattle for Chisum, they are turned over to him; and he, with Morton, Baker, and McCloskey, take them to Las Vegas. McCloskey alone returns to camp and tells the Kid that Chisum, Morton, and Baker have double-crossed them and are planning to turn them over to the authorities. It is then the Kid makes the vow to kill Chisum, his cattle, and his cowboys until the debt is paid. And thus legends are born.

While the stolen cattle are being loaded into cattle cars at Las Vegas, the Kid overhears Chisum plotting with Morton and Baker to do away with him. When the latter two leave town to try to find the Kid's camp, he and McCloskey follow and capture them. As they are being taken back to camp in bonds, McCloskey tries to defend Morton and is shot in the back by the Kid. Then, because he fears leaving living witnesses to his cowardly act, he shoots the other two. All this bloodshed creates great excitement in Las Vegas, and the chapter closes with a wordy proclamation of a reward made by Governor Wallace—which is solely a product of the author's imagination.

Next Sheriff Brady and Deputy Hindman are pointed out to the Kid in a saloon, and he is told they are after him. When the two start after him, he backs behind the corner of a house and kills them both. This particular account has the Staked Plains embracing portions of Lincoln and Doña Ana counties, New Mexico, and describes them as a place where most white men fear to go on account of the Apaches. Here, in a peculiarly cone-shaped house, the Kid makes his headquarters.

After the killing of the two peace officers, when the Kid decides to organize a gang, he sends for "Tom O'Phaller". While the latter rides to Lincoln to recruit members, the Kid goes back to Colorado to pick up some of the men he met when he first came West. (All the early dime novels seem determined to put the Kid in Colorado.)

On his trip to Lincoln, O'Folliard hears about the will of Mr. Fritz, and that his sister in Indiana has appointed the lawyer "McSwain" as executor. He tells the Kid of the trouble between McSween and the Dolan faction. He reports that Dolan had seized the cattle belonging to Fritz and that McSween with fifteen cowboys had ridden out to Dolan's ranch, run him off, taken the cattle into Lincoln, sold them, and hidden the money in his house. Upon hearing this news, the Kid and his gang join McSween, and the Lincoln County War is on. This book is filled with such half-truths, but never is the whole truth told.

To continue with the story, when the Kid and his gang get to town, they go into a saloon and invite everyone to have a drink, and since everyone is afraid to refuse, they all line up at the bar. When the Kid is asked what he will have, he says, " 'Give me something from that decanter there,' drawing his revolver and designating the particular bottle by clipping the glass stopper from it with a well directed shot." No cowboy would use such a word as "decanter," nor would he be likely to shoot at a bottle from which he expected to pour a drink.

The account of the fight at McSween's home is equally fantastic. In this story McSween is the first to fall, "and as he was carried from the front of the house, *where he had taken an active part in defending his house* from the sheriff, the sight of his almost lifeless body seemed to unman a great many of the band, and one after the other deserted, stealing their way from the house until but a handful of men remained to aid the Kid." Now it is well known that McSween refused to handle a gun under any circumstances—he relied upon his Bible. Here is one early novelist, however, who does not have Mrs. McSween playing her piano. He does not even mention the lady. He does credit the Kid with killing thirteen men during this fight.

Of the killing of Bernstein, he relates that the Kid and his gang ride up to the Agency to steal cattle. Only a handful of men are at the fort, no one with any authority except a government clerk named Bernstein and a man named Al Roberts, who had once held a commission as captain, but who had been asked to resign because of intemperance. When Roberts starts to obey Bernstein's order to get the soldiers, he is shot by the Kid; then Bernstein secures a rifle and takes a shot at the Kid, the bullet going through the brim of his hat. The Kid is a better marksman. The gang then takes the cattle and drives toward their hideaway. On the second day of their journey they are ambushed by Sheriff Turner's posse and there is a stiff fight.

"The outlaws," writes author Fable, "were pushed hard, and had it not been for their superior knowledge of the country would have been exterminated. When they were in their worst plight, and when it seemed almost impossible for them to escape capture, Tom O'Phaller appeared on the scene with reinforcements, and, encouraged by this aid, they made a stand against the sheriff." He has O'Folliard killed in this battle, and when the Kid tries to ride away, he is surrounded on all sides. By swinging his rifle as a club, he crushes the head of the sheriff, but is himself hit on the head with a revolver. When he recovers consciousness, he is tied hand and foot in the camp of Colonel Dudley. All of this, of course, is pure fiction.

This writer says that Pat Garrett was a deputy sheriff, but "with the death of Sheriff Turner, Pat was elevated to that position." In truth Garrett was elected by a vote of the people, not by any promotion through death or any other means. Like so many others, Mr. Fable confuses his geography. He declares that Lincoln was too full of the Kid's friends to be safe and it is deemed advisable to jail him in Mesilla. After he is jailed, a special term of court is called at Lincoln to try him. Actually the Kid was jailed at Lincoln and tried at Mesilla. And instead of Fable's Judge Dyer, of Santa Fe, Judge Bristol is the presiding judge.

Although Pat Garrett had gone to White Oaks to purchase lumber for the Kid's scaffold or, as Pat himself said, to collect taxes, and was there during the Kid's escape, Mr. Fable puts him in the jail listening to the hammer strokes as the scaffold is built. The fact is that the Kid had escaped before Garrett ever got back from White Oaks. And although it is common knowledge that Olinger and the Kid hated each other and that Olinger did everything he could to make the Kid's life miserable, this author writes, "The constant companionship of Olinger showed a disposition to *temper his official duties with as much kindness as he could permit.*"

Differing from all other writers, Fable has the Kid pretend he cannot drink his coffee at breakfast with the handcuffs on his wrists and so persuades Bell to take them off. In this account, Bell is the man who goes "down town." While Olinger is standing looking out the window, the Kid swings his handcuffs, hits him on the head, then takes his pistol and shoots him. After this, the Kid gathers up all the pistols he can carry and starts downstairs.

"On the way he looked through a window and saw Bell, the other guard, who had heard the shot, hurrying back to the prison.

" 'Hello, Bell!' shouted the Kid.

"The former looked up and saw his prisoner standing at the window pointing a *revolver* at him through the bars. It was too late to retreat and in a moment Bell had met the fate of his comrade."

The Kid proceeds to the kitchen, where he forces the cook to "remove the shackles from his limbs." When he mounts a horse to escape, the animal becomes unmanageable and throws him off, so "picking himself up *he mounted another horse.*"

Then the Kid rides to Fort Stanton to kill Colonel Dudley, whom he blames for his capture, although in reality it was Garrett who captured him at Stinking Springs, not Dudley at his Staked Plains hideout. After he leaves Fort Stanton, where two men talked him out of killing Dudley, he meets four of Chisum's cowboys. He kills three of them and sends the fourth to tell Chisum how he is collecting his debt. This story became a legend early in the writings about the Kid.

Garrett now asks for a leave of absence so that he can do nothing but hunt for the Kid. Week after week he searches, until he grows weary and rides into Fort Sumner to rest. During the second week of his stay at Sumner, Garrett sees a Mexican come in to purchase some cartridges, and he is "certain it was the Kid who had come in the store, and who had resorted to the old dodge of tanning his face to the copper colored hue of a Mexican, the better to elude officers."

He inquires of the storekeeper, but the only information he gets is that the man works on the Maxwell ranch, which appears to be some distance from Fort Sumner. Arriving at the ranch house (in reality it was no ranch house at all, but one of the buildings at Fort Sumner being used as a residence by Pete Maxwell), Garrett stations one man at the front door and *the other at the back* with instructions to shoot down anyone who tries to get away. The story of the actual killing is much the same as in most other accounts.

I cannot refrain quoting at length from Fable's description of the Kid's dress just to show how ridiculous is his conception of things western.

"His dress," he writes, "was arranged with view to attract attention. [And from his description it surely would have!] He wore a blue dragoon jacket of the finest broadcloth, heavily loaded down with gold embroidery, buckskin pants, dyed jet black, with small tinkling bells sewed down the sides. . . . Underneath this garment were his drawers of fine scarlet broadcloth, extending clear down to the ankle and over his feet, encasing them like stockings. But his hat was the most gorgeous and the crowning feature

of his getup. . . . And this whole structure of a hat was covered with gold and jewels until it sparkled and shone in a
dazzling and blinding manner when one looked upon it.
There was a gold cord around the crown as large as a man's
thumb, and a great bright rosette at the left set it off in all
its glory. The shoes worn by this young prince of the plains
were low-quartered, with patent silver spurs in the heels,
which took the place of the common clumsy arrangements
that ordinary equestrians use." Who ever heard of a cowboy wearing shoes, especially low-quartered ones? Or of
built-in spurs? This proves again how little such writers
knew of actual western customs and how well equipped
they were with imagination.

Because this book is exceedingly rare (I know of but one
copy, the one I examined in the Athenaeum Library in
Boston), I have gone into the story it gives in some detail.
In the confusion of truth and fact and in the exotic spelling of characters' names, it is a typical example of the western novels of the period.

The following year, 1882, Pat Garrett's book was published. Garrett said in his introduction: "I am incited to
this labor, in a measure, by an impulse to correct the thousand false statements which have appeared in the public
newspapers and in yellow-covered cheap novels. Of the
latter, no less than three have been foisted upon the public, any one of which might have been the history of any
other outlaw that ever lived, but were miles from correct
as applied to 'the Kid.' These pretend to disclose his name,
the place of his nativity, the particulars of his career, the
circumstances which drove him to his desperate life, detailing a hundred impossible deeds of reckless crime of
which he was never guilty, and in localities which he never
visited."

45

Although his own book is far from the truth, there is no doubt that the three novels described earlier in this chapter are among the ones he refers to in this quotation.

A Chicago publisher, catching the fever, issued a book in this same year entitled *Cowboy's Career; or, the Dare Devil Deeds of Billy the Kid,* "by One of the Kids." This account is quite similar to the one by Don Jernado. Both make the statement that the Lincoln County War began when John Chisum and Alex McSwain [sic] tried to monopolize the cattle business in New Mexico.

The account of the killing of McCloskey, Baker, and Morton in *Cowboy's Career* is anything but correct. In it, the Kid killed "McClusky," then "chaining the two men [Baker and Morton] together by the wrists and carefully securing them to the saddle, he placed them both on McClusky's horse and started back at a slow trot toward Chisum's ranch." When they tried to slip their handcuffs, the Kid killed them both with a rifle.

Furthermore, the Kid killed Sheriff Brady and George Hindman not on the streets of Lincoln, as in reality, but when they came to arrest him at John Chisum's ranch.

". . . raising his rifle to his shoulder, and pulling the trigger, with the barrel aimed at Brady's heart, there was a quick flash and another report. The south wind quickly cleared the air, and stepping forward, with *derringer* drawn, the Kid saw Brady and Hindman at his feet, the one dead, the other breathing faintly and asking to be put out of his misery.

" 'You shall go as quick as I can send you,' the cowboy said. 'Give Baker my love,' and he placed the muzzle of his *derringer* at Hindman's right temple and finished the bloody work."

There is also a lengthy account of a battle between Sheriff Turner, with thirty-five men, and the Kid, with sixty-five men, only forty of whom escaped alive. Colonel Dudley sent his cavalry troops to assist Turner, and they chased the Kid into Lincoln, where he took shelter in the house of McSwain. (Note that not only were these writers copying each other's stories, but they were even using the same misspelling of proper names.) Here, too, "during the battle Mrs. McSwain encouraged the garrison by playing martial airs on her piano, and singing inspired battle songs. . . . The besieging posse soon got the range of the piano from its sound, and shot it to pieces with their heavy buffalo rifles, the wife of McSwain narrowly escaping." During the rush from the burning house, "Tom O'Fallaher," a "pard" of the Kid's, young, and from San Antonio, Texas, saw a friend fall. Although a storm of bullets and buckshot rained around him, he coolly stopped, picked up his comrade, and was about to carry him out when he noticed that he was dead. Throwing the body down, *he drew a sword* and fought his way out. I am indeed surprised to learn that western outlaws in America carried swords as a part of their accouterment. How ridiculous can a writer get?

Down through the years these cheap novels were published, using the Kid as the chief character, until the public grew tired of them. No situation was too remote from the facts for these writers to incorporate in their stories. One more example of one of the later ones, *Old King Brady and Billy the Kid; or, the Great Detective's Chase* (1890), by Francis W. Doughty, will suffice. This one, like others before it, makes the Kid a stage robber and has him kidnap a girl passenger after killing her father. Pat Garrett, *"hidden under Pete Maxwell's bed for that purpose,"* finally kills him.

As examples are given of the various accounts of the Kid

down through the years, please keep in mind the absurd exaggerations, of names and incidents, that have just been pointed out, and judge for yourself how much influence these cheap novels have had on later attempts to tell the story of this young outlaw. As a collector of books on western outlaws and a researcher into the facts of their lives, I fail to understand why so many writers are content to accept the legends that have been handed down as actual fact without investigation. Perhaps they themselves believe the legends or want to believe them; perhaps they do not wish to take away from their heroes the glow of romantic glamour with which the public has invested them; or perhaps they may accept the legends without believing them merely to tell a good story.

3. Newspaper Reporting

IT WOULD BE both useless and tiring to discuss more than a small number of the various newspaper accounts of the Kid which appeared over the entire country during his lifetime and immediately after his death. They were legion, and some were just as unreliable as the dime novels current at the time. As a rule, the newspapers published in the Lincoln County War territory were trustworthy, depending upon the editors; yet even some of these, like the Las Vegas papers, were often unreliable. Sides were chosen, and very few newspapers were impartial.

The *Las Vegas Optic* of Monday, May 2, 1881, published the following: "Advices from Lincoln bring intelligence of the escape of 'Billy the Kid,' the daring young desperado, the murderer of Bob Ollinger and J. W. Bell, officers in charge. As near as can be ascertained 'Billy the Kid' was in an upstairs room *in the hotel* at Lincoln, and watching his opportunity, slipped his handcuffs. He then knocked Deputy Sheriff Bell down, and snatching his revolver, killed the gallant young officer dead. Bob Ollinger, one of the guards, hearing the shot, and with the remark, 'the Kid tried to escape and Bell has shot him,' *rushed upstairs.* The moment he reached the *top of the stairs* the Kid fired, killing him instantly. He then went down stairs and at the muzzle of the deadly six shooter *forced the landlord* to saddle the fastest horse in the stable, on which he mounted and made his escape. Several men were at the house at the time but dared not offer any resistance. This is the report on the street, and I think it is in the main correct."

To show how some of the wild tales about the Kid got started, the *Las Vegas Optic* is again quoted—Monday, May 9, 1881: "It is reported on the streets this morning that Billy Bonney, 'the Kid,' had been killed by Marshal Studemier [*sic*], of El Paso, Texas, but as yet the report has not been confirmed, nor do we give it much credence. It is hardly probable, in the first place that a man of the Kid's known shrewdness in such matters would go into a place like El Paso, knowing that the officers were in after him, and secondly, it is barely possible that he was killed in a fight without woulding [*sic*] his captors, as is reported."

On the next day this same paper quoted from the *Denver Times:* "The question of how to deal with desperadoes who commit murder has but one solution—kill them and be prompt about it. Some nice people are so horrified at the thought of a hanging that they forget all about the murderer's victims. They forget the widow, the fatherless children or brotherless sister he has made. They only see a good man purified by affliction led upon a scaffold and executed, while saints are shedding rivers of tears. This section of the country is full of men who ought to be hanged before sunrise—men driven from every other quarter of the globe for their crimes and who came here to continue their evil practices and war upon society. When one of them is caught a smart lawyer succeeds in baffling the law and justice entirely, or puts the public to an extraordinary expense, when twenty-five cents for a rope is all the prisoner deserves. The escape of 'Billy the Kid' at Lincoln, N. M., on the 28th ult., is due to the fact that he contained more active deviltry than the officers in charge gave him credit for having. His crimes are too numerous to count, and nothing from petty thieving to murder was beneath him. His capture was only effected by the utmost skill and bravery, and after a stubborn and protracted fight *in which an officer was killed.* Once captured he became penitent and fearful. He begged not to be taken to Las Vegas for fear of lynching. [This is untrue.] Taken to Santa Fe he was expensively tried, convicted and sentenced to be hanged on the 13th inst., and was taken to Lincoln for safe keeping and *religious consultation.* [He was tried in Mesilla, not Santa Fe.] On the 28th ult., when alone with Officer J. W. Bell, the Kid slipped his handcuffs, knocked the officer down, and snatching his pistol shot him. Officer Robert Olinger hearing the difficulty *rushed in and stopped a bullet.* The Kid then *forced the landlord of the house* where he was confined to saddle his best horse, and colly [*sic*] rode away. But soon meeting with William Mathews [*sic*], who had been prominent in his efforts to break up lawlessness, quietly shot him and also another man. [This is also untrue.] That is all he had killed at last accounts, though should he meet any of those philanthropic men who have labored so hard to have his death sentence commuted, he might kill them just to keep his hand in. The Kid is no worse than many others who are running around Wyoming, Colorado and New Mexico, though a little bolder; and not quite so particular about committing murders in the dark. There is only one way to deal with outlaws; offer rewards for them dead or alive, the former preferred."

Perhaps the tale that Billy the Kid killed Chisum's employees to get even with Chisum for an alleged debt got its start from this account from the *Las Vegas Optic* of Friday, June 10, 1881:

51

"Billy the Kid has been heard from again, this time near Roswell, in Lincoln County, and three more murders are set down against him. About dusk a few days ago he rode up to a cow camp of John Chisum, in which there were four men, three sitting around the fire engaged in preparing supper and the fourth some distance away hobbling horses. Approaching the last mentioned man he asked, 'Are you working for old John Chisum?' and receiving a reply in the affirmative, he remarked, 'Well, here is your pay,' and killed him. The remaining three seeing their comrade thus ruthlessly murdered jumped to their feet but, before they could draw their pistols, the Kid had killed two of them, and levelling his pistol at the fourth one commanded him to throw up his hands; the order was promptly obeyed and, after informing him that his life had been spared so that he could deliver a message to Chisum, the Kid told him that he fought for Chisum all through the Lincoln County War and that Chisum had agreed to pay him therefor $5 per day and that he had never received one cent from him. 'Tell him I am living now to get even with my enemies; I shall kill his men wherever I find them and credit him with five dollars for each man I kill. Whenever I see him I will kill him and call the account square,' said this incarnate fiend. The county is thoroughly aroused over this heartless triple murder, although no organized effort as far as we can learn is being made to capture him.

"He expressed the intention of remaining in that country until he has gotten even with his enemies, and at the rate he is now going, he will soon depopulate Lincoln County."

The same newspaper, on Thursday, July 28, 1881, quotes the *New York Tribune* in this wise: "The *New York Tribune* shows a delicate appreciation of the situation of affairs on the frontier hardly to be expected of a newspaper published in the East. Speaking of the death-dealing outlaw and tiger in human form known as 'Billy the Kid,' it says:

" 'The inhabitants of New Mexico do not stand upon technicalities of the law in dealing with desperadoes. A certain Mr. McCarthy, formerly of New York and better known as Billy the Kid, a promising young man of twenty-one whose proud boast it was that he had killed a man for every year of his life, has lately been pursued and shot on sight, by a sheriff near Las Vegas. The coroner's jury which sat on his body thus energetically furnished for its use, rendered a verdict of justifiable homicide, and passed a vote of thanks to the sheriff for ridding the community of this remarkable young man, who seems to have made himself a terror of the region. Furthermore, the sheriff will receive a handsome reward from the state, and be the recipient of a popular subscription. In all of which there is more of justice, rude as it is, than many of the decisions of the courts, aided as they are by all the machinery of civilization.' "

Again the *Las Vegas Daily Optic*, of Saturday, July 30, 1881, published an exchange from the *Kansas City Journal* which is a good example of the confused information common in connection with the early western outlaw:

"As [*sic*] exciting controversy is going on in certain police circles and newspapers as to the nativity and identity of the notorious murderer recently killed in New Mexico. Seven cities contended for Homer dead, through which the living Homer begged his bread. In this respect the New Mexican hero surpassed the blind old bard of three thousand years ago. Springfield, Ill., puts in a claim to being his birth place, and so does Philadelphia, Cincinnati and New York. St. Louis as yet has made no sign, but she is sure to come forward in the end and claim his [*sic*] as a product of the classic locality known as Kerry Patch. A New York policeman says the renowned 'Billy the Kid' was no other than little William McCarthy of the Fourth Ward, who, four or five years ago, *when but seventeen years of age,* committed one of the most provoked and atrocious murders known to the criminal records *of that city.* He was not captured, because it is alleged his father *smuggled him off to Ireland,* with a view of having him join the patriots of the 'old Sod' in their struggles against British tyranny. The 'Kid's' blood had become corrupted, however, and he evinced no inclination to right anybody's wrongs but his own, so he came back to the land of the free, and hies himself to the far Southwest to grow up with the country. In his new home he grew and flourished for a time beyond all precedent. In New Mexico, where the old and the new civilization had just come in contact, he found a magnificent field for his peculiar operations. *In less than three years he dispatched into eternity over twenty of his fellow mortals.* Having in that brief space of time made for himself a name that carried terror throughout New Mexico and *Colorado,* Sir William McCarthy, alias 'Billy the Kid,' began to presume somewhat on the fear he had inspired. Then a plain practical sort of fellow named Pat Garrett, *who happened to be sheriff* of one of the counties of New Mexico, concluded to go for the rampant 'Kid,' and laying in wait for him at one of his haunts, he soon put an end to his lamb like sports! On sight he sent a bullet straight through his heart, and the illustrious 'Kid' was dead in a minute, like the commonest cur that ever fell before a bullet of the municipal dog killer."

On Monday, September 19, 1881, this article is found in the same paper: "Billy the Kid had a sweetheart, so we have just learned. The young lady's name is Kate Tenny and she lives on Fifteenth Street in Oakland, California. She read in the newspapers that THE OPTIC had the index finger of the Kid in pickle, and she had written for it, with a request to send also a photograph of the young killer. We have written Miss Tenny a sorrowful epistle, full of touching condolence and broke the news gently that we had just sold our relic of her lover for $150 cash, and that 'Billy' was such a contrary fellow that he wouldn't sit still long enough for a photographer to get his camera turned loose upon him, hence the photograph she craved must ever be forthcoming. We will see that physician who was fortunate enough to secure Billy's 'stiff' and will present a request for some part of the Kid's skeleton—a shank bone, or something of that kind, which we will send to the broken-hearted maiden as a lasting memento of her dead lover's former greatness."

A little less than a month after the Kid's death, the *Laredo* (Texas) *Times,* of August 10, 1881, carries the statement that after the Kid's escape from Lincoln he had added three more victims to his credit.

"About the 5th of June," it says, "the escaped desperado rode to the cow camp of John Chisum, the well known cattleman of the Panhandle [!], in which there were four cowboys. Three of these were seated around the fire cooking supper, while the fourth, Bennett Howell, was hobbling his horse about twenty yards from the fire. Riding up to the latter, the Kid inquired, 'Are you working for old John Chisum?' 'Yes,' was the reply. 'Then here's your pay!' and a bullet from the Kid's pistol pierced the man's brain at the same moment. Seeing the murder of their comrade, the other boys sprang to their feet, but before they could draw their six-shooters that of the Kid exploded twice again, and two more of the cowboys fell. Pulling down on the remaining one, the murderer shouted, 'Hold up!' The command was promptly obeyed. 'Now,' continued Billy, 'I want you to live to take a message to old John Chisum for me. Tell him during the Lincoln County War he proposed to pay me $5 a day for fighting for him. I fought for him, and never got a cent. Now I intend to kill his men wherever I meet them, giving him credit for $5 every time I drop one until the debt is squared.' " Note that this is practically a repetition of the report in the *Las Vegas Optic* of June 10, 1881.

Such statements as these, coming from western newspapers and so soon after this range war, were taken in good faith, especially by outsiders. This last account further states that the Kid had "killed over thirty men." Regarding the Kid's visit to the Maxwell home, it says, "The belief is that the Kid received intelligence of Pat's presence, and was searching for him at the time, or that he had gone to *murder Maxwell in his bed.*"

The *Dallas Morning News* of June 28, 1925, contained a story in its Sunday feature section which I put into my collection of false accounts of this outlaw.

"Billy the Kid," says the author, "the most notorious bandit and gunman who ever ranged over the Southwest during the wildest of early days, started on his career of crime *to avenge a raid on his parents' home by guerrillas during the Civil War.*

"This is the story related by Billy the Kid to A. A. Prince, of Sweetwater, Texas, who knew the young desperado at *Fort Griffin, Shackelford County, Texas,* before he had become one of the most feared characters in Texas and New Mexico." Billy the Kid was never near Fort Griffin. But tales like this make us wonder why it is that old men in their dotage try to convince others they knew famous or, rather, notorious men personally.

"Before he was twenty years old," continues Mr. Prince, "he had killed twenty-one men, not including Indians, who he said 'didn't count.' He was himself killed by Sheriff Pat Garrett of Lincoln County, New Mexico, on July 4, 1881." The date of the killing was the fourteenth. This gentleman knew there was a four in that date somewhere and with characteristic carelessness gave the wrong one.

The teller of this tale admits that his account of the Kid's first killing is different from Charlie Siringo's, which identified the Kid's first victim as a Negro soldier who had cheated him in a crap game when he was twelve years old. Mr. Prince declared that he had a saddle shop in Fort Griffin and that he and the Kid boarded at the same hotel; that Billy used to visit his shop frequently and sit around cleaning his gun. But let Mr. Prince tell this fantastic tale in his own words:

"One day he became confidential with me and told me how it had happened he had killed a couple of men. He said that during the Civil War, when he was with his parents in Missouri or Kansas, I don't remember which State it was, a group of five Jayhawkers went to the home, turned out the family and burned the house to the ground." Billy recognized the men in the raiding party and swore vengeance. Even if this incident had happened during the last year of the war and the Kid had really been born in 1859, he would have been only four years old, which, it seems to me, is rather a tender age to be swearing vengeance.

". . . and when he grew up," continues Mr. Prince, "or rather reached an age when he thought he was about grown up, he killed two of these men and skipped the country. He told me he was going back to his old home and get the other three men, who he had heard were still alive. I advised him not to go, but he said he must. He was gone two or three weeks. He spent a short time in Fort Griffin after his return and then went west. I read in a newspaper where three men had been killed in Missouri and I always figured out that Billy the Kid had done the job." Nearly all the rest of Mr. Prince's account is a direct quotation from Siringo's book, *The History of Billy the Kid.*

In 1882, the same year that Pat Garrett's *Life of Billy, the Kid* appeared, there ran a serial in the *Las Vegas Optic* typical of the biographies of the Kid at that time. It was published anonymously, but its author certainly knew, or thought he knew, that the public was avid and ready to gulp down anything about this most talked of outlaw. At any rate, he left behind an excellent example of the farcical accounts written in those days as history.

The narrator makes a personal visit to the Kid at his rendezvous and learns from him what he wants to know by "investigating questions." The Kid likes his interviewer from the start, and invites him to join his band. The Kid tells him: "I was born in County Limerick, Ireland, about 1859. My father's name was William. He was a poor Irish peasant, and like all poor classes of peasantry suffered much and did not escape persecution." But what finally drove the Kid away from Ireland was the "ruin of my two sisters by a son of our landlord." This blow killed his father, and his mother took the children to Canada. From Montreal they went to Nova Scotia, where his mother married "an old reprobate named Antrim, and soon afterward accompanied him to New Mexico." This happened in 1869, so the account reads. It will be seen before this work is finished that the Kid's mother married Antrim in New York, Canada, Kansas, Texas, Colorado, and New Mexico.

In chapter IX of this serial the Kid tells how he had worked in a kitchen where he helped himself "to a keg of butter and sold it to a Chinaman." He was not punished for this theft because he promised to pay for the butter by letting the landlord take so much money each week from his salary. Later he stole the overcoat of the Chinaman who had first given him away, and for this he was put in jail. He was sentenced to a year, but soon escaped up a chimney and went to the Chinaman's home and "cut his throat from ear to ear." This story has been told by others, no doubt capitalizing upon this writer's imagination and demonstrating how these falsehoods are copied and handed down as actual facts. The Kid claims that this was his first murder and "he felt a little scared" at what he had done, so he stole the Chinaman's horse and beat it to Arizona.

At the Arizona border he got a job as a blacksmith's helper, but the smith "was an ugly drunken brute whom nobody could get along with," and the Kid killed him. In the final installment the writer tells a wild tale about a man dying and leaving $12,000 to his heirs. (He had evidently heard of the Fritz insurance money.) There was a woman, who claimed to be the only sister of the deceased, coming to New Mexico to claim the estate. However, the sheriff, who was the administrator and an ambitious fellow as well, was also trying to appropriate the money, so the Kid decided he would try to get some of it, too; and before it was all over, he had killed thirteen men.

When the Kid was captured, tried, and condemned to death, he was guarded by two "murderers of note," so writes this author. One day one of the guards went to town "to fill his whiskey jug," and the Kid got the other one to loosen one hand so that he could eat with more freedom. He "got the other talking, and getting up behind him, I raised my hand holding *two* [!] handcuffs, and hit him on the head, dropping him like an ox." He then took his pistols and shot him in the head. The other guard, hearing the shot and suspecting something had gone wrong, came running back. When he got near, the Kid opened the window and said "Hello, *Bill!*" and shot him through the heart *with a rifle*. When this writer parted with the Kid, the latter gave him "a beautiful revolver" to remember him by!

Could anything be farther from the truth? Yet it is a typical example of some of the all too common newspaper reporting of that day.

4. Magazine Historians

I FIND THAT DURING PAST YEARS the magazine writers were especially careless in writing factual articles on the West. Perhaps this was due to the fact that very few of them were historians, but of that breed which sought sensationalism and glamour rather than dry facts. Further, early magazine writers rarely did the conscientious research commonly undertaken by writers of books, although, as is apparent, the writers of the books listed herein seem to have done very little research upon their subject, either.

In the September, 1901, issue of *Everybody's Magazine,* there was an article by Emerson Hough entitled "Billy the Kid, the True Story of a Western 'Bad Man.'" Like so many other so-called true stories of the Kid, this one is far from "true." Although Hough lived in the Billy the Kid country soon after the Kid was killed and wrote a great deal about the young outlaw, he seems to have had a talent for getting everything wrong. It was not until many years later, when he went back out to that country and spent some time with Pat Garrett, that he seemed to gain a maturer perspective and to get his facts straightened out to a certain extent.

In this article he has the Kid buried in Las Cruces, though where he got his information is hard to imagine. It only goes to prove how careless a writer can be. He repeats the story of the Kid's killing seven Mexicans which he told in his book, *The Story of the Cowboy* (1897), a very careless piece of writing. Martin Chavez told former Governor Miguel Otero, "In all his career Billy never killed a native citizen of New Mexico, which was one of the reasons we were all so fond of him."

Throughout this article Hough depicts the Kid as a depraved killer and declares, "Billy the Kid killed because he liked to do so. By the time he was sixteen the groan of a victim, the sight of his writhings upon the ground had ceased to affect him. . . . Not all the wild West has ever produced his equal in sheer inborn savagery." In telling of the Kid's escape from his Lincoln prison, Hough says that the Kid persuaded Bell to unfasten the handcuffs on one hand, and when Bell *leaned out of an open window*, the Kid hit him in the back of the head, jerked his gun from its holster, and killed him. Then he shot "Orrendorf" (Olinger) with a shotgun.

The April, 1905, issue of *Outing Magazine* included an article under the authorship of Arthur Chapman entitled "Billy the Kid, a Man All 'Bad.' " It was evidently based on Hough's *The Story of the Cowboy,* as it makes the same errors. About the only departure is that only three Mexicans were killed by the Kid "just to see them kick," while in the Hough version there were seven. The author spells Chisum's name "Chisholm" and contends that several hundred men lost their lives in the Lincoln County War.

Evidently he had read Morrison's dime novel, also, for he uses the incident of the Kid's shooting down three of Chisum's cowboys and sending a fourth back to Chisum with the message that his account had been credited with five dollars for each man killed—thus the legends created by the dime novelists were beginning to take hold. Chapman also places an exaggeratedly large posse with Garrett at the capture of the Kid at Stinking Springs, and says that

Garrett's right-hand man in this posse was the "ever-loyal" Olinger, who was not with the posse at all. The version of the escape at Lincoln is the one of the Kid's hands being loosened from the handcuff to let him eat with more comfort, whereupon he hit Bell over the head with them.

"Some of the gun-fighters of frontier days killed in self-defence," writes Chapman, "and others killed when they were in liquor or inflamed with anger—but Billy the Kid was the *only white man* who slew out of pure wantonness. . . . If he ever had a grudge against a man he never harbored it long, but simply confronted his victim and slew without making explanation." More of the Hough theme.

In this version it is said that the Kid spent his early boyhood as a street waif in New York City, "from where he *was sent* to Silver City, New Mexico." Chapman also states that the Kid was serving as an apprentice to a blacksmith at *Camp Apache* when he killed his employer. His account of the mob at Las Vegas is all wrong; he says that Garrett placed his prisoners *in a box car,* and repeats the growing fable regarding the judge's sentencing of the Kid at his trial at Mesilla, " 'I thereby sentence you to be hanged by the neck until you are dead—dead—dead!' " and the Kid's impudent answer for the judge " ' to go to hell—hell—hell!' "

In spite of the fact that this article was entirely made up of incidents which never happened, it was chosen as a chapter in an anthology, *Frontier Days*, published in 1928 under the editorship of Oliver G. Swan.

Nearly six years after the appearance of this first article in *Outing*, there was another, under the title "A Cowboy War," by the same author. It dealt primarily with the Lincoln County War, which the author blames on Chisum and the undesirable element associated with him, saying that the better element rallied to the side of Dolan and Murphy, "two fine young men." He has a reward of $1,000 posted for the capture of each member of the gang who killed young Tunstall. Most of his information follows closely that in his first *Outing* article of 1905.

During the year 1906 there were many articles published about Billy the Kid. A few examples will suffice to show that there was no improvement in telling the truth with the passing of time. In July of this year there appeared in the *Pacific Monthly* an article by William MacLeod Raine entitled "Billy the Kid." It is an early effort of Raine's, written before he had made a serious study of western history, and is not reliable. Heretofore he had written fiction. His later factual articles were much more accurate, and he was generally a reliable historian. In this first article, however, he repeats many of the tall tales of his predecessors, including the story about Chisum's riders being killed by the Kid, as well as the one about the Kid's killing the Mexicans "just to see them kick," though he, too, cuts the number to three. In addition, he gives the Kid credit for inventing the trick of twirling a six-gun by the trigger guard and says he once killed a deputy by this contrivance. I feel this idea must have come from the fact that Curly Bill Brocius was the first to use this trick, on Marshal White, at Tombstone, Arizona.

In July of this same year there was an article entitled "Billy the Kid" in the *Overland Monthly*, written by J. E. Sligh, a man who had settled in White Oaks in 1880. From a man living in the center of the area where these things were happening, we should expect a certain amount of accuracy, and the editor even states that Sligh "wrote the truth" about the Kid's life, yet the account is anything but reliable from beginning to end.

Sligh makes the statement that the Kid's father was a

soldier at Fort Bayard and that when he died, the Kid, then fifteen years old, had to go to work to help support his mother and two younger children. Even his description of the Kid is wrong, for he says that the Kid was dark, with raven black hair and very black eyes.

His account of the Kid's meeting with the Apaches is wrong, too, and he seems to be quite confused about the incident at the home of Greathouse when Carlyle was killed. He has a Texas desperado named Jim Saunders held as hostage by the Kid and killed when he tried to escape through the window.

The following month the same magazine published a sequel to this story. This one, too, is full of errors and reveals the author's ignorance of his subject. He claimed to have met Garrett and held extensive conversations with him, and so should have known more about what really happened than he apparently did. He claimed Garrett was so illiterate that he could not run his own office.

The Kid's escape from his Lincoln imprisonment is rather garbled, with Olinger killed first and "Charlie" Bell killed as he returned from across the street to see what the shooting was about. Of course, the facts were just the opposite. When the Kid went to Maxwell's house on that fateful night in July, this writer has both the Kid and Garrett shoot at the same time, but "the Kid missed and Garrett did not."

The following month of this same year (1908), *Harper's Weekly* contained an article entitled "American Bandits; Lone and Otherwise," written by Barton W. Currie. Among the other outlaws mentioned is Billy the Kid, who the writer says killed thirty men at a conservative estimate. He makes the Kid a newsboy in New York or Chicago (he can't remember which) and says he did not get to Silver City, New Mexico, until he was twelve years old, when he went there with his mother when she appeared there as a pretty music hall singer. Here seems to be a man trying to create a new legend of his own.

Now, let's skip seventeen years and see how Billy the Kid is faring in print in 1925. The issues of *Collier's Weekly* for November 14 and 21 contain a two-part serial by Owen P. White on Billy the Kid. Anyone with a knowledge of both history and the writings of Mr. White never expects reliable information on the western outlaws from him, but we will not go into details here. This account was incorporated into his *Trigger Fingers* the following year and will be discussed in the last chapter of this book. Suffice to say at this time that he lists the Kid's first killing as that of a "black nigger" whom he killed in a card game, and he repeats the fable that he killed Bernstein "because he didn't like Jews nohow." He calls the Kid's guard in the Lincoln jail "Dave Wall" instead of J. W. Bell, and he says that the Kid killed "twenty-six men, not counting Indians."

Harvey Fergusson, in an article in the *American Mercury* of June, 1925, follows Garrett's account closely. He quotes George Coe on the killing of Tunstall, to the effect that Tunstall, the Kid, and two other cowboys were riding the range when they were approached by a posse of thirty men. The Kid tried to get Tunstall to ride away, but he was stubborn and refused to run, whereupon the Kid and the others deserted him and left him to his death. Fergusson also says that old-timers in New Mexico didn't think much of Garrett because he had killed so many men, most of them from cover.

The April 10, 1926, issue of the *Saturday Evening Post* carries a story by Fred Sutton, entitled "Fill Your Hand." Again, the reader cannot expect anything other than fantastic tales from the pen of this writer. In this article he claims to have saved the life of Billy the Kid in Hays City, Kansas. There is no other record of the Kid's ever having been in this Kansas town. Sutton has his own brother, Clyde, help Garrett capture the Kid *in the Panhandle* of Texas, which must be startling news to historians everywhere. Furthermore, the Kid shortly afterward escaped from jail at Santa Fe, and when the sheriff's posse passed Sutton's ranch, Sutton joined it and was with Jimmy Carlyle when Jimmy was shot trying to escape the Kid at Greathouse's ranch. Sutton told this tale earlier, in *The Trail Drivers of Texas,* volume I, which will be discussed more fully later.

The spring issue, 1929, of *The Southwest Review* contains an article by Philip Stevenson, "Prelude to Murder," in which the author states that at the age of three the Kid witnessed his father's death during a fit which followed a quarrel he had had with his wife. At the age of five the Kid punched Mr. Antrim in the nose because he found out that he was going to marry his mother. After they moved to New Mexico, he became quite a street fighter and learned all about the bad men from a boarder in the family home, Ash Upson.

Although the author gives no dates, he has Antrim moving his family to Silver City when Billy was eight years old. And in his story Billy gambled in the saloons when he was still a mere child, his mother visiting these saloons to watch her son play, hoping he would take her home. Now in those days a lady would not walk on the same side of the street on which a saloon was located if she could help it, and saloon keepers still had some scruples about serving minors or allowing them in their places of business. They were more particular then than now.

In this account the Kid played stud poker with Kirk, the

blacksmith he was later supposed to have killed, strictly a piece of imaginative writing, the author even identifying each card dealt. Another time, when Billy was taking his mother home from the saloon, "They had gone only a few steps from the saloon doors. Kirk, the blacksmith was striding toward them, walking steadily enough, and yet plainly—well—feeling good. He had the air of being up to something.

"Sure enough, he planted himself squarely in front of Kathleen, hands on hips, a wide yellow grin spread over his face, hat tipped insolently back.

" 'So you're the mother o' the little bastard! Ah've heard of you,' he said with his loud swaggery drawl. 'Say, but you're a mahty nache-lookin' heifer, you are. Ah'd sure lahk to spread mah loop over you en lead you to mah corral....' [Now it is doubtful that any western man would have spoken in this fashion to a lady, nor would he have used the exaggerated vernacular recorded here.]

"A rock the size of his fist caught his tilted hat and carried it crashing against an adobe wall. Billy hadn't waited for the end of an obvious insult to his mother. With a bound into the muddy street he had picked [up] and hurled the rock in one movement. His aim for the man's forehead had proved perilously true in the crisis; only a mock-solicitous bow had saved Kirk from an ugly crack."

Then the author repeats that threadbare tale about Ed Moulton's coming to the Kid's rescue, with all the trimmings, for later, in a saloon fight, when the blacksmith tried to hit Moulton over the head with a chair, the Kid repaid his friend by stabbing Kirk to death.

He concludes with this imaginative piece of writing: "A knife was in Billy's left hand. The point of it was slowly scratching through buckskin; then it cuttingly pierced the rubber-yielding flesh, glanced grinding off a bone, and gave—soft and deeply sank—into the core of a human life. As slowly it withdrew—without command, without will, and yet without hesitation. Surely, accurately, it sought another spot; scratched, pierced, ground, plunged; withdrew and plunged again. A warm, slippery, rubbery stream trickled down Billy's doubled-up little finger, along the edge of his left palm and wrist." Stevenson brings his account to a close when the Kid had killed his first man, the man who insulted his mother.

In June of 1930, there appeared in *The Westerner*, a magazine published in Salt Lake City, an article by Dennis H. Stovall, entitled "The Kid Kicks In." This writer makes the Kid's first victim a Negro soldier "from the army post," and "immediately he had Uncle Sam's fighters on his trail."

"Tunstall," he continues, "like all other prominent cattlemen and ranchers of the Southwest, had enemies. The worst of these was the murderous 'Morton gang,' whose leader was 'Noddy' Morton. This outfit had been creating terror throughout the county of Lincoln, and farther south to the Texas line. Through the late seventies, the Mortons waged almost unbroken warfare on the Tunstall riders. One after another of the ranch punchers were slain. And in 1878, Tunstall himself was killed by a member of the gang."

He intimates that the whole Lincoln County feud was between Billy the Kid and the Morton gang, and says that one after another the Morton men were slain, and "the list of killings reached such length that the law-abiding citizens of Lincoln County decided it was time to call a halt. A price was placed on the head of the 'Kid.' He and his followers became hunted outlaws."

Of the killing of Brady, he writes: "Then came the day when he and Bob Brady [his name was William] met on the streets of Lincoln. Reports differ as to just what happened. Some say it was a fair enough fight. Others declare the sheriff was shot from ambush—from behind, while he rode out of town. Anyhow, the 'Kid' killed him—shooting him twice."

Since killing a sheriff was a serious business, a posse of forty men calling themselves the "Seven Rivers Warriors" and "two companies of United States soldiers from the nearest military post" went after the Kid. But the Kid "brazenly took refuge in Lincoln, the county seat—and in the house of Lawyer McSween."

This mob surrounded the McSween home and set it afire. Those inside stayed until forced to run for it. "Deputies and soldiers had their rifles trained on every door and window as they came, all were killed, McSween included, except the 'Kid' himself. As if possessed of a charmed life, he dashed from the flaming house and across the yard, while a score of riflemen fired at him—and still he got away." Garrett "took the belt and star of Bob Brady" and took up the chase.

After the capture and imprisonment of the Kid at Lincoln, Stovall comments: "It was but two days till the 'Kid' would hang. Sheriff Garrett, *who himself stood watch over the prisoner at regular hours every day,* had to leave for White Oaks *where the scaffold was to be built.*" Here is more carelessness and confusion—the Kid was to be hanged in Lincoln.

"Investigation revealed how cleverly the 'Kid' had worked to effect his escape," continues Stovall, in telling of the killing of Bell. "For nearly two weeks he starved himself. His hands had become so thin that he could, by tight squeezing, draw them through the manacles. He had practiced the trick lying in bed, while his arms were beneath

Drawing from Garrett's *The Authentic Life of Billy, the Kid.*

Billy the Kid

Photograph purported to be of Billy the Kid's mother

the blankets. When the final test came, he had drawn them free of the steel cuffs and struck the guard an unexpected blow over the head. Then he had snatched the latter's gun and finished the deadly work. This was the report that brought Bob Ollinger scurrying from the restaurant."

And of the Kid's end: "Then came the tip that the 'Kid' had a girl. Love plays queer tricks, and has been the downfall of countless men, clever and bold, wicked and just, with no choice or favor." He says the girl was "the daughter of a wealthy sheepman whose place was out Fort Sumner way."

According to this version, Garrett went to the sheepman's home and had scarcely been admitted to his bedroom when footsteps were heard in the hallway and the "other door" opened. "Garrett pulled the sheep man with him *into a dark corner, where they waited in breathless silence.*" This is different from any other version I have seen. When the Kid approached, Pat was afraid to shoot for fear it would be the wrong man. Then the shadow called, *"Buenas dias, Señor."* Why should Stovall have the Kid say, "Good day, sir," when what he actually said was, *"Quien es?"* ("Who is it!")

In the *Frontier Times* of August, 1930, we again run across an article by Fred Sutton, entitled "Dr. Hoyt, Panhandle's First Doctor." Expecting anything but the facts, we are not surprised to read that the Kid was wounded in the Panhandle of Texas during a great gun battle in which four men were killed. Sutton evidently had in mind the fight at Tascosa which occurred nearly five years after the Kid had been killed. Nevertheless, as he tells it, Dr. Hoyt nursed the Kid back to health; and to show his appreciation, the Kid rode all the way back to Lincoln, stole Sheriff Brady's horse, returned with it to Tascosa, and gave it to the doctor with a bill-of-sale. He makes Jim East the sheriff of Tascosa and says that he, himself, helped East track down one of the wounded cowboys. As it happened, East was not sheriff until several years after the Kid's death, and the Kid did not drive a band of horses to the Panhandle and give Dr. Hoyt one of them until after Sheriff Brady had been killed in New Mexico.

For the January, 1934, issue of *The Voice of the Mexican Border,* Jack Shipman (Mrs. O. L. Shipman) wrote an article entitled "Brief Career of Tom O'Folliard, Billy the Kid's Partner," which, like so many others, is unreliable. While she does not have Mrs. McSween play the piano during the fire, she does include a piano-playing scene: "Regardless of the threat of death by fire inside the house and man-killers outside, the Kid and Tom played the piano and sang to keep up the courage of the men. . . . In discussing a break for freedom Tom O'Folliard said he would play the piano and keep up the noise so those outside would not suspect their plans. The heat was intense and they could wait no longer. Someone threw the door open. At this move one of the Mexicans in the house became frightened and called out that they would surrender. The Kid laid him low with a vicious blow from the butt of his rifle.

"When the Mexican had called out his intentions to give up, Robert W. Beckwith and John Jones stepped around the corner of the house. Someone shot Beckwith in the hand: then Beckwith shot McSween, though it was not a fatal shot. Again Beckwith fired, killing Vicente Romero. By this time the Kid's gun was barking, and he killed Beckwith, who fell in front of the door.

"Tom quit his position at the piano when the last man had left the house, and made a run for freedom through the rain of bullets . . . though he was badly burned."

Another two-part serial appeared in the March and April

issues, 1934, of *Blood and Thunder,* entitled "Billy the Kid, True Life Story of the Boy Bandit," under the name of Frank T. Fries. He has the Kid rescue the wagon-train emigrants from a band of Comanches instead of Apaches as Upson has it, and says that the Kid "charged them with an ax," killing five of them and scaring the rest away. After this the Kid became a professional hired killer, but retained a great weakness for women; in fact, he hid out in Maxwell's home just to be near his sweetheart. According to Fries, the common story about the killing of the Kid was that Garrett hid under the bed on which the Kid's girl lay dressed in a negligee, and when the Kid came in for a visit, Garrett killed him.

A few years ago there was published in *Big-Book Western Magazine* an article, "Boothill Battle Song," written by Harry Van Demark, who is the author of a number of fairly dependable articles which have appeared in magazines from time to time, but it seems that when even a reliable author writes about the old outlaws, he begins to romance. He starts out thus: "Flames crackled at her back, bullets hissed around her, but Susie McSween kept on playing. Like the voice of tragedy the tones of her piano filtered through the smoke, while Billy the Kid and his men pumped lead into the Murphy gang and Susie's husband knelt in prayer."

Sometimes when I think of the thankless task it is to straighten out historical facts and of the frowns cast my way for destroying the romantic legends people really want to believe, it makes me wonder whether it would not be better to abandon the whole project. Yet when I continue to read statements like this year after year, written by people who would know better if they took the time and trouble to investigate their subject more closely, I feel that

I must do what I can to separate these myths from the facts for the benefit of a new generation.

Many early writers on western outlaws relied too heavily upon the old dime novels, as has been pointed out. Although the majority of these accounts were declared to be "true and authentic," any real historian or biographer should avoid them as he would the plague. They were not written as fact, but solely for entertainment. Imaginary incidents like the one of Mrs. McSween playing the piano, gave their stories dramatic suspense, a common tool of the novelist. Mr. Van Demark dwells unduly upon this dramatic situation, even picturing the men moving the piano from room to room as the McSween home burned.

"She sat down," he writes, "and ran her hands over the keys. Snatches of old tunes took form beneath her delicate touch. Before she knew it she was playing 'Home, Sweet Home.' It was like the voice of tragedy, for her home was nearly destroyed."

After she had visited Colonel Dudley and met with his refusal to stop the shooting, she again returned to her home, says this romancer, for another piano concert. "Mrs. McSween's eyes," he writes, "rested again on the piano that would soon be a charred wreck. She sat patiently down on the stool. She still had faith in Billy the Kid. Her one last effort might save the day. She plunged into the stirring notes of 'The Star-Spangled Banner.' The Kid began to whistle the tune. O'Falliard [*sic*] beat time with his gun." Shades of Walter Noble Burns!

Most writers have been satisfied to have Mrs. McSween play the piano once or twice, but Mr. Van Demark adds that after she had left the burning building for the last time, "the Kid seated himself at the piano and with bullets whistling through the room, cheered his men with a stirring tune, after which he prepared for a final dash."

Then the writer proceeds to get the facts really confused. As the men tried to escape the burning building, "Bowdry [*sic*], Coe, French and Scurlock were each in turn mowed down by a withering fire from the Murphy gang." When it was O'Folliard's time, "he was met by a Murphy volley. He turned, his hand pressed to his chest, and stepped back into the room.

"'They've got me, Kid!'

"The Kid said, 'You'll roast in here. Go back and see if you can get one of them before you go.'

"'Okay—Kid!' The pallor of death was on O'Falliard's [*sic*] face as he stepped outside again, two blasting guns in his hands. Then almost with his last breath, he accounted for two Murphy men."

Mr. Van Demark evidently was thinking of the time the Kid sent Bowdre back to kill some of the attacking party and Garrett's posse shot him as he stepped outside the stone house at Stinking Springs, long after the burning of the McSween home. Neither he, nor Coe, nor French, nor Scurlock was "mowed down" as they left the building. In fact, Bowdre, Coe, French, and Scurlock were not in the McSween home, but in a warehouse, farther down the street. And so the distortion of fact continues.

Max Coleman, in an article in the *Frontier Times* in January, 1936, states that the Kid was killed in *June, 1882*. This, of course, is a month earlier and a year later than the actual date, and the error is no doubt due to carelessness.

In the September, 1937, issue of *Personal Adventure Stories*, A. P. Anaya, who was a personal friend of the Kid's, declares that the Kid killed Grant because Chisum had sent

him to kill the Kid. He also claims that the Kid shoved a gun in Chisum's mouth and made him give him a check for $5,000. Furthermore, the Kid's sweetheart smuggled him a knife in a *tortilla* while he was in the Lincoln jail. This article is perhaps the source of J. W. Hendron's story in his book on Billy the Kid, which will be discussed later.

The March issue of *The Cattleman* (Vol. XXXII, No. 10 [1946]) contains an article by Georgia B. Redfield, entitled "Billy the Kid Rides the Chisum Trail." Shortly after the opening of her discourse she writes: "The gun shot of retribution which ended the Kid's lurid career as a killer was fired at Fort Sumner, on July 15, 1884, by Pat Garrett of Roswell, sheriff of Lincoln County, New Mexico."

She repeats the legend of his having been born in New York of William and Kathleen *Bonney* and their moving to Coffeyville, where the father died. "The mother," she says, "with her two small boys drifted on to Colorado, where she married a man by the name of Antrim, *to whom much of the blame was given for his stepson's life of crime.*"

She continues with the information that the Kid at twelve years of age stabbed the blacksmith "whom he claimed made slurring remarks to his mother. On another occasion, he again became his mother's champion, when he felled her abusive husband with a chair. Believing Antrim dead, Billy is said to have bidden his mother a sad farewell, and left home never to return."

She follows Upson's account by having him kill Indians and gamblers in both Arizona and Old Mexico. "There are no records," she says, "of any shooting at Mesilla, but in all, by the time the eighteen year old kid outlaw had reached Seven Rivers, the numbers of his killings had considerably grown toward the twenty-one notches on his gun he claimed stood for that many men he killed before he was twenty-one, with alibis a-plenty for all his killings, in the name of chivalry, and revenge, for murder."

She makes one statement I have not found in any other account: "The Kid did not fight in the cattle war on Chisum's side for the very good reason, that although the Cattle King had grievances enough . . . he took no part in the bloody cattle feud, and gave strict orders that his cowhands stay away from the fighters and the fighting zone."

In two different places she says that George Coe and Frank Coe were brothers, although they were cousins. And in mentioning the killing of Sheriff Brady, she tells of the "Kid's leaping from over the wall, and with bullets flying around his head, disdainfully, with his foot, turned the body of Sheriff Brady from his gun and made way with it." Since this murder was committed from behind a swinging gate, why should he take the trouble to leap over a wall?

Of the fire in the McSween home she writes: "Billy the Kid, last to leave the burning building, awaited the distracting moment of the falling of the roof, suddenly sprang from the doorway, with pistols blazing, and with his usual luck made it over the rear adobe wall to safety, where he was joined by his pal, George Coe, and others who managed to escape." As has been said before, George Coe was not in the McSween home during the fight.

For the killing of Bell she uses the card-game version: "Billy managed to brush a card from the table, and when Bell stooped to get it, he rose to find himself looking into the muzzle of his own gun the Kid had slipped from his scabbard." No westerner ever calls a holster a "scabbard," this being the receptacle for a saddle gun.

In the January, 1950, issue of *The Cattleman* (Vol. XXXVI, No. 8), is an article by Nell Murbarger entitled "Battle of Blazer's Mill." The first sentence reads, "In a lonely boothill cemetery near the little Indian town of Mescalero, New Mexico, the mouldering bones of two implacable enemies *occupy a single*, unmarked grave." Miss Murbarger, of course, intimates that Brewer and Roberts were buried in the same grave, but this is untrue, as will be seen in a later chapter. She states further on that she interviewed the "Coe brothers—George and Frank." Toward the end of the article she says: "Soon after Billy the Kid and the remaining possemen—or assassins, as you choose—had taken their departure, a single coffin was made from Dr. Blazer's lumber and Roberts and Brewer—duelists to the death—were laid in it, side by side."

In his own magazine, the *Frontier Times*, of February, 1950, J. Marvin Hunter makes the statement that Ash Upson finished writing *The Authentic Life of Billy, the Kid*, credited to Pat Garrett, in Uvalde, Texas. This book was published in 1882, and Upson did not go to Uvalde until 1889, seven years later. He died there October 6, 1894.

A few more citations will be sufficient to demonstrate the prevalence of wildly inaccurate accounts of Billy the Kid and his associates in magazines. Moreover, even in our supposedly enlightened age, the legends still persist. For example, there is Jeff Adams' account in *True West* (Vol. I, No. 2 [1953]). His story of the Kid's escape from the Lincoln jail uses dialog freely, and the Kid's winning poker hand—queens and treys—is described, although no one knew what he held except the Kid himself, and he never told. Indeed, it has never been proved that a card game was actually in progress when the Kid seized Bell's gun. This writer has the Kid stumbling over the threshold and "sprawling on the narrow platform at the top of the stairs" when Bell went through the door trying to get away from the Kid after he had grabbed his gun from its holster.

Seeing his chance, Bell plunged down the stairs, but his "chance in a million" failed as the Kid fired.

The Kid delayed his escape long enough to "kill the man he had come to hate during the bitter weeks of his imprisonment in this bare, bleak room." While in reality he had hated Olinger long before his imprisonment, there is a kernel of truth here, for Olinger did goad him unmercifully during his confinement. According to this version, Olinger went across the street to get a drink of whiskey, although actually he took some other prisoners to dinner.

While the Kid was searching the armory for a supply of weapons, the story continues, "he chuckled in sardonic amusement as he selected a fine new Winchester rifle." I ask you, who was there to know whether his amusement was sardonic or otherwise? Or if he chuckled at all? As he rode out of Lincoln, he again "rattled out his sardonic chuckle and turned his pony's head toward the distant mountain." This seems to be a favorite expression. When the author says, "the kid rode untroubled by any nagging fear for the future," he is treading the dangerous ground of expressing another's thoughts, something rarely known except to one's self. When an author creates a fictional character and makes him live and breathe, this is all to the good, but a poor device in writing of an actual man, especially when there is no evidence that he had such thoughts. One more detail—this writer has Garrett sitting in a chair beside Maxwell's bed when the Kid entered the room to his death; Garrett himself says he was sitting on Pete Maxwell's bed.

In *Arizona Highways* for February, 1954, there is an article by Edwin Corle entitled "Billy the Kid in Arizona." "Little is known," writes Mr. Corle, "about the early life of William Bonney, who was first called Billy the Kid about his seventeenth year, other than a few sparse facts." He then repeats the date and place of the Kid's birth and the story that he went to Coffeyville, Kansas, with his family "at the age of three or four"; that his father died there, and his mother then moved to Colorado, where she "married a man named William Antrim, and the family finally settled temporarily in Santa Fe, New Mexico."

Although he makes their stay in Santa Fe a temporary one, he says it was at this place that "Billy had his formative childhood years, and learned to read and write both Spanish and English." He then states that when the Kid was about ten, the family moved to Silver City and the Kid "learned how to deal monte and stack cards." The Kid would have been ten years old in 1869, several years before his family moved to Silver City.

"In Silver City," continues Corle, "some time in 1872 between his twelfth and thirteenth birthdays, Billy committed his first crime. Legendry likes to say that it was motivated by the defense of his mother, and possibly it was. Uglier rumors suggest that he and Jesse Evans, another wayward juvenile product of the frontier, killed a Chinese when the Celestial caught them stealing litchi nuts." He doesn't seem sure about either of these killings and admits that they were probably rumors, and he is wrong about the date, for we know that Billy had no trouble in Silver City until two or three years after his mother's death in 1874.

About his source, he writes: "Since Garrett knew the Kid personally, even intimately, from his eighteenth year to his death, there is no gain-saying the 'faithful' and 'interesting' commentary on the part of the book's publisher, and the book is the cornerstone upon which a whole superstructure of Billy the Kid literature has been built.

"Garrett, however, did not know Billy during the Kid's early days, and most of his information about the Kid's activities in Arizona stem from a man by the name of Marshall Ashmun Upson. This man, known generally as 'Ash' Upson, was a newspaper writer and editor and, coincidentally enough, boarded with Billy's mother in Silver City before Billy hit the outlaw trail, and was living in Garrett's house at the time Garrett killed the Kid. Thus, between the two of them, Garrett and Upson were able to supply as clear a picture of the Kid's life as could conceivably be put together."

Perhaps one of the greatest pitfalls in connection with the Kid is that too many people, like Mr. Corle, believe that Garrett's book tells the true story of the Kid's life. There is no doubt that the latter part of the book, after Garrett became sheriff, is fairly accurate, but Upson's account of the Kid's boyhood is completely untrustworthy. Although he was a newspaperman, Upson seems not to have read the newspapers; likewise, he seems to have learned nothing about the Kid's boyhood during the time he boarded at the Antrim home.

"Upson," continues Corle, "was able to report only from hearsay about Billy's life in Arizona, but he is certain that the Kid first entered the territory sometime in 1872." The records show that he did not go to Arizona until 1877. Corle admits that most of his "scanty facts" about the Kid's adventures in Arizona were gleaned from Garrett's and Otero's books.

"But the records," he adds, "have been embellished by remarks dropped by the Kid himself from time to time, and remembered by some of those who were his contemporaries. These help to fill in the blanks. If Billy the Kid rode into Arizona leaving one dead man behind him in Silver

City, he rode out of Arizona a year or two later leaving, as a minimum, three dead Indians and one dead soldier. Thus his record for murder began to gain momentum. Nevertheless, he left the territory virtually as unknown as when he arrived, and it was only in view of his later exploits that these lost years began to take on any significance."[1]

Otero followed Upson's account of the Kid's early years, though he criticized that book throughout his own, and Corle follows them both closely regarding the Kid's early escapades; but repetition cannot make these incidents any truer than they were when Upson invented a boyhood of sorts for the Kid out of whole cloth. Corle admits, when Upson quoted the Kid's thoughts regarding the Indians he intended robbing and murdering, "that these were Billy's very words is doubtful; but that they were approximately what he said is probable. More to the point is the fact that Billy and Alias rode off with the property of the three good Indians—made 'good' by Billy's six-shooter."

He has Billy kill five different men in Arizona, the last a Negro soldier, and says "This fifth killing of Billy's took place in 1873, or not later than 1874." Since the Kid did not go to Arizona until after his mother's death, this statement cannot be true. Of this killing, however, he writes further: "But the incident was serious enough to Billy's mind in 1873 to cause him to flee the scene. He was then not more than fifteen years old. He was still a boy and he was afraid of the consequences of his act. Killing a soldier of the United States Army was his greatest crime yet," but

[1] In the September, 1929, issue of *The Texas Monthly,* there appeared an article entitled "Billy, the Kid's Lost Years," written by myself, in which I tell something of the Kid's life in Arizona as it was told to me by Cyclone Denton, with whom he worked as a cowhand.

he is not sure whether this killing took place in Tucson, Fort Bowie, or Fort Grant.

In the September, 1954, issue of *True West* there appeared an article, "Buckshot Roberts, Fighting Man," by Eugene Pawley, which, according to all I have been able to discover about this incident, is entirely unreliable and confused.

"Just about every man in Lincoln County, except Buckshot Roberts," he writes, "lined up on one side or the other. Roberts said that he had no quarrel with either faction and would stay neutral." Evidently he failed to stay neutral long, for he was in the posse which murdered Tunstall. Billy the Kid knew that he was, and that is one reason he was on the lookout for him when their paths crossed at Blazer's Mill.

This writer says that the Kid sent word to Roberts that he had better line up with one side or the other and made dire threats about what he would do if he failed to join the Brewer side. I have dug into many books, newspapers, records, and other sources, but have never seen this statement elsewhere. Pawley also says that Roberts then put on all his artillery and rode to town, "not looking for trouble but ready for it if it came." When he got to town, three of Brewer's men stepped out of a saloon and opened fire on him. But "just as they fired, Roberts' horse reared and leaped sideways, thus saving his life. By the time the bronc settled down, Buckshot's .45 was out, spouting flame and lead. Two of the desperadoes went down, one stone dead, the other dying. The third was shot through the right arm; he dropped his gun and scurried for cover."

He portrays Roberts as a peace-loving man who, when he saw that he would have to get into the Lincoln County troubles, decided to sell his ranch and cattle and leave New

Mexico. "But before he could close this deal, however, a rider came quirting a foam-flecked horse up to the ranch house one afternoon. An old army pal of Roberts, Kitts by name, had been shot, badly wounded, up beyond Doc Blazer's sawmill. Brewer, Billy the Kid, and their men were due to arrive at Kitts' place any time to finish off the wounded man. Would Roberts come to his rescue?"

So Buckshot Roberts again buckled on his artillery and rode forth to battle. "But Buckshot Roberts never got to Kitts' place," Pawley relates. "As Roberts rode up to Blazer's Mill . . . a mob, paced by Dick Brewer, rode in from the opposite direction. Alongside Brewer rode Billy the Kid and behind were George and Frank Coe, Charlie Bowdre, Doc Middleton, Jake Scoggins, 'Dirty Steve' Stephens, and others to the number of thirteen." I think Mr. Pawley will find that Middleton's name was John, not "Doc."

And I think Mr. Pawley will find, if he searches the records, that Roberts went to Blazer's Mill to do some bounty hunting. After Brady and Hindman were killed, the Lincoln County commissioners held a special meeting to authorize a reward of $200 for each of the men connected with the slaying of the officers. News of this reward was interesting to Roberts, especially when it read "dead or alive."

One of New Mexico's most dependable historians, William A. Keleher, in his recent and splendid book *Violence in Lincoln County*, tells it this way: "On April 4, 1878, Roberts rode from his home to Lincoln, where he obtained official assurance and confirmation of the report he had heard in the mountains that the county had offered to pay $200 for the arrest of each of several men suspected of having killed Sheriff Brady and Deputy Hindman. Officers in Lincoln told him that Dick Brewer, Billy Bonney, and other suspects might be located in the vicinity of Blazer's Mill. Within a matter of hours, Roberts rode into Blazer's on a mule, a conspicuous figure in a country where there were many horses and only a few mules.

"Armed with rifle, pistol, and plenty of ammunition, it was only too apparent that Roberts was not on a mission of peace or an errand of mercy."

Although Pawley builds up his hero to high proportions, most of his account of the fight is wrong. Further, he says that after Brewer was killed, Billy the Kid took command, called his men together, and led them away, "the whole outfit soundly licked by a single little lead-thrower who didn't know when he was beaten and who had the heart to fight it out no matter what the odds."

Most of the truth about this battle came to light during the Dudley Court of Inquiry at Fort Stanton, where eye-witnesses testified to what happened.

In March of 1955, there was published in the little Gun Collectors' magazine, *Great Guns* (Vol. IV, No. 3), an article on Billy the Kid. It is one of a series entitled "Famous Gun Fighters I Knew," by Roy J. Scates. It merely repeats the well-known legends which have been handed down for years, including the killing of the man who insulted his mother, etc.

Another installment of this series (in Vol. IV, No. 4) concerns Pat Garrett, and in the course of the account the author says the Kid killed Bernstein "in cold blood" and repeats the fable of the Kid's killing Chisum's cowboys. "Garrett," he writes, "thrust the Kid in the old Lincoln County Courthouse where he was guarded day and night by deputy Olinger and deputy Bell. This measure was continued before, during, and after the Kid's trial and subsequent conviction and sentencing to death on the gallows."

A Fitting Death for Billy the Kid

Since the Kid was tried in Mesilla, he was not guarded in the Lincoln County Courthouse until after he was sentenced.

The April, 1956, issue of *Saga,* one of the many men's magazines found on the news stands, carried an article on Pat Garrett by Clair Huffaker, and once more fiction replaced fact. The account of the Carlyle killing, for example, is all wrong: "A posse led by J. W. Bell [an error] had closed in on the gang, and after a sizeable gun battle the outlaws had split up, some of them taking refuge in a nearby ranch house. Carrying a flag of truce, Pat's young blacksmith friend, Jim Carlyle, went to the ranch house and told Billy the place was surrounded and he had better surrender if he knew what was good for him. That kind of talk didn't sit well with the Kid and he refused to let Jim return to the posse, apparently intending to hold him as a hostage. At any rate after some wrangling back and forth, Carlyle suddenly decided to make a break for it, and jumped out of the window, taking the sash and pane with him. Billy must have had his eye on Jim all the time because he managed to whip his gun out quick enough to shoot the blacksmith in the back before he hit the ground."

There follows a fantastic tale about Charlie Bowdre's sending Pat word that he wanted to meet him and talk surrender, and when they met, Pat couldn't promise anything except to help get him released on bail. This incident never happened. Furthermore, there is a character named Brazil who briefed Garrett on the lay of the land and advised him. The author is also mistaken in saying that the Maxwell home was "a large one-room house" into which Garrett went and carried on a conversation with Pete Maxwell. His account of the killing of the Kid is also garbled.

Again, in the April, 1957, issue of *True West,* there is an

Hendry Brown

Blazer's Mill, in the Ruidoso country, where Buckshot
Roberts was killed.

Courtesy Ed Bartholomew
Rose Collection, Ruidoso, N. M.

Old county jail and courthouse at Lincoln, N. M., from
which Billy made his famous escape.

article entitled "Killer Kid," by Norman B. Wiltsey. No doubt Mr. Wiltsey made an honest effort to give a true history of Billy the Kid, but he failed to do the proper research and the whole article has an air of careless reporting. In telling of the blacksmith's insult to Mrs. Antrim and the later fight involving Ed Moulton, he calls Moulton "Andy" instead of Ed. It is notable that recent serious historians, those who have searched the records carefully, do not mention this fight, nor has any account of it been found in contemporary newspapers. It did not happen.

Mr. Wiltsey follows Upson in saying the Kid was born in New York, November 23, 1859. Here attention should be called again to the fact that no one has ever been able to document the birth date of the Kid, and some of the contemporary New Mexico newspapers emphatically state that this date is in error. It should be recalled, too, that in the early years of the Kid's life, when the fight with the blacksmith was supposed to have taken place, the kid did not go by the name of Billy Bonney, but was known in Silver City as Henry McCarty, Henry Antrim (after his stepfather), or Kid Antrim. All the records I have seen of this period refer to him under one of these names. He later took the name of Bonney of his own accord.

Wiltsey goes on to say that the Kid's father was William Bonney, and "Bill Junior" was three years old when his parents took him and his brother "Edward" to Coffeyville, Kansas, in 1862. In reality, his brother was named Joseph, not Edward, and the town of Coffeyville, as has been said repeatedly, was not in existence in 1862.

The author is also wrong about Mrs. McCarty's marriage to "Jack" Antrim, which he says took place in Denver. The place of the marriage was Santa Fe, and the groom's name was William Henry Harrison Antrim.

"After three years in Santa Fe," continues Mr. Wiltsey, "the Antrims moved to Silver City." According to records recently unearthed, the marriage took place March 1, 1873, and Mrs. Antrim died September 16, 1874; thus she was married only about eighteen months before her death, and most of this time was spent in Silver City.

The account goes on: "At noon on the 13th, Tunstall had set off for Lincoln accompanied by his foreman Dick Brewer, and Billy the Kid." According to the statement of Robert A. Widenmann, who was with the party, they started from the Tunstall ranch about eight o'clock in the morning on February 18, not noon of the thirteenth. Also in the party, besides Tunstall, Brewer, and the Kid, were Widenmann and John Middleton. The circumstances of the killing as given by Mr. Wiltsey are incorrect. He says that Billy Morton and Tom Hill both fired at the same time and killed Tunstall, but Widenmann related that "Jesse Evans shot him through the chest, which shot felled him to the ground. Morton then jumped off his horse, drew Tunstall's pistol from its holster, shot Tunstall through the head, shot Tunstall's horse in the head with the same pistol, returned the pistol to its holster, and then mashed Tunstall's skull with the butt of his [own] gun." They later swore that Tunstall fired first; hence the firing of his pistol to make it appear thus.

Much of the information in this article on the killing of Baker and Morton is wrong. The account of the fight at the McSween home contains much dialogue, and I am always doubtful about repeated conversation unless it can be substantiated by records or living witnesses. It is related that the Kid killed Beckwith after he himself had reached the wall, but Beckwith was killed earlier at the door of escape.

The author is also mistaken in saying that the Kid's gang went to the Mescalero Indian reservation to steal fresh horses, where they killed Joe Bernstein, a clerk, for, as he puts the words into the Kid's mouth, "not minding his own business." The facts about this killing were given in Chapter III above.

This writer is another who thinks George and Frank Coe were brothers, when in fact they were cousins. He names the Kid's lawyers in his trial at Mesilla "Ball" and Fountain, whereas the former was Bail, not Ball. He has the Kid yell at "old man Geiss [*sic*]" for a file after his killing of Bell and Olinger, but Gauss himself said he threw a little prospector's pick in to Billy, who succeeded in freeing one leg with it. Wiltsey continues to get proper names wrong when he calls Poe "Jack" instead of John. And he has Poe, in answer to the Kid's "*Quien es?*," say, "Put down that gun you locoed *peon!* What the hell's the matter with you?" I'm afraid Poe never uttered these words.

Also in 1957, in a magazine called *Showdown For Men,* there is an article entitled "Showdown at Fort Summer," by Edwin V. Burkholder. Surely the word "Summer" is a typographical error. Preceding the article itself is an editor's note several columns long in which are repeated the legends of Billy the Kid's birth, the move to Coffeyville, the killing of the blacksmith for insulting his mother, and other tales which have lately been found to be legends and nothing more.

Of the Carlyle killing, the author says: "The Kid wounded Greathouse, killed deputy Jim Carlyle, who had been foolish enough to act as an emissary with a white flag, and then the Kid and his men shot their way through the posse, leaving five of them dead." We know all this to be untrue, except the fact that Carlyle was killed. And we know that

Greathouse was not killed but was held by the attacking party.

In giving the account of the Kid's incarceration in the Lincoln courthouse, Mr. Burkholder says the two guards were Bob Olinger and "Ben" Bell. Nowhere else have I seen Bell's Christian name given as Ben.

"For two months," he writes, "the Kid was *chained to the wall*. At night Bell had to help him onto his cot and the iron balls on his legs forced him to sleep in an uncomfortable and cramped position. Bell protested against such cruelty. Ollinger laughed at his protests, taunted the Kid about how the noose would feel around his neck. As the day of the hanging approached, the workmen were busy building the scaffold and Ollinger moved the Kid close to the window where he could see everything."

When the Kid said he'd like to stretch his legs, the sympathetic Bell "unlocked the chains to the wall, took the iron balls off the Kid's ankles," and then proposed a game of cards. Then comes the old story that when the Kid dropped a card and Bell leaned over to pick it up for him, he snatched his gun from its holster. After the killing of Bell and Olinger, "Old Bill Goss [*sic*], the jail cook, was hugging the wall, his body trembling with terror." The Kid ordered him to cut the leg irons with an ax, and also the handcuffs, all of which he did. And so it goes to the end.

"The Secret Life of Billy the Kid," by Dave Markson, appeared in the *Male Magazine* of July, 1957, and it is surprising at this late date to find writers still giving the public such frivolous and unreliable accounts as fact. The author of this article certainly works his imagination overtime. He has Olinger hear a shot while eating in a restaurant across the street from the Lincoln jail. When he went to investigate, he saw, too late, that Billy the Kid "*stood on the roof* of the jail porch" with his manacles and leg irons on. Why should he climb to the roof when there was a long porch on the building? And how did he accomplish this feat with leg irons and handcuffs? As a matter of fact, the Kid did not even come out on the porch at this time, but killed Olinger from an upstairs window.

One of the spectators in the restaurant declared that he would go over and get a file for the Kid, and another said he "reckoned he might saddle him a horse, too."

"Across the way," writes the author, "the boy [Kid] disappeared, then returned once more before his hands and ankles were finally freed from the cuffs." Billy was not entirely freed of his leg irons before he left.

The Kid's life was a mystery which had grown with the years, says the author, "for of all the legends to come out of the American West, that of Billy Bonney, alias Billy the Kid, is the strangest. When he died at the age of 21 he had slain a man for every year of his life." Believe me, it is writers like him who make the Kid's life a strange one. They do nothing to correct misconceptions and continue not only to strengthen the old legends but to create new ones of their own.

This writer also gives a fantastic account of the fight at the McSween home. "It was pitch-black," he says. "Any time a shot was fired from within, a heavy volley answered, centered at the giveaway spot where the powder had flashed. This meant that none of those in the house could run and fire at the same time without being spotted, and if they didn't keep firing the men on the outside would quickly understand what was up. It was an impossible situation, and a murderous one—until the Kid set himself up as a decoy.

"He loaded six separate pistols, setting them at various

windows. Then sprinting from gun to gun, his boy's face gleaming in their flashings, he deliberately drew the outside fire to himself as the others tried to slip away."

Markson tells many fanciful stories about the Kid's love affairs and makes him quite a Casanova with the women of Spanish blood. On the night of his death, there is a passionate love scene with a fictional sweetheart called Celsa: They "came together fiercely. Her fingers were tearing at the shirt across his shoulders as he drew her toward the bed. It was an hour later that they shot him."

Each and every year there are more and more ridiculous tales written about Billy the Kid. It seems as if writers get more careless as time passes, or perhaps they are interested only in the profit to be gained and care little for truth or history. One of the last examples I found before this book went to press is in *Man's Action* magazine of July, 1958. In an article entitled "The Man Who Killed Billy the Kid," by Leo O. Miller, I find some of the most ridiculous statements yet encountered in print. He opens his story in a saloon in Capitan, New Mexico, where two men are drinking beer. One is Billy the Kid, whom he describes as "a young man with sandy-red hair. His eyes were blue but suggested evil; his nose was pugged, face chubby and flushed, accentuating the ugly pock-marks, and his mouth was marred slightly from yellow-stained bucked teeth. His name was William H. Bonney, alias Billy the Kid."

The friend with whom Billy was drinking beer was Pete Maxwell, and they were carrying on quite a conversation. Pete was trying to get the Kid to leave the country after he had killed Bell and Olinger, but the Kid was arguing against going. Of Maxwell, the writer says: "He hated this ugly young killer, but was afraid to draw on him. Several had tried already, and they were buried. No, he would play it smart and leave before the Kid's sudden temper exploded and gunplay started. Besides, while he [the Kid] was playing up to the Spanish bar-maid, Pete just might be able to let someone know that Billy was in town and bunking in his shack at the edge of town. And with that thought in mind, he departed and left Billy in the saloon.

"Just who Pete told and how they got the word to Pat Garrett, is uncertain. But the real reason that Pete Maxwell feared Billy so much, even hated him, was because of a robbery he had helped the Kid pull off just prior to the latter's capture at Stinking Springs."

In reality, Maxwell was not the Kid's enemy but a friend, and, as I have said repeatedly, the Kid was not a robber. Moreover, Maxwell was never accused of such law breaking. The author also errs in stating that when Pete ran into the Kid outside of Tucumcari shortly before the beer episode at Capitan, he "had heard of the Kid, [but] *he had never seen him,* and never dreamed that this dirty, sweating young man could be the cold-blooded killer."

In another paragraph the author declares that "Billy's friendship with Pete is known to many an old-timer in New Mexico," although he has just said that Pete had never seen him. Why Maxwell helped Billy hold up an express office in Vaughn and escape with him, is not made clear. The hold-up netted them $500, hardly worth the outright boldness of their daylight attack. Pete, however, was not known in Vaughn, and though seen by the express company's agent that day, went unidentified as the accomplice of the Kid. The Kid held this robbery over Pete's head to force his aid.

This author has the Kid bring a "shapely" Spanish girl to Maxwell's room and leave her there while he went to a saloon for some tequila. While he was gone, Pat Garrett arrived and made Maxwell consent to help him carry out a plan to kill the Kid. "Pete nodded his assent. Pat outlined his plans and while the señorita lay on the bed, posed seductively, inwardly scared out of her wits, *both* Pat and Pete hid *behind* the bed. It was getting dark outside now and was thus accentuated inside the shack. Only the low breathing of the three occupants mingled and betrayed their presence."

When the Kid came into the room with his arms loaded with bottles of tequila, "Pat and Pete both raised up on their knees, aiming at the vague figure in the darkness. The girl silently slid off the bed to the dirt floor near them, and lay flat."

" 'Billy!' Pat's voice thundered in the room. Before he could say more, Billy's startled grunt was drowned out by the roar of two six guns. Billy fell, whined a moment, then was silent."

The author of this fantastic tale claims that the Kid was killed in Pete Maxwell's shack in Capitan, not Fort Sumner, and that his body was later taken to the fort for burial. "To this day," he writes, "state records offer proof that Pete was a hero and assistant to Pat Garrett—not a former friend, hold-up man and partner of the Kid! And the Spanish prostitute and heroine—right in the line of fire until the last moment—is not even known!" Indeed she is not except in the imagination of the writer.

In support of my contention that magazines will publish anything written about Billy the Kid, no matter how unreliable, the very next month (August, 1958) there appeared in *Real West Magazine* an article entitled "The Cattle Baron Who Wouldn't Fight," by Carelton Mays. He starts his story off with the killing of Tunstall:

"The rider came to a sharp turn on the mountain trail

that led down into the Bonita Canyon in Lincoln County, New Mexico. It was late in the afternoon of February 13, 1878. The rider saw the horsemen coming toward him. He stopped his horse, and watched them with a pleasant smile.

"He was a tall man, with the marks of education in his gracious manner and face. When the twenty horsemen got near him, he exclaimed with an English accent, 'By Jove, boys, you up to some prank?'

"His answer was a shot from a rifle in one of the men's hands. He lurched forward, fell across the horn of his saddle and then tumbled to the ground. The horsemen surrounded the body. One of them jumped off his horse, placed the rifle against the head of the man, and pulled the trigger. The bullet tore most of the top of his head away.

"The other horsemen dismounted. They were drunk, wild with the lust of killing. *They danced around the body,* while one of them, a Mexican, hammered the head with a jagged rock. A rifle cracked and the horse of the murdered victim went down."

This victim was, as he says, J. H. Tunstall. (Later in the article he calls him "Jim," but his name was John.) There were not twenty men in the posse, as he says. He states that during this year "Lincoln was a bawdy, wide open town of the old West, where six guns roared day and night and men died without anybody giving it a second thought," but I'm afraid the town was not quite so callous as that.

He tells us further that Boots Angeleo, Jim Coons, and Red Loomis were arrested for stealing Chisum's cattle and taken to Fort Stanton, where they were tried and convicted, but I find no mention of such names anywhere and they certainly do not appear in the records of Fort Stanton. He writes: "The night after the three cattle thieves had been taken to prison, John Riley, Murphy's chief hench-

man, rode to the McSween home. Riley didn't find Mc-
Sween and his wife alone. They were giving a small party
for five men. The men gave Riley the bum's rush out of
the house. As they did a note book fell from Riley's pocket."

This notebook, revealing the names of Murphy's rustlers,
the cattle he had stolen, and the prices received, *was* lost
by Riley, but not under such circumstances. It was lost
when he went to McSween's right after Tunstall's funeral
to try to convince Tunstall's friends that he had nothing
to do with the murder, emptying his pockets to show them
he was unarmed. It was then that he lost the notebook.

In one place Mays says that the town and county took
sides after the killing of Tunstall and "no one was neutral."
Yet farther on he has Roberts claim to be neutral. Comment: being a member of the posse that killed Tunstall
was certainly a strange way to show neutrality. The author
does not mention that the battle between Roberts and
Brewer's force took place at Blazer's Mill, but says the posse
stopped to eat near the Mescalero Indian reservation. Here
is his account of the battle:

"Frank Coe rode out to meet Roberts, told him they had
a warrant for his arrest. Roberts said, 'The hell you're
aresting [*sic*] me. I ain't dying like Morton and Baker. I
know them skunks, Billy the Kid and Charlie Broddie [*sic*].

"The battle started. Old Bill fell off his horse with a bullet through his side. He stood up weakly, his six gun roaring. Jim Middleton went down with a bullet through his
chest. Another bullet from Bill's guns blew off the right
hand of George Coe."

In these brief paragraphs we find several errors. Roberts'
name was not Bill, but Andrew, and he did his shooting in
this battle with a Winchester, not a six-gun; Middleton's

name was not Jim, but John, and Coe's hand was not blown off, only a thumb and trigger finger.

"Jimmy Frost, one of old Bill's cowboys, came riding to his rescue. A bullet knocked him off his horse. He huddled close to old Bill, whose left hand rested on his head. Another bullet hit old Bill. He swayed but kept on his feet. His six gun jumped in his right hand. The bullet got Dick Brewer between the eyes, blowing most of his head off. A fourth member of the posse lunged forward as old Bill fired.

"Old Bill stood there, looking over the carnage. The ground around him had the appearance of Custer's massacre. A third bullet hit old Bill and he went down. He never got up. Five minutes later he was dead."

This whole account is erroneous. There is no record of a Jimmy Frost's having taken part in this fight, and Roberts did not stand where he had first been wounded and absorb that much lead; we know that most of his fighting was from a building where Doc Blazer slept. Here he doubled up a mattress from the bed, rested his Winchester on the window sill, and did some damaging shooting.

Earlier Mays is wrong about the circumstances of the killing of Morton and Baker, saying that after their horses had been shot from under them, they sought shelter in a dugout where they held off the Kid's posse for two days, or until they were weak from hunger and thirst, before they hoisted the white flag.

He writes that Sheriff Brady formed a posse to get the Kid, the members of which went to Murphy's saloon to have a round of drinks before starting out. "The sheriff and his men walked out of the saloon. They marched to the McSween home. Nobody was there. They went to the McSween store. Only a few Mexicans were lounging on the porch. The posse continued down the road, got fifty yards beyond the McSween's store. They were talking and laughing about the Kid. They didn't see six heads slowly rise above an adobe wall.

"The crack of rifles broke the stillness. The sheriff grabbed his throat, fell face downward to the ground. Deputy George Hindman and Dad Peppin dashed for a small house across the road. Hindman went down with a bullet through his back. The other members of the posse were *fleeing in every direction.*

"Billy the Kid and six of his gunmen walked out from behind the adobe wall, sauntered casually down the street for the McSween home."

Again here are misstatements of facts, on and on *ad nauseam.* In the first place there was no posse, only Sheriff Brady and George Hindman, and, a little way behind them, Billy Matthews, Jack Long, and George Peppin. They were not after the Kid, but were going to the courthouse to change a notice of the next session of court.

Of the fight at the McSween home, this author writes: "The flames burst high. The McSween house was afire. McSween and his men rushed inside, trying to stop the flames. They were not successful, but they were able to slow down the flames, if not to extinguish them. The fire from the Murphy men poured into the house. Mrs. McSween's piano was in the back bedroom. It was a baby grand, her prize possession. It was pushed into the front room, away from the flames. Bullets whizzed over the top, as she sat down and played. There was a crash as one wall fell in. She continued to play. A bullet cut down a man standing near her." Of course, this is ridiculous.

Mays also has many more men killed in this battle than actually were; and of McSween's death he writes: "Orange flames leaped out from the darkness. He went down on one knee. Other flames were coming at him. His head snapped back as a bullet him [*sic*] him between the eyes. He slumped forward, his Bible under his lifeless body." And when Murphy's men saw this happen, they "let out a demoniac chorus of screaming shouts. They fired at the lifeless body of McSween. Bullets thudded into the body. It jumped and jerked weirdly." All this is imagination.

Mays says that Beckwith killed McSween and the Kid then killed Beckwith. The facts are that McSween called out his name and said he would surrender to an officer. Beckwith stepped forward, saying that he was a deputy and would accept his surrender. When Beckwith stepped into the light, some of McSween's men shot him, although Mays reports that "Bob Beckwith, leader of the Murphy men, yelled, 'I got him. . . . I killed the old bastard,' " speaking of McSween, of course.

After the Kid had escaped and the fighting ceased, this author has the Murphy men kicking and mauling the body of McSween, "that strange Christ-like character, the man who read his Bible and yet innocently fomented a war to be fought by murderers and desperadoes, a Sir Gallahad who had a child-like understanding of men and the brutal realities of life.

"The celebration that night was a bacchanalian carousal. Guitars, banjos and fiddles supplied the music. The revelers danced and twisted and yelled drunkenly around the dead. The dying flames of the McSween house cast a reddish glow over the white men gyrating like savages. Their uncouth antics, their horseplay and loud buffoonery floated afar through the night air. In the early hours of the morning the drunken revelers stopped."

Nothing could be farther from the truth, yet such "history" continues to be handed down. Even one illustration of this article is wrongly titled: it shows a man and woman on horseback with the legend, "Daughter of John Chisum at rodeo many years after end of cattle war. She was a child when six guns roared and men died to save Chisum." It is a picture of Sally Chisum, who was a niece of John, who never married and as far as we know never had a daughter. Sally was a young lady in her late teens during the Lincoln County War.

The June, 1959, issue of *Double-Action Western* contained an article entitled *"The Real Billy-the-Kid,"* by Carl Breihan, which follows the common legends created by Upson. He has the Kid born a son of William H. and Kathleen Bonney and says, "From all available records it appears that he was the only child," although it is fairly common knowledge that he had a younger brother.

This author also has the family moving to Coffeyville, Kansas, in 1862 in spite of the fact that there was no town there at that date. Shortly afterward the father died and "Mrs. Bonney found that it was next to impossible for her to support herself and her small son," so she married a man named Antrim.

"The magic call to Silver City, New Mexico," he writes, "also beckoned to the Antrims, and there they traveled from Coffeyville. Billy was now twelve years old; and it was here he killed his first man." He leaves the impression that Billy's mother married Antrim in Coffeyville and that they went directly from there to Silver City.

He repeats that old legend about the blacksmith's insulting the Kid's mother and Billy's later stabbing him with a knife. He then ran home to bid his mother farewell and left, and "that was the last time mother and son saw each other." The writer says he "has been unable to locate any record giving subsequent events in the life of Mrs. Antrim, but knows she died in Silver City." He follows the legends created by Upson in having the Kid go to Mexico, rescue the wagon train, and deliver his friend Segura from a Texas jail.

"Most people," he writes, "who came in personal contact with Bonney considered him the fastest living man on the draw," and admits that this "was never contested by anyone so far as available records show." There is no record of the Kid's having to prove his speed on the draw.

He states that Morton and Baker "were both killed by Billy the Kid." In writing of the fight at the McSween home, he says that "Colonel Dudley at Fort Stanton *was summoned by Mrs. Mills.*"

He is also mistaken when he says the Kid met Governor Wallace for a conference "at the Ellis House." He also has Carlyle "shot through the body" by the Kid, and shot again as he was "crawling away in the snow." He uses the card-game legend in the killing of Bell. On the night the Kid was killed, the author has him *stumble* over John Poe on the porch of the Maxwell home, and says Pat Garrett was sitting in a chair near Maxwell's bed when he shot the Kid. Although this is a fairly long article, most of the incidents are glazed over, all of them following the common legends which of late years have been disproved.

5. The Old-Timer Thinks He Remembers

ONE OF THE MOST PROLIFIC sources of misinformation is the old-timer who writes his memoirs. Rarely is he a writer to begin with, and seldom does he decide to write a book before he is in his dotage. He then depends upon a faulty memory, hearsay, or the tall tales he has heard around the campfire. If he places his completed effort in the hands of an editor, the latter is frequently utterly ignorant of the West, its language, and its history, and like the average public, usually thinks the author's statements must be true because he is writing about his own experiences.

It was when old-timers began to tell what they remembered, or thought they remembered, that responsible people began to believe the garbled accounts. Perhaps some naïve persons had taken the dime novels for truth, but the majority of people knew that they were written for entertainment only and looked on them with healthy skepticism. But why shouldn't they accept what a man had to say about his own life and times and believe the stories he told about a popular outlaw whom he had known, or claimed to have known, personally?

When one knows the facts about a subject, it is a great shock to his belief in the integrity of his fellow man to read some of the preposterous accounts written by these men "who were there"—who were acquainted with historic or notorious persons and events, and who should have known better than to make some of the statements they did unless they were simply counting upon the reader's ignorance to let them off without challenge. It is disappointing to discover that the men who help make history often cannot record it accurately. Perhaps the most charitable view is that most of them are elderly, their minds are hazy, and their memory of what they did and what they heard as rumor or conjecture is so mixed that they really do not know when they depart from truth. Characteristically, they are careless with facts; they spell the names of people and places by ear; and dates have little significance for them. To demonstrate my point, I will cite a number of examples from the writings of these old men, largely in their own words, and let the reader judge for himself.

Without date of publication, some years ago there was printed a little book by J. L. Hill entitled *The End of the Cattle Trail.* The author did very well as long as he stuck to his experiences as a cowboy on the trail, but when he got on the subject of outlaws like Billy the Kid, he quickly convinced me he did not know what he was writing about. For example, he writes (pp. 43–44): "Billy the Kid, one of the most dangerous outlaws that ever harassed the border, stole one thousand or fifteen hundred LX cattle, drove them over the Goodnight Trail to New Mexico and disposed of them to old Chisholm [*sic*], owner of the Lightning Rod brand [usually called the Long Rail]. The Kid was the hired gun man of Chisholm during the famous Lincoln County War. This war *originated between the sheep men and the cattle men.* It seems the cattle men had the right to the range by priority, the sheep men were determined to graze their sheep over the ranges of the cattle man, and as cattle will not graze where sheep are kept for any length of time, the war was declared." Of course this statement is not true since the war was between the Chisum-McSween faction and the Murphy-Dolan faction, neither of which were sheepmen.

"Chisholm with his gang of rustlers carried it to war," he continues. "The first man the Kid killed at the request of Chisholm was a Black Smith, whom the Kid had nothing against but Chisholm had some little trouble with and wanted him out of the way. . . . The Kid was said to be a little weak minded, for that reason, he was feared. He would not wait for cause to murder, he murdered without cause. He was killed at the Maxwell ranch, New Mexico, by Pat Garrett, then sheriff of Lincoln County. The Kid was a friend of the Maxwells or some of the boys at the ranch. It was planned, or made known to Garrett that Billy would stay there at the ranch on a certain night and would sleep with one of the boys. After dark Garrett, with two deputies, went to the ranch. They found that the Kid had not arrived. The deputies lay down flat on the ground a little way from the trail that led to the house. Garrett went in and *got in bed with the boy* the Kid was supposed to sleep with, after everything was still and quiet the boy outlaw came. He saw through the dim starlight some un-usual object lying on the ground near the trail. He entered the *cabin* quickly and as he approached the bed in the dark-ness asked in the language of the Mexican of the man in bed, what it was out there on the ground? As he was then near the bed that gave Garrett his chance to locate him. He raised his six-shooter and fired, the bullet pierced the heart of the hunted kid outlaw, [and] he dropped dead in his tracks. Thus ended the wild life of the most dreaded kid outlaw that ever terrorized the border lands of the West."

It is noticeable in all the passages I quote from their

books that these old-timers had heard versions of the Kid's life and death, of the "war," and of various other events, but with age dimming their memories, they did not recall clearly just what they had heard about these events in their younger days. Mr. Hill, for example, here remembers that the Kid was an outlaw, that there was a war, that Garrett had some deputies with him when he went to Maxwell's house, and that Garrett shot the Kid. Of other than these facts he was not sure, and so his account, like most of these old-timers' memoirs is filled with half-truths.

Another little book published without date was written by an old man named J. M. Parker and called *An Aged Wanderer*. Mr. Parker wrote this book in his late years, after he was more or less crippled by paralysis, and sold copies of it for a livelihood as he wandered over the country. Perhaps Billy the Kid was a favorite subject of conversation and here was a chance to arouse interest by telling the people that he was a personal friend of the Kid and thus sell his books and make himself a person of importance. Of course, I am conjecturing here, but judging from the little he seems to know of the Kid, even as a personal friend, this could be what happened.

He gives us this astonishing information: "I had reached my nineteenth year and in the meantime I had formed the acquaintance of 'Billie the Kid.' . . . He and I were great friends so I decided to go with him to Lincoln County, New Mexico, and help him have a good time. Right here I will say that since I have become older and learned the way of righteousness more perfectly, this was a sad mistake when I decided to join Billie the Kid in his wild, reckless life. He was an outlaw of the first order, and had he not been killed, there is no telling what he would have led me into. At that time Billie was in a great deal of trouble; that is, he was on the dodge. As for trouble nothing ever seemed to bother him, and I tell you, my good reader, that boy was as brave a man as ever lived or died, and as good a man in a sense, although he killed many a man. But the poor boy was driven to his meanness to begin with. He would not stand by and see anyone mistreated if he could help it. The first man he killed was his step father because he was abusing his mother. The next one he killed was a blacksmith. Billie thought more of his horse than he did of life itself, and when the blacksmith was shoeing Bill's horse, he got mad and hit the horse with a hammer. Billie asked him not to hit the horse again and the man asked him who was shoeing the horse. Bill said, 'That's all right, but don't strike him any more.' The blacksmith hit the horse again and Billie shot him dead and got on his horse, and then rode away with only one shoe on his horse, and then made his escape. There was a strong lookout for him, but all in vain. Before we reached Lincoln County, Billie and I had gotten in with some more of his friends, making seven in number, and the officers got after us and we went into a house on the banks of the Penasque [Penasco] river and some forty armed men surrounded the house trying to capture the Kid. We entered the house about 3 o'clock in the afternoon and the men tried to get Billie to give up, but he told them he would never give up as long as he lived. They finally told him they would burn the house, and Billie told them to burn and be d——d. So they set fire to the house and Billie played the piano that was in it *and I danced to the music.* There were seven of us in the house at the start, but five of them gave up when the house got too hot for them. Billie and I stayed until it got too hot for us and then he said, 'Follow me' and I did so.

"As he opened the door a man was standing just outside.

Bill killed him and both of us reached Penasque river and made our escape. About forty shots were fired but no one of them struck either of us. All Bill said was 'Roe stick to me, old boy, and you'll never get hurt.' We traveled all night, but little did we care. The only thing I hated was that the horses had to be left, but we soon got them. Little did the people know when, on the next night, Billie got back to his old stomping ground, and before daylight had secured our horses and left with them for he would have died for his horse and I thought lots of mine. So before day Billie came riding, bringin' my horse. . . . So we stopped for a couple of days and then proceeded on our journey to Lincoln County and there spent the remainder of the summer. Along about September Billie became involved in more trouble and we had to scamper to the far West and remained in the Rocky Mountains until the spring of 1872, after which Billie the Kid and myself started for Lincoln County, New Mexico. [According to the Kid's supposed birth date, he would have been thirteen in 1872]. Down in Lincoln County Bill found a pretty Mexican girl whom he would have married if he had lived long enough. So this is the way it all came about. After our return from the Rockies we had been there for some time when one afternoon several of us boys were out in front of a cabin where some of them stayed, shooting at a mark that we had set up. Someone thought of it being Sunday, so Billie said to me, 'Let's go to see our girls, if it is Sunday.' So we quit shooting and were soon on our way to see two Mexican girls who lived some miles away. When we reached the house we found that the girl's father had gone and left an old Mexican man there to see that Billie did not come to see his girls. When we went upon the gallery the man would not speak, but threw himself before the closed door to prevent us from entering. The conduct of this one was the death penalty. Bill shot him and dragged him off the gallery to die. While he was doing this I went into the house and found the girls much frightened. I sat down on a bench by Billie. The other girl was standing by the window watching the Mexican die. When Billie came in neither of the girls would talk to him although they were friendly toward me. The girls were no longer angry at Billie, and Billie's bravery or daringness at last caused his death.

"While the girls knew nothing of it, their father had arranged with Pat Garrett, *the drunken sheriff*, to kill Billie, so Garrett watched his chance and *killed him while he slept*. This ended the life of a boy I loved like a brother, although he killed twenty-one white men, and he never kept any account of the Indians, Mexicans and Negroes he killed. There was a reward offered for him dead or alive of $500 at the time of his death, so it was no wonder everybody was on the lookout for him."

John J. Callison, an old-timer with whom I often corresponded before his death, wrote a book called *Bill Jones of Paradise Valley, Oklahoma, and the Great Southwest.* Like so many of the old westerners, he had something to say about Billy the Kid, and, like most of them, too, he had the majority of his facts garbled. Mr. Callison claims to have worked as a cowboy on a ranch which he at first thought was owned by Dave Pool, an old member of the James gang, but which he subsequently discovered was really the property of the James and the Younger brothers. When the James brothers came to visit the ranch, they found out that Billy the Kid was stealing their cattle. They trailed the Kid's gang and had quite a battle, only the Kid and one other rustler getting away.

"Although Billy the Kid escaped our clutches," writes

Mr. Callison, "he did not live to a ripe old age. His ambitious career was nipped in the bud some time after this by an unromantic sheriff, Pat Garrett, of *Las Cruces*, N. M., who was afterward shot to death by a kid less than twenty years old. The sheriff had sent word to Billy that the world was too small to hold both of them, and that one or the other would have to get off. . . .

"There is no telling to what heights of eminence Billy the Kid might have reached had his life been spared. He was only *twenty-three* when he died. . . . Committing his first murder at fourteen, he had *twenty-three* killings to his credit—an average of one a year for his busy life."

No matter how old or young various writers say the Kid was when his life was ended, they invariably credit him with killing a man for each year of that life. I can recall but one or two exceptions.

Another example of the careless writing of these old-timers is the autobiography of Nat Love, a Negro who claimed he was known as Deadwood Dick. In *The Life and Adventures of Nat Love*, the author says he first met Billy the Kid "in Antonshico [Anton Chico], New Mexico, in a saloon, when he asked me to drink with him, that was in 1877." The Kid "was hired by John Chisholm [*sic*] to rustle cattle for him. Chisholm agreed to pay the Kid so much per head for all the cattle the Kid rustled. When the time came for settlement, Chisholm failed to settle right or to the Kid's satisfaction, then the Kid told Chisholm he would give him one day to make up his mind to settle right, but before the Kid could see Chisholm again, Chisholm left the country going east where his brother lived. The Kid then swore vengeance, and said he would take his revenge out on Chisholm's men, and he at once began killing all the employ[ees] of John Chisholm. He would ride up to a bunch of cowboys and enquire if they worked for Chisholm. If they replied in the affirmative, he would shoot them dead on the spot.

Love was coming back to Silver City from Holbrook, Arizona, with Billy and some companions in 1880. "The Kid," he writes, "showed me a little log cabin where he said he was born. I went in the cabin with him, and he showed me how it was arranged when he lived there, showing me where the bed sat and the stove and the table. ... He told me he was born and raised in Silver City, New Mexico, which is near the Moggocillion [Mogollon] Mountains, and at that time the Kid was badly wanted by the sheriffs of several counties for numerous murders committed by him mostly of John Chisholm's men in Texas and New Mexico."

Love also has Garrett place the prisoners he captured at Stinking Springs in a boxcar at Las Vegas when the mob was trying to get at them; and, like many others, he repeats Judge Bristol's sentence and the Kid's mocking reply.

Another old-timer who claims to have taken part in the Lincoln County War and knew the Kid thinks he remembers a lot about him and has written it down in his book, *History of the Chisum War; or, Life of Ike Fridge.* Just *how* he remembers is illustrated by the following excerpts:

"Billy the Kid, one of the most noted and among the most dangerous of all New Mexico outlaws, joined with the rustlers in a crusade against our ranch [Fridge was working for Chisum]. They organized and began a series of well planned cattle raids.

"The Kid's career of crime started when he was quite young, and he literally grew up to kill—and to be killed. He was sixteen when his faher died. Billy was a great lover of his mother but when she married again he began to drift.

He bought the best horse that could be found, and secured the very best in firearms that existed in that day. [He does not explain how such a young lad managed to secure these expensive luxuries.] Long rides over the country alone followed and his mother talked to him time and again in an effort to settle him down but all to no avail.

"Billy went into a Mexican sheep herder's camp one day and found it deserted at the time. It was the custom of the times to make yourself at home if in need of food or shelter, whether the owner was at home or not. In keeping with that custom the Kid began the preparation of a meal. Just as he had it ready to eat the Mexican came in and began to abuse him. The Mex ran at Billy with a knife, but was stopped by a bullet from the Kid's gun.

"This was the first man Billy had ever killed, and though he went home and was not suspected of having killed the Mex, he was put on the war path. His murderous career was definitely begun and though the first killing was probably justifiable, and in self defense, others followed that were not.

"Soon after this incident the Kid saw four prospectors in the mountains. They had good horses and Billy thought they had plenty of money. He laid a plan to kill them. Stealing into their camp one night while they were asleep, he brutally killed the four of them. He took what money they had and hid the horses in the mountains.

"The Kid then returned home but his frequent absences and roaming disposition attracted attention and the cloud of suspicion settled upon him. His mother's home was surrounded at night and the Kid demanded. Instead of surrendering, he fixed up a kind of dummy and put it in the doorway. Firing a few shots from near the dummy to attract the officers' attention in that direction, he whirled and ran out the back door. However, he was discovered and fired upon as he ran, receiving two bad wounds. The faithful mother made trips to his mountain rendezvous daily and nursed her outlaw son back to health. There could be no more deceiving the public. The die was cast. So as soon as he could ride, 'Billie the Kid,' as he was ever afterward known, took the trail. Hiding out in Colorado for awhile, then boldly returning to his old haunts, he joined hands with the cattle rustlers of the district, where his skill with firearms and his reckless daring won him the leadership.

"A period of raiding followed that was never equaled and frequently United States troops had to take a part to defend the ranchers and their property."

Farther along he writes: "*A United States marshal*, Pat Garrett, was sent to help quiet the outlaws and stop cattle rustling. He soon decided that the best way to break the backbone of the gang was to get the leader.

"After several battles with 'Billie the Kid's' gang and the death of some of his most prominent fighting men, Billie was finally trapped and captured, but after being sentenced to hang he killed two of his jailers and made his escape. Everyone knew then he would never be taken alive as his deeds were so bloody and the hanging sentence was over his head. He could expect nothing except to die if he should be captured, and his guns had carried him through so many tight places that if he should be cornered no other thought would even enter his mind except to fight his way out or die trying.

"It was he that Pat Garrett intended to get as the leader of the bunch of lawbreakers. So many were the deeds of daring and of cruelty that had been accredited to Billie that everyone figured peace would reign if he were eliminated. Still in some sections he was admired for his bravery and daring exploits and he had the sympathy of the ranchers. These ranchers, of course, were the ones who had not suffered from the rustler raids, and who shielded the Kid for the protection of their herds as much as anything else.

"An outlaw never gets so bad but that a girl cannot enter his life and win his affections. Billie, though a hardened criminal, was a flashy knight of the saddle, and went strong for showy garb of the Mexican Caballero type. This gave him the idea that the ladies should all be attracted to him. Being a frequent visitor at the Maxwell ranch, he became deeply in love with a señorita there.

"His love was not returned however, and it was through this girl that the U. S. marshal laid his plans to get the outlaw into his meshes. It was next to impossible to locate him out on the range, and harder still, to get into a position to kill or capture him there. Garrett went to the Maxwell ranch and holed up out of sight of all comers so that no word of his presence would be conveyed to the Kid by his friends. *After a period of patient waiting* he was rewarded by a signal from the girl that the outlaw *was in her parlor.* Billie had pulled off his boots and made a silent entry into the house.

"The marshall and Maxwell were in an adjoining room. Billie heard them talking and asked the girl who they were. She told him that it was only Maxwell and a friend of his. Soon after the girl had let them know by a pre-arranged signal who her visitor was, Maxwell got up from his chair and left the house. He purposely made quite a bit of noise as he was leaving to make the Kid believe he was the visitor and was quitting the place. The girl then told the outlaw that Maxwell's friend had left. Billie, thinking it was Maxwell who had remained in the room, started in to talk to him.

113

"As he came through the door Pat Garrett had him covered. Just as soon as the Kid discovered the marshal he went for his guns. But Garrett had only to pull the trigger and the most dangerous outlaw and desperado ever on the western Texas and New Mexico ranges was no more. He fell to the floor dead as the man of the law had done a good job.

" 'Billie the Kid' had gone the route of so many criminals. He had fallen for a woman and given the officers the clew that led to his destruction. The marshal asked the government for troops to aid in running down the rest of the bunch and when the U. S. soldiers interfered the outlaws were without a leader."

It is useless for me to point out the absurdity of Fridge's statements. We know that Garrett was not a United States marshal and that he did not call for the aid of soldiers. We know that the circumstances of the Kid's killing were not as he related them. All in all, it appears that Fridge was exercising a well-developed imagination in many of his other assertions as well.

In 1926, John Lord recorded his memoirs in a book he called *Frontier Dust*. The full import of his fantastic tale can be gained only through examination of a whole chapter, which shows how muddled some old-timers can get, even when they are supposed to be telling their own experiences.

"I first saw Billy the Kid (William H. Bonney)," he writes, "as a small boy, playing around the streets in his step-father's harness shop in Silver City, New Mexico." [His stepfather was a miner, not a harness maker.] "Later I saw him as a cowboy working for John Chisholm [*sic*]. He was then sixteen or seventeen years old, a tall, good looking, athletic chap, an expert rider and roper, and a fine shot with a six-shooter.

The Old-Timer Thinks He Remembers

"I was holding a trail herd of cattle on the south side of the Arkansas River where the town of Rocky Ford now stands. I was waiting for the water to go down so I could cross without danger of quicksands. John Chisholm, one of *Texas'* biggest cattle raisers, was holding a herd for sale twelve miles up the river. One evening Chisholm's foreman came to my camp and wanted some help in delivering thirty-six hundred head of cattle to some buyers. Our cattle were glad to eat, drink and rest, so we had little to do. I took five men and the necessary saddle horses and went to help. When I got to Chisholm's camp I was introduced to two gentlemen, the Thompson brothers. They appeared to be men of good manners, polite and sociable, but not talkative. I soon discovered that they were not experienced cattlemen. I also found that they were experts with the six-shooter as well as good horsemen. Every evening after supper the boys would engage in a little pistol practice which consisted of putting a tomato can on the ground, stepping off twenty steps, and with a forty-five in each hand keeping the cans jumping. They also shot a hat thrown in the air. There is where I saw Billy the Kid do some fancy shooting. The Thompson brothers were simply artists. They afterwards *turned out to be Frank and Jesse James.* Billy the Kid was a very likable boy, with little to say, but a willing, pleasant and reliable worker.

"The next summer Billy was still working for Chisholm. He and the camp cook got into a row. The cook had a frying pan on the fire with a lot of grease in it. He grabbed it and either struck or threw it at Billy and some of the grease burned the Kid severely. Billy didn't do a thing but jerk out his pistol and kill the cook—get on his horse and rode away, an outlaw.

"Officers and posse men chased him around for nearly

a year and finally captured him. They had him in jail for a few days when he smashed the jailer on the top of the head with the handcuffs, knocked him senseless, took his pistol and cartridge belt and keys, made the jailer's wife get a file; then he dragged the jailer into an empty cell, made his wife go in with him, locked them up, went to the living room, got something to eat and all the cartridges the jailer had; then made a Mexican prisoner file the handcuffs off; then he walked out, locked the door behind him and put the keys in his pocket. Court was in session and plenty of good horses, with saddles on, were tied everywhere. He took the best looking horse he could see. Everyone was at the courthouse and Billy rode out of town. You can rest assured that there was no grass growing under that horse's feet.

"The officers and deputies chased him for about another year. He killed a number of men during that time, mostly officers and their deputies who were out to capture him, though he killed several men whom he met on the roads and trails—killed them so they couldn't tell they had seen him. By this time Billy had established a headquarters *in the sandhills of the Panhandle of Texas,* and had got together between *eighty and ninety* men, every one of them a man with a price on his head. They had all the good horses they wanted, for they didn't hesitate to take one wherever they found him. The sandhills are a big waste of sand blown up into big hills that are constantly on the move, with water only in one place. That is sixty miles from any other water, and if a man didn't know the sandhills he would be almost sure to get lost and he and his horse both die of thirst. There were no roads or trails to guide anyone as every little wind obliterated every track, so the officers didn't venture into the sandhills. Billy and his gang didn't

have to come out very often, as there was plenty of game
—buffalo, deer and antelope. But there was no fun in staying in there all the time, so the boys came out occasionally
and held up a train, a bank or two, a few stage coaches and
individuals. The local authorities had simply failed, but
while holding up the trains and stages they had robbed the
mails and that brought Uncle Sam into the game and he
sent a company of cavalry to capture the outlaws."

Whatever else the Kid might be accused of, he, as I
have said repeatedly, could not truthfully be called a highwayman, who robbed trains, banks, and stagecoaches. A
cattle thief, a horse thief, yes. But a robber, never.

The account of the Kid's escape from jail given in this
volume is one of the most absurd I have read. But then
it is a good rule never to be surprised at anything you read
concerning the Kid. If this book seems outlandish, I can
call your attention to even more outlandish accounts.

"The gang heard of it," Mr. Lord continues, "and came
out in full force. They met between Fort Sumner and Los
[*sic*] Vegas and the outlaws whipped the cavalry in an
open fight. That made Billy and his men pretty bold. They
rode over the country in squads doing pretty much as they
pleased until the cattlemen and other frontier men formed
a company to assist the cavalry. They got a buffalo hunter
to guide them to the outlaws' camp in the sandhills. The
outlaws had been posted and had scattered and gone.

"In going into and out of the sandhills they came to
Pecos River at old Fort Sumner, an abandoned frontier
military post. There were buildings enough there to make
a good sized town. A wealthy half-breed Mexican by the
name of Pete Maxwell had arranged with the government
to look after the property for the privilege of using the
reservation as a sheep and cattle range. The nearest white

settlement was Los Vegas, one hundred miles away. Billy and his men went back and forth quite regularly, and all the protection Maxwell had was to be friendly with them, which he did. About this time my parents and I, through Senator Teller, of Colorado, got a bill passed ordering the sale of Fort Sumner Reservation and everything on it. We bid the land, twenty-four thousand some hundred acres, at one dollar and twenty-five cents an acre. That included the buildings and everything in them.

"In the meantime a new sheriff had been elected and he put up posters notifying the outlaws that it was war to the death and that he was appointing plenty of deputies —all men that would shoot to kill. Among his deputies was a man by the name of Pat Garrett. After the election of the new sheriff Billy and his gang had kept pretty well under cover." How is it possible to be so completely wrong in every detail?

"I had to go to Fort Sumner," he continues, to close a deal with Maxwell for eight hundred head of cattle and twenty-five saddle horses. When I got there I found Maxwell leaving for his home ranch thirty-five miles distant; he said he was obliged to go but would be back the next morning and for me to occupy his room and make myself at home. There were several Mexican families living there, and the man working for Maxwell. In one of the families was a señorita. She and Billy the Kid were very much in love with each other. There was a young Mexican, Maxwell's foreman, who was very much in love with the señorita also. The girl and her mother favored Billy, but her father was bitterly opposed to Billy's coming to see her. The girl and her mother never told anything, but the old man could tell when Billy was expected by the cleaning and straightening up around the house. He would post the foreman and the latter would manage through his Mexican friends to get word to the sheriff and in that way they hoped to get the drop on the Kid.

"This time it worked. About an hour after Maxwell started to his home ranch Pat Garrett arrived disguised as a Mexican. He spoke Spanish as well as a native. His disguise was perfect but I soon detected him by his voice. He told me that the Kid was expected that night. He said he had met Maxwell, who had told him I was there occupying the room. The Kid always came to Maxwell's room about half past ten or eleven o'clock to sleep until morning, as that was as late as the old folks would let the girl stay up.

"Garrett and I went to bed about half past nine. The bed stood out from the wall and was rather high off the floor. I undressed and went to bed on the front side, Garrett lay down on the back of the bed with his clothes on. We had lain there about half an hour when we heard Billy coming. Garrett slid off the bed and squatted behind it with his forty-five in his hand, full cocked. The moon was shining bright, which made it light in the room. Billy stepped into the room and left the door open behind him and said, 'Who is here?' in Spanish. Just as he spoke Garrett raised instantly and fired over me and Billy fell dead, shot through the heart. He had expected to find Maxwell in bed; I was lying purposely so he couldn't see my face and had to put my clothes where he couldn't see them. But the instant he stepped in the room he suspicioned there was something wrong. Garrett's raising and firing was as quick as thought, but Billy had pulled his pistol almost entirely out of the holster.

"Billy was *twenty-four years old* and had killed *twenty-four men* single handed. The outlaw gang lost its brain power when Billy was killed and soon went to pieces. Some were captured, some were killed, and some left that neck of the woods to find safer territory."

Had I not read this story with my own eyes, I never would have believed that anyone would think the world so gullible as to swallow such wild tales, especially when so many books on the subject had already been published, including Garrett's own account. Mr. Lord could not even get the Kid's age right, though he did, like most of the others, have him kill a man for each year of his life.

In the publisher's preface to Thomas Marion Hamilton's book, *The Young Pioneer* (1932), the statement is made that "this narrative, and others of a series to follow, is told by Thomas Marion Hamilton, Captain U.S.A., Retired, and is a *true story of his experiences* since the age of eleven." Yet, when one reads this book, he immediately feels that it was written as a tall tale for the entertainment of the Captain's grandchildren. If it is intended for history, then I must label it the most preposterous account it has been my privilege to examine.

The author claims he met Billy the Kid for the first time when he, the writer, was only fourteen years old and was already a cowpuncher on a ranch—men must have been scarce. He says the Kid was arrested in *Tombstone, Arizona,* and taken before the judge, and just as they were about to turn him loose, in walked Pat Garrett. There followed a terrible fight, in which the Kid was overpowered. He was put in jail, but in the daytime was taken through a trap-door to the roof and kept up there with guards watching over him. The guards were changed two or three times a day, and food was brought up to them by a stairway leading to the trap-door.

The Kid's sweetheart, Maria Monette, came to town and got a job as a cook in the hotel across the street. She had a horse which she kept tied to a hitching post on the side of the jail lot. She soon let the Kid know she was there. It was her job to cook the meals for the jailers and prisoners. The guards' food was sent up in regular dishes, but the prisoners had theirs served in tin dishes. One day the Kid found a note in one of his biscuits telling him that the next day the guards' food would contain a sleeping drug, which she had obtained from a Yaqui Indian doctor, and that her horse would be waiting. After the guards ate their food the next day, they fell fast asleep. Then follows a fantastic account of the Kid's escape and flight to Old Mexico, where he hid out.

Albert J. Fountain, a prominent New Mexico lawyer, and his young son, Henry, disappeared in the White Sands of that state on January 31, 1896, and were thought to have been murdered, although neither the killers nor the bodies of the victims were ever found. In spite of the fact that Billy the Kid was killed in 1881, this author states that Billy followed Fountain to El Paso, Texas, to warn him of impending danger as Fountain started on his last journey. At this time the Kid had been officially dead for fifteen years; yet Mr. Hamilton says he followed Fountain and saw him murdered by the Tate gang—whoever they were. According to his account, Billy caught up with this gang, gave them a lecture on their dastardly deeds, and, as time passed, killed them one by one. *Billy the Kid told the author all this personally.*

The author later went to Mexico, where he soon discovered a gold mine, and Billy the Kid arrived just in the nick of time to save him from the Poe gang of robbers.

The final chapter is absurd. It seems that Garrett was anxious to make a bargain with the Kid to give himself up, serve a few years, then go free to marry his sweetheart and lead a straight life, or so Garrett told the Kid's sweetheart. He persuaded her to get the Kid to come out of Mexico and meet the sheriff at her home. She wanted Garrett to come into the house to wait for the Kid, but he said he preferred to remain outside while smoking. The Kid had hardly entered the lighted parlor and greeted his girl when there was a crack of a rifle from outside and the Kid fell with a bullet in his brain. Not only did it seem impossible for Hamilton to get any of his facts straight, but neither could he get the names of his characters right. He called A. J. Fountain, "Robert" Fountain; Charlie Bowdre, Charlie "Bowder"; Tom O'Folliard, "Tom O'Foulard"; Wayne Brazil, Wayne "Bonzel"—to cite a few.

James S. Guyer, in his book, *Pioneer Life in West Texas* (1938), makes a claim I have never seen anywhere else. He says that he first met the Kid while he was on the trail to Dodge City, Kansas, with a herd of cattle, and that he helped him gather some lost horses, and that, later on this same drive, he helped him cross Red River at Doan's store. He also states that Pat Garrett was with the Murphy faction in the Lincoln County War, which is untrue.

He relates that after the battle at the McSween home, "the survivors of both factions called a mass meeting. A plan was mapped out satisfactory to all concerned. The idea was to 'let by-gones be by-gones, the past is to be wiped out and forgotten,'" but, as we know, this was not the end. "The new sheriff was Pat Garrett, one time friend and cattle rustler with Billy the Kid. But now the alluring title of sheriff had brought about a change of heart as to peace and order."

His account of the killing of Bell and Olinger reads thus: "While playing cards Billy purposely dropped a card. Bell stooped to get it, and Billy with shackled hands snatched his pistol, shot him dead, walked to the window and, as the other guard, Ollinger, passed by, sent a shot into his heart." He says that a man named George Graham, formerly a well-to-do rancher but now a drunken bum, offered to tell, for two drinks of whiskey, where they could find the Kid after his escape.

He claims that the Kid had many girl friends and sweethearts, but that Lucia Maxwell was the only girl he ever loved. "For more than a month," he writes, "Billy and Lucia had been meeting at her home in old Fort Sumner, and so well did they keep their meeting concealed that the law, just at their door, never suspected it."

Then the fateful night came, and, as the author says, "Billy walked slowly into the Maxwell yard, called softly, 'Lucia! Lucia!' Bang! A flash from a Colt's revolver, in the hands of Sheriff Pat Garrett, *hid behind a small table in the hall,* snuffed out the life of William B. Bonney." It is indeed irony that this author complains bitterly because so much false and misleading matter had been published about the Kid.

Tex Moore, in his little book, *The West* (1933), is another old-timer who claims to have known the Kid. He says that Mrs. McSween was finally persuaded to leave her burning home while there was yet time. "She went," he writes, "the tears streaming down her face, but not until she had one last look at her treasured piano, which she so dearly loved. To the surprise of all present, this brave woman stopped and played a strain of the *Star Spangled Banner* before facing what was thought to be almost certain death."

He declares that Morton killed Tunstall, Tom Hill blew his brains out with a Winchester, and a Mexican beat his head in with a rock. Afterwards they rode back to Lincoln and "celebrated again with several rounds of drinks at Murphy's saloon." Billy the Kid, he writes, "stood bareheaded at the grave, silent, but swearing in his soul to avenge the death of his friend by shooting every man of the posse as he found them."

He continues with the time-worn legends of the Kid's killing the blacksmith who insulted his mother when he was twelve and his having killed twenty-one men by the time he was twenty-one years old. He is another who has Morton and Baker hole up in a dugout for two or three days until forced out by hunger, adding that the Kid admitted killing them both. Like many others, too, he relates that Mrs. Mills ran to Fort Stanton to seek aid from Colonel Dudley during the attack on the McSween home. All the way through his account he shows partiality for the McSween faction and goes to some length to tell how crooked Murphy and his henchmen were.

In telling of the Kid's escape from Lincoln, he writes: "As to the card game which was fatal to Bell, nobody knows what was said or done prior to Bell's death. There were no eye witnesses. There were none to hear the conversation. It would be pure fiction for any person to state what was said while the last game was being played. The fact remains, however, that by some lightning move, the Kid got hold of Bell's gun and Bell ran and was killed before reaching a distance of ten feet. His body rolled down the stairway *into the street* after being shot.

"Ollinger, hearing the shot, walked over there, but seeing the Kid sitting unconcerned at the window, thought everything was all right—'till coming closer, he heard the Kid speak to him."

The author claims he heard the shot that killed Bell while he was eating dinner at the Wortley Hotel. Then, going out on the porch, he saw Olinger cross the street, look up at the window, and get shot by the Kid.

Another example of an old-timer's memoirs is the biography of Jeff Ake, written by James B. O'Neil under the title *They Die But Once.*

"Billy the Kid," says Jeff, "was friends with me what time I knowed him. I drove cattle to Fort Sumner a couple of years before the Kid was killed. He would borrow a hoss of me sometimes and always brought him back. I remember the Kid went riding in a hack in Sumner with two other fellers. They was all a-drinkin' and after a while the Kid come back with the other fellers dead in the hack. He said they had started a fight. . . .

"Billy had a ranch down on the Pecos, at Big Sandy, I think, just above the Bar V. That was the hangout for his gang. Pat went down and rounded it up once, but the gang shot him off. . . .

"Pat was deputized by Sheriff Poe, of Lincoln County. They said that old Pat Coghlan had agreed to buy all the cattle that Billy could steal out of the Panhandle. . . . Pat [Garrett] went down to Lincoln. The Kid was wounded, and they jailed him. When he got pretty near well, he killed his guard, and broke into the courthouse armory, with his handcuffs still on. He got guns of the armory, and sent a Mexican trusty after his hoss. Word got around that the Kid was loose. Ollinger, the deputy, come a-running with his gun in his hand. The Kid shot Ollinger's head off, and made his getaway. Then Pat killed him afterward, at Fort Sumner."

We know that Poe was not the sheriff, but a deputy under Garrett. Although mistakes in such minor details in themselves are not especially important, they testify to careless reporting by men who were on the ground, or claimed to have been, and should have known better. It should be added also that the Kid was not wounded when he was in the Lincoln jail.

A page from Jim Cook's book, *Lane of the Llano* (1926), provides us with a typical example of how just the old-timers "remember."

"It was while I was working for Uncle John Chisum," he wrote, "that trouble between rival cattle gangs started over at Lincoln. A band was stealing from Uncle John, and Chisum hired Billy the Kid to fight for him. Uncle John had fifty men in his fighting squad. He promised Billy fifteen dollars a day as a fighter. The Kid rode in to Uncle John one day and said, 'Come on and go up to Lincoln with us. We're going to shoot up the town.' He had Tom O'Folliard and five or six others with him. They didn't mean any real harm. Uncle John didn't go, but Billy and the rest of us did. When we got into Lincoln, the soldiers came in there with orders to get Billy dead or alive. We had to barricade ourselves in the McSween house. Mrs. McSween wasn't there. The boys *played her piano* and sang during the day while the bullets were coming into the house. Mc-Sween was killed when he stepped out of the door to talk to the commanding officer of the soldiers. Eventually the soldiers set fire to the roof, and about twilight the Kid decided to make a break. There was a long adobe wall which ran to the house and down to the creek. We broke out along this wall—Billy, Tom O'Folliard, myself and some others. The Negro soldiers had placed themselves around two sides of the wall, and they couldn't fire at us without shooting each other. When Billy started out he said, "Don't shoot any of the soldiers if you can help it. We don't want to have any more Government murders to account for. Shoot your guns in the air to scare them niggers."

It is strange how many old characters wanted their readers to think that they had known the Kid personally and had been with him during many of his escapades. Were they so vain that they failed to consider that readers would sooner or later discover that their accounts were simply braggadocio? This whole account, for example, is absurd. Men fighting for their lives would have no compunction in shooting a "nigger soldier" if it meant the difference between life and death. And in the first place, this was not a battle between the Kid's gang and soldiers, but between the McSween faction and the Murphy followers.

It seems that for a time every man or woman who wrote a book about the West felt obliged to bring the Kid into the picture. He made good copy and his name was still on everyone's tongue. Having heard or read the various tales created about him, they felt capable of giving some of his "history."

Benjamin S. Miller, a prominent cattleman and one of the early presidents of the Cherokee Strip Live Stock Association, wrote a little book, now quite rare, about his ranching experiences. Entitled *Ranch Life in Southern Kansas and the Indian Territory*, it was published in 1896. On a trip to New Mexico, Miller happened to be in the smoker of the railway car into which Garrett brought Billy the Kid and his other prisoners at Las Vegas. This was the time the mob was after Rudabaugh, and Miller told of the mob's actions much as it had been told before. Why he thought it necessary to include any other information about the Kid is conjectural—but he did, and that carelessly. He knew very little about the Kid, perhaps cared less, and therefore made no investigation concerning the circumstances surrounding his death. Yet in the last paragraph of his book he writes: "I read in the papers that Billy the Kid, of Las

Vegas and Santa Fe fame, had been shot by the same *marshal,* Pat Garrett, who had him and his two men in charge when I ran across them some months before. It seemed they escaped from the prison in Santa Fe, assisted by one of Billy's female friends, and immediately made their way to their old stamping grounds. Garrett took up the trail once more, never resting until, some months later, he found the Kid *in bed* at the home of a friend called Maxwell. Garrett didn't wait to take him prisoner, but *poured a load of buckshot into him as he raised up in bed,* and that settled it, Billy taking some of the medicine he had been accustomed to administering in such liberal doses to others."

As we know, the statements about the Kid's escaping from the Santa Fe jail, being assisted by a girl, being in bed when killed, and being filled with buckshot, all are untrue.

In 1905, William Hale Stone wrote and had privately printed a little book entitled *Twenty-Four Years a Cowboy and Ranchman in Southern Texas and Old Mexico,* under the pseudonym of Will Hale. This book seems to have disappeared and is exceedingly rare. The copy I examined is in the Library of Congress. (Since that time the University of Oklahoma Library secured a copy, and the University of Oklahoma Press reprinted it in the Frontier Library Series). The author says that when he and a friend went to Fort Sumner, they found there a notorious outlaw who had "killed three of Chisholm's [*sic*] men." He says the reason the Kid came to Fort Sumner so often was that "he was smitten on a part Mexican and English girl," and once when he got back to the ranch after visiting her, he found his English friend (Tunstall) murdered.

Of the Kid himself, he writes: "This young fellow's nickname was Billy the Kid. Cowmen call boys kids. . . . The Kid, so I heard, was born in New York, and at the age of seventeen his parents moved to Silver City, New Mexico, and put up a boarding house. After staying there awhile, the kid shot and killed a negro soldier in self-defense. The next man he killed was a blacksmith, and not according to law. He left Silver City and went to the western part of Arizona, where he soon learned to be perfect with cards. After staying in Arizona awhile he went to Old Mexico and began to work for a cattleman, in the state of Chihuahua."

He relates that after the Kid came in from Fort Sumner and "heard of Tunsal [*sic*] being killed by a lot of men from the Rio Pecos, he swore he would kill everyone. The kid killed them before the stockmen's or cattlemen's war ended." He says that "Norton [Morton] and his men made their escape. This started the Lincoln County War."

According to the author, he and his friend Dixon became involved in the war with Chisum against the Kid, and he states that the Kid killed two of the men who had murdered Tunstall and then rode to Lincoln, where "he was corralled in a building by some of our own men. They set fire to the building, which was surrounded by a lot of soldiers and some Seven River Indians, also our men. The reason us and Dixon did not like the kid was because he had murdered the sheriff of Don [Doña] Ana county. While the building was burning the kid played on a piano all the while. He said he did that to entertain the crowd on the outside. When the house was all afire the kid and his crowd came out facing lead and fire. Everybody was killed but Tom Ophollard [*sic*] and the kid. They seemed to have charmed lives. The war ended that fall, and many a cowhand and ranchman was placed under the sod. The kid killed every man that murdered his friend."

He tells a story of the killing of Grant similar to accounts in the dime novels of that day. Although he calls no names,

I feel sure it was the Grant killing he had in mind when he said, "After getting back to Fort Sumner he had to kill a man, to give anyone an idea how rapid he was with a revolver.

"I will tell about this killing. After the kid and his men came back from Tascosa, they spent their idle time around Sumner. They had a great many enemies at this place, caused by the war, and, as I was going to say, the kid was leaning against the wall of a house, when a man said to another, 'I will bet the drinks I can kill a man before you can.' The other fellow said, "I will take that bet.' The first man out with his revolver and snapped it twice at the kid. The kid out with his revolver and shot him six times before he touched the floor."

He claims that he was in the posse under Jim Caralyle [*sic*] and that they chased the Kid to the *Great House* ranch. He tells quite a story of what went on in the house between the Kid and Carlyle, and when Carlyle jumped through the window, "the kid shot him several times before he touched the ground."

This author was also in the crowd with Garrett when O'Folliard was killed in Fort Sumner, or so he says. He puts himself with the posse which captured the Kid at Stinking Springs, but says nothing of the mob at Les Vegas. He merely says that "next day the kid was taken *toward Lincoln,* and from there was taken to Don Ana and tried before Judge Bristol for the murder of the sheriff during the Lincoln County War, and was sentenced to be hanged in April."

After the Kid was captured, Hale left with a herd of cattle for the Black Hills, and he devotes several chapters to his adventures on this trip before resuming his account of Billy the Kid. Although the Kid made his escape while

Hale was on his way to the Black Hills, he tells all about it, using the version that Bell was reading a newspaper when the Kid slipped his handcuffs and hit Bell over the head with them.

"Bell looked up from his newspaper," he writes, "and came very near fainting. He started downstairs after receiving a stunning blow on his head from the handcuffs. The kid reached forward and pulled his revolver. He had made no effort to draw it. Bell fell dead out in the yards with a bullet hole through his body." His account of the killing of the Kid is fairly accurate, but adds that after he was killed, no one would go back into the room again until "Maxwell's half-sister went in and found him dead. She was in love with the kid, and mourned over his grave many a time."

In 1912 there was published a book of reminiscences written by an F. W. Grey, an Englishman who had come to America to make his fortune, entitled *Seeking Fortune in America*. Grey had spent some time in the West and it was only natural that he felt obliged to bring the Kid into the picture. We have but to read a couple of pages to discover how very little he knew about his subject:

". . . He [the Kid] was a *halfbreed Indian*," he writes, "or at least had Indian blood in him. When he was finally killed, it was proved that he had killed more than one man for every year he had lived. He is supposed to have originated, or at least brought to perfection, the art of whirling a gun and shooting. On two occasions when arrested, he pulled out his gun and handed it butt first to the sheriff, holding it by the barrel with the butt up and with his first finger in the trigger guard. As the sheriff on each occasion reached for the gun, the Kid would whirl it on his finger, and as the butt reached his palm, shoot. Finally . . . Sheriff

Pat Garrett . . . and Kipp McKinney went after him. They found out a Mexican girl whom the Kid used to visit, and lay in wait for him there *after tying and gagging her.* Garrett stayed in the house *behind a sofa,* and Kipp was to stay outside to see that the Kid did not get to his horse again after the shooting commenced. The Kid rode up when night fell and walked into the house; but, like all hunted animals, his suspicions were easily aroused, for he had hardly entered the dark room when he drew his pistol and asked who was there. As he called out, Garrett rose from behind the sofa, and, sighting the Kid against the light of the doorway, fired twice, killing him instantly. This was not showing much sporting spirit in Garrett, but the man was a murderer of the worst type, killing men *just for the sport of it.*"

Occasionally we find an author who lays claim to having known personally all the outlaws of the early West, no matter how scattered their haunts. Such a one is Raymond Hatfield Gardner, who wrote that fairy tale, *The Old Wild West* (1944). Perhaps the fact that he was the nephew of the notorious Belle Starr (so he claims) gave him the privilege of seeing how tall he could spin his yarns.

"A lot has been said and written," he writes, "about a very capable and fast working badman, Billy the Kid. I knew Billy the Kid and once had drinks with him, together with General Lew Wallace, the writer, and Billy listened while we swapped yarns about old frontier days. [Wallace was no frontiersman, and I doubt that he had many tales to swap]. Billy hadn't killed more than half a dozen at that time and nobody knew what a bad hombre that youngster was."

He says that Billy, "like thousands of other youngsters, was playing around the streets of New York with wooden guns, imagining he was shooting Indians. [He doesn't seem to know that it is claimed the Kid's parents left New York when he was only three.]

"He was one of the very few men," he continues, "that I ever knew who could stand at a bar and by looking in the backbar mirror aim backward over his shoulder and hit his man." Another feat, which even the author admits is an "almost impossible trick but accomplished by the Kid," was to shoot with a gun in each hand at two different targets at the same time and hit them both. And, of course, the Kid could fan a six-shooter so fast it sounded like a submachine gun.

When Governor Lew Wallace invited the Kid to come see him, Mr. Gardner, Johnny-on-the-spot for everything, was called in to take part in the conference, so he says. Right here it might be well to cite Governor Wallace's letter to the Kid requesting this interview. Sent on March 15, 1879, it reads as follows:

"Come to the house of old Squire Wilson (not the lawyer) at nine (9) o'clock next Monday night *alone*. I don't mean his office, but his residence. Follow along the foot of the mountain south of the town, come in on that side and knock at the east door. I have authority to exempt you from prosecution if you will testify to what you say you know.

"The object of the meeting at Squire Wilson's is to arrange the matter in a way to make your life safe. To do that the utmost secrecy is to be used. *So come alone.* Don't tell anybody—not a living soul—where you are coming or the object. If you can trust Jesse Evans you can trust me."

Thus we see that, with the Governor's insistence on secrecy, it is not likely that Mr. Gardner would be invited to accompany the Kid, even though Gardner goes on to relate that during the conference with Governor Wallace, the Kid told His Excellency that he was broke and hoped it wouldn't be held against him if he held up a few people that evening. "General Wallace," Gardner reports, "promptly 'lent' him $40."

He also makes the statement that the cattlemen of Lincoln County had hired the Kid to kill sheepmen. He says that "Billy fought for the McSween side, with fifty men, which included forty Mexicans who were not worth counting as gun fighters, against a Murphy army of sixty first-class gunmen. After a few killings Governor Axtell ordered the *Mexican aliens* with the McSween outfit to quit the country, leaving Billy with only ten men against Murphy's sixty."

He states that in the battle at McSween's home, only Billy the Kid and a Mexican named Salazar escaped, the Kid without a scratch and the wounded Mexican because he shammed death.

This writer further says that the good people of Lincoln County grew tired of the Kid's robbing and murders, so Constable Longworth was outfitted with a posse of forty men, who surrounded the "lone bandit" in a house at White Oaks. With the odds "forty to one," the Kid shot his way out without receiving a scratch, though he killed many men himself.

In telling of the killing of O'Folliard, the author does not name this outlaw, although he had evidently heard something about the incident, which he describes thus: "All the fighting cowboys along the Canadian River were enlisted for the duration of this war to wipe out Billy the Kid. With a bunch of these fighters Sheriff Pat Garrett laid an ambush near Fort Sumner, where he expected Billy to visit a Mexican woman. After dark they saw a shadowy form sneaking up to the Mexican woman's house and they pumped the shadow full of lead. But it was only a small-time murderer, one of Billy's pals. At the last minute Billy had gone back for his tobacco." The last sentence is about the only truthful one in the whole paragraph.

"But a woman betrayed Billy's last hide-out," he continues, "and the sheriff was soon on his trail.

"A cocked revolver in one hand and a knife in the other, and in his stocking feet, Billy sneaked at night into a house where Sheriff Garrett happened to be watching. The sheriff had an idea that the bandit would do that very thing, and as the shadow crept toward the only *lighted* room, Garrett's *guns* roared from the *darkness* and Billy the Kid's career was over." Note the discrepancy in the last lines—one second he has the room lighted and the next dark.

He says that Garrett personally told him just how he had killed the Kid, but he has even the date wrong, as he has Garrett say, "On the night of July 12, 1881 . . . ." Farther down the same page he quotes Garrett thus: "When he came back to the ranch-house [Maxwell's], he saw my two men and spoke to them in Spanish. They made no answer and he darted into the house and *upstairs* in his stocking feet. My face was in the shadow when he appeared in the doorway, and he darted over to me with his knife in one hand and his gun in the other. He had his gun within a foot of me when he *laid his hand on my knee* and demanded, 'Who are you?'" Surely the Kid must have laid one of his weapons aside to have a free hand to place upon the sheriff's knee! "He sprang back instantly and fired. But I had fired first and the ball went through his heart." My reaction is, why would Garrett tell him such a preposterous tale?

Still another old-timer, Jesse James Benton, who "remembers," wrote a little book entitled *Cow by the Tail* (1943), which shows the influence of the early dime novels on Billy the Kid accounts. While the author and a friend were quarantined in the home of Pete Maxwell—because of an outbreak of smallpox—they were quartered in the very room in which Billy the Kid had been killed. Seeing a large blood stain on the floor, they asked a Mexican boy about it, and he told them it was the blood of Billy the Kid. Apparently they had never heard of an outlaw called Billy the Kid, but when the boy told them that some of the cowboys called him Billy LeRoy, they both remembered him as a cowboy they had met in Texas and "pardnered" with a lot in the Panhandle.

"I knew Billy LeRoy very well," writes Mr. Benton. "My first time to see him was some time in 1878 or 1879, can't say exactly. Him and Gus White had come up the trail together with a herd of cattle from a cattle ranch down in Uvalde County, Texas. The herd was bound for some point in Kansas. Billy and Gus quit at Fort Mobeetie in the Panhandle where I was working for Odem." One cannot help wondering why cattle should be driven hundreds of miles out of the way through the Panhandle from Uvalde County to get them to the markets then existing in Kansas. Further, if Mr. Benton had worked at Mobeetie, he should have known that it was not a fort, even though it was near Fort Elliott.

The author repeats the oft told tale of the Kid's escape from the Lincoln County courthouse, of the card game with Bell, his killing, and the subsequent shooting of Olinger. Of Billy's death he says: "One night Billy came in from a ranch, and he saw two men on the porch of the Maxwell house. He stepped into Pete Maxwell's room from the side door, and asked Pete who the two men was. Pat Garrett was *in the next room,* and when he heard Billy's voice he knew who he was. *He stepped in and shot Billy dead before Billy even seen him."*

The publisher's editor adds a footnote that Benton's account "does not always agree with other published versions," and informs us that "Billy the Kid was sometimes known as Billy LeRoy in Texas." Does this editor, like many others, believe what his writer says simply because he is writing of his own life? Perhaps both the editor and the author had read that fantastic book, *Billy LeRoy,* published by the *Police Gazette* sixty years before.

Nearly ten years after the publication of Benton's book we find old-timers still telling fantastic tales about the Kid. In 1952 there appeared a book entitled *Injun Summer,* the reminiscences of Bill Walker, as told to Mrs. D. F. Baber. As long as Walker dwelled on his own experiences, he did very well; but when he strayed to subjects which were not within his personal observation, he lost the confidence of his readers.

"Mrs. Bonney worked in the mining camps," he says, "cooking for the miners, washing clothes, doing all sorts of odd jobs that showed up, and was looked upon as a good, straight woman. So, when a man walked up to her and made a personal sort of remark, and wouldn't take no for an answer, the buttin [Billy] blew him apart. This man was a prominent duffer, with some sort of a pull in town, so the little shaver took it on the lam. He hid away in the hills, and they didn't catch up with him for several years. By the time the law did get their clutches on him, he had killed so many men that he had lost all count; and all the men he had killed were not lawmen, either. He had turned into a plumb outlaw; *robbing banks, holding up stages,* killing right and left!

"Bill Bonney had sure got off on the wrong foot! He was on the dodge from the posse when he hit Loveland [Colorado], and he didn't stay there long. The law made it too hot for him, such law as there was!

"He was riding a fine black mare, and the lawmen got to thinking they should own her. Billy the Kid was sure to get killed sometime, and they figured they might as well fall heir to his horse!

"No matter what they say, no man who loved his horse as Bill Bonney loved Bess, can be all bad! He loved her enough to keep her out of the lawmen's hands.

"They might ride her till she dropped dead, just because the Kid loved her, they might covet her just because she was good, but he didn't take any chances! When the posse was about to close in on him, and he knew his gun was going empty, 'Billy the Kid' took a high dive into the *Missouri River* [the author has confused his geography] but he saved one last shot for Black Bess!

"After the Kid made his nervy leap into the drink a report of the story got around; then it wasn't long till it was being written up into a song. . . .

"It must have given the Kid some satisfaction to know that the loss of his 'Partner,' his pet horse, was appreciated by someone, at least.

"Bill Bonney didn't drown in old Mizzou that night. He lived a few more years, killed several more men, and died with his boots on at the hands of Pat Garrett, a young, unknown law officer. There was some mighty tall grieving over the case. Bill was a great favorite in Lincoln County, N. M. Even outlaws have their good points, and their good friends.

"If anyone is inclined to disagree, a little scouting around the libraries will show my claim is correct. Governors, lawmen, Gen. Lew Wallace, and others took too much interest in Billy the Kid for him to be classed with the rusties, without one good point!

"Pat Garrett might have had plenty of cause to kill the little outlaw; but he didn't have to hide in the dark, and *behind a curtain,* to do it. A rattlesnake will give warning before it strikes; and even an outlaw is entitled to some sort of break. Pat Garrett stacks up as somewhat less than a 'man of the West,' according to my way of thinking. 'Shooting from a sneak' just isn't in my books. . . .

"They say that neither grass, flowers, nor trees will grow above the Kid's grave. Was it because he was a killer? . . .

"Pat Garrett was a friend of Billy the Kid. They ran in the same crowd; took in the same dances; entertained the same Mexican *señoritas.* They played poker together; they drank each other's health—and then the sheriff shot him down.

"Pat Garrett was small-time and small-town before he shot Billy the Kid. He rose to a big-time sheriff when he did that."

It was because many persons took this attitude toward Garrett in his own day that he decided to write a book to try to justify his killing of the Kid.

Teddy Blue Abbott, in *We Pointed Them North* (1939), wrote that "the Lincoln County troubles was still going on, but you had to be either for Billy the Kid or against him. It wasn't my fight and I wasn't for or against, though cowpunchers as a class never had any use for Billy the Kid —it was the Mexicans that made a hero of him. He had fell out with Chisum the year before, after being on his side in the war, over $500 the Kid claimed Chisum owed him. The talk there at the time was that the Kid told Chisum: 'I will kill one of your men for every fifty dollars you owe me,' and that he had already killed three and sent Chisum the receipt." Again, here is evidence of the way in which this fable continues to be kept alive down through the years.

Even the usually reliable James H. Cook proved that he knew very little about the Kid when he wrote *Fifty Years on the Old Frontier* (1923). "Men like Billy the Kid," he says, "who made such a record in New Mexico during the days about which I write, caused a number of weak-minded young men to try and imitate him; and the reading of trashy novels had, I think, much to do with starting young men on the wrong path. Billy the Kid had the reputation of being one of the most desperate criminals of the Southwest. Yet he was, to begin with, not a western product, but a *New York City tough*. Doubtless he had read some very yellow novels about the bandits of the West before he started on his career of crime in New Mexico."

6. *"Billy Bonney's" Biographers*

THE VERY FIRST WORK which could be called a biography of Billy the Kid was written by the man who killed him. Or rather it was, in modern parlance, "ghosted" by his friend, Ash Upson. Garrett was feeling the barbs of the gossip that he had taken unfair advantage of the Kid, and he wanted to give the world his side of the story. Since his friend Upson was a good and experienced writer, he turned the chore over to him with the understanding that the book would be published under his own name. There is no doubt that Upson had the opportunity to learn the facts about Garrett's connection with the chase and death of the Kid, but he knew little of the Kid's boyhood and therefore had to call upon his imagination. Although he claimed to have boarded with Mrs. Antrim, the Kid's mother, in both Santa Fe and Silver City, he seems to have gained very little information on the Kid's life prior to the Lincoln County War that can be termed authentic.

Upson, like most frontier journalists, was fond of quoting the classical poets, was adept at using flowery words and phrases, and frequently wrote with tongue in cheek. His imagination supplied incidents from the Kid's boyhood which future historians and biographers would find hard to believe yet would have difficulty disproving. Certainly his inventions have never received corroboration from any other source.

Before Upson and Garrett started to write this book, there had appeared several "true lives" of Billy the Kid which were fantastically untrue and Garrett wanted to correct the impression these dime novels were creating. But he wanted principally to vindicate himself. As a friend, Upson, gave Garrett all the best of it and painted the Kid in the darkest colors. The West did not censure a killing if the killer had given his enemy a chance, but the Kid was killed in the dark without knowing who was in the room. People were talking, some saying the Kid was not even armed. The two deputies on the porch said he was carrying a knife and a pistol. but it was near midnight and dark outside. Garrett said he was carrying a pistol, but it was dark inside, too. The first persons to enter Maxwell's room after the killing, Jesus Silva and the old Navajo woman, Deluvina, both stated emphatically that the Kid had no gun.

Did Garrett realize he had killed an unarmed man? It has been suggested many times that he proposed writing this book to salve his conscience, to build up a super-gunman for his own purposes. He declared, "It was either him or me," but I think that deep down he was trying to convince the world that his act was justified.

Although the book contains many facts, especially for the period after Garrett's election as sheriff, there are, in addition, many highly colored incidents, primarily in the first chapters, which were likely written in their entirety by Garrett's collaborator. Upson apparently could not resist the richness of his own imagination and the florid phraseology which he felt was needed to give his work the proper literary style. Above all, however, he was trying to convince his readers that his friend and bed-fellow was justified in his every act. In the introduction, to build up the Kid's reputation as a bad man and thus Garrett's prowess, he writes: "This verified history of 'the Kid's' exploits, devoid of exaggeration, exhibits him as the peer of any fabled brigand on record, unequalled in desperate courage, presence of mind in danger, devotion to his allies, generosity to his foes, gallantry, and all the elements which appeal to the holier emotions, whilst those who would revel in pictured scenes of slaughter may batten until their morbid appetites are surfeited on bloody frays and mortal encounters, unaided by fancy or the pen of fiction."

There are many things in the early chapters of the book which seem doubtful, but they have created a legend so often repeated that it will be hard to correct them. Here are a few of the doubtful "facts": the Kid's being an expert at card dealing at the age of eight; his knife-killing at the tender age of twelve of the blacksmith who insulted his mother; his conflicts with the various Indians; and his ride of eighty-one miles in six hours to rescue a Mexican friend from a jail in Texas. These are all the offspring of Upson's vivid imagination. His accounts of the killings of Buckshot Roberts and Bernstein are inaccurate.[1] He also incorrectly labels the Lincoln County War as being between the cattle king, John Chisum, and the small ranchers of the county.

It is strange that Ash Upson, who claimed to have written every word of the Pat Garrett volume, who lived on the ground and was, moreover, a newspaperman himself, apparently failed to read the frequent news items referring to the Kid as Henry McCarty, Henry Antrim, or Kid Antrim, and should declare him born a Bonney. The very first paragraph of the first chapter states that "William H. Bonney, the hero of this history, was born in the city of New York, November 23, 1859." From this time until very recently every writer on the subject of Billy the Kid followed in this

1 See Chapter I above for the correct version.

old itinerant newspaperman's footsteps. As I have said, earlier, Upson himself was born on November 23, and by some strange coincidence chose this date for the Kid's birth.

My friend Jeff C. Dykes, who has long investigated the Kid's history, writes in his introduction to the University of Oklahoma Press reprint of Garrett's book: "This book, far more than all the dime novels written about the Kid, is responsible for the perpetuation of unverified tales about his early life. Ash Upson claims to have boarded with the Kid's mother at both Santa Fe and Silver City and to have been personally acquainted with the facts of the Kid's boyhood. If Ash knew the facts, they evidently did not fit the purpose of the book and were laid aside in favor of trying to outdo the writers of those three 'yellow-covered cheap novels' in creating 'the peer of any fabled brigand on record.' "

In spite of the search by several historians in the vital statistics of New York and the newspaper files of New Mexico, no records have been found to substantiate the place and date of the Kid's birth.

Garrett's, or Upson's, book can be picked to pieces, paragraph by paragraph. "But little is known of his father, as he died when Billy was very young, and he had little recollection of him. In 1862 the family, consisting of the father, mother and two boys, of whom Billy was the oldest, emigrated to Coffeyville, Kansas. Soon after settling there the father died, and the mother with her two boys removed to Colorado, where she married a man named Antrim, who is said to be now living at, or near, Georgetown, in Grant County, New Mexico, and is the only survivor of the family of four, who removed to Santa Fe, New Mexico, shortly after the marriage. Billy was then four or five years of age."

There are several misstatements of fact in this one paragraph. Coffeyville, Kansas, had not been founded in 1862, but in the 1870's. The widowed mother did not marry Antrim in Colorado, but in Santa Fe, New Mexico, and so naturally did not "move to Santa Fe *shortly after* the marriage." This marriage took place in 1873, which, according to Upson's own birth date for the Kid, would make him fourteen years old instead of "four or five."

To quote from Frazier Hunt's recent splendid and accurate book, *The Tragic Days of Billy the Kid:* "The roving Ash apparently had boarded for a time with the boy's mother in both Santa Fe and Silver City, and obtained from her certain facts regarding the lad's early years. Later they were to be fattened by the printer's own imagination.

"The various youthful adventures concocted and elaborately described by Ash Upson in the Garrett book have long been accepted as gospel facts. Yet the first valid date and incident in the early days of the Kid's life was unearthed as a result of the research of Robert N. Mullin and Philip J. Rasch almost eighty years after the event took place. Their findings blew to bits many of the accepted 'facts' which clearly were the creations of Upson's romantic imagination.

"In both the 'Book of Marriages' of Santa Fe County, New Mexico, and the records of the First Presbyterian Church in the capital, there was found a notation of the marriage on March 1, 1873, of William H. Antrim and Mrs. Catherine McCarty, performed by Rev. D. F. McFarland. Among the witnesses were the bride's two sons, Henry McCarty and his older brother Joe McCarty."

Here is a record, the accuracy of which we have no reason to doubt, that gives the lie to frequent statements that that the Kid's brother was named Edward and was younger than the Kid.

145

A few paragraphs farther on, Upson states that the Antrims moved to Silver City in 1868. This is also an error, for Silver City was not founded until after the silver strike in that locality in 1870, and, besides, they would certainly not have moved there as a family until after the wedding. A newspaper notice of Mrs. Antrim's death also confirms the fact that the Antrims did not move to Silver City until 1873. In the September 19, 1874, issue of the Silver City *Mining Life* is this obituary: "Died in Silver City, on Wednesday the 16th inst., Catherine, wife of William Antrim, aged 45 years. Mrs. Antrim with her husband and family came to Silver City *about one year and a half ago*, since which her health has not been good, having suffered from an affection of the lungs, for the last four months she has been confined to her bed. The funeral occurred from the family residence on Main street, at 2 o'clock, on Thursday."

It seems strange that Upson, as a citizen of this same town and a newspaperman, had not read this item or did not check the newspaper files before preparing his account.

Another legend which Upson created and which continues to bob up concerns the killing of the blacksmith who insulted the Kid's mother. He says the Kid was twelve years old at the time, although Billy was twelve before he ever moved to Silver City. Since Mrs. Antrim lived only about eighteen months in Silver City before her death and the last four months of this time were spent in bed, the blacksmith would have had to insult her soon after her arrival. Ed Moulton, the man whose life the Kid was supposed to have saved by killing the blacksmith, declared that such an incident never occurred. No old-time resident can recall any such incident, nor is there any newspaper account of it. Here, sad to say, is but another legend for historians to check and refute. Here was also drama which

Upson could not resist, and in telling of the stabbing of the blacksmith by Billy, he wrote: ". . . once, twice, thrice, his arm rose and fell—then, rushing through the crowd, his right hand above his head, grasping a pocket-knife, its blade dripping with gore, he went out into the night, an outcast and a wanderer, a murderer, self-baptized in human blood." Very heroic and dramatic indeed to avenge one's mother and banish one's self to save a friend.

Upson seemed to think the Lincoln County War was between John Chisum and the smaller cattle owners. In Chapter VIII, he wrote: "This bloody war originated about as follows: The smaller cattle-owners in Pecos Valley charged Chisum with monopolizing, as a right, all this vast range of grazing country—that his great avalanche of hoofs and horns engulfed and swept away their smaller herds, without hope of recovery or compensation—that the big serpent of this modern Moses, swallowed up the lesser serpents of these magicians. They maintained that at each 'round-up' Chisum's vast herd carried with them hundreds of head of cattle belonging to others."

Other writers have adhered to this line, some even saying it was a war between cattlemen and sheepmen. But, like Jeff Dykes, I believe that "this was not a war between the cattle king, John S. Chisum, and the smaller cattlemen. Chisum was hardly an innocent bystander, since he was a partner of Tunstall and McSween in the bank at Lincoln and a bitter enemy of the Murphy-Dolan crowd and its backers, the 'Santa Fe Ring.' On the other hand he was not an active participant. This writer fully agrees with Colonel Fulton that the brutal killing of Tunstall precipitated the actual fighting. Back of that killing was greed and fear of loss of both economic and political power in the county on the part of the Murphy-Dolan clique of former army officers."

The Murphy-Dolan faction could not stand competition or interference with the way they had been conducting their business since the establishment of their trading post They were getting rich off the government in Indian contracts, furnishing beef which had been stolen from Chisum. When McSween and Tunstall decided to establish a store and a bank, where before there had been no competition, the Murphy crowd could not take it. McSween had worked for Murphy in a legal capacity, but being a Christian gentleman, he could not countenance the way Murphy conducted his business.

It is true that the killing of Tunstall brought the trouble to a head, but it is also true that Tunstall signed his own death warrant when he wrote a letter to the editor of the *Mesilla Independent* which was published in the January 26, 1878, issue: "Major Brady [sheriff under Murphy's control], as the records of this County show, collected over twenty-five hundred dollars, Territorial funds. Of this sum Mr. Alex A. McSween Esq., of this place [Lincoln], paid him over fifteen hundred dollars by cheque on the First National Bank of Santa Fe, August 23, 1877. Said cheque was presented for payment by John H. Riley, Esq., of the firm of J. J. Dolan & Co., this last amount was paid by the last named gentleman to Underwood and Nash for cattle. Thus passed away over fifteen hundred dollars belonging to the Territory of New Mexico. With the exception of thirty-nine dollars, all the taxes of Lincoln County for 1877 were promptly paid when due. Let not Lincoln County suffer for the delinquency of one, two or three men. By the exercise of proper vigilance the tax payer can readily ascertain what has become of that he has paid for the implied protection of the commonwealth. It is not only his privilege, but his duty. A delinquent tax payer is bad; a delinquent tax collector is worse. J. H. T."

Tunstall was thus publicly accusing the Murphy crowd of openly stealing the county's tax money. No doubt that is just what they were doing, but no one wants to be openly accused of such a crime, and publicizing such an accusation was perhaps the biggest mistake Tunstall ever made, for now his enemies would stop at nothing, not even murder.

I quote Upson's account of this murder, because Pat Garrett's book has long been looked upon as the one authentic source for what really happened.

"In the month of February, 1878," writes Upson, "William S. Morton (said to have had authority as deputy sheriff), with a posse of men composed of cow boys from the Rio Pecos, started out to attach some horses which Tunstall and McSween claimed. Tunstall was on the ground with some of his employes. On the approach of Morton and his party, Tunstall's men all deserted him—ran away. Morton afterwards claimed that Tunstall fired on him and his posse; at all events, Morton and party fired on Tunstall, killing both him and his horse. One Tom Hill, who was afterwards killed whilst robbing a sheep outfit, rode up as Tunstall was lying on his face, gasping, placed his rifle to the back of his head, fired, and scattered his brains over the ground."

The truth of the matter is that Tunstall was on the trail driving a bunch of horses when he was killed. Brewer, his foreman, and Robert A. Widenmann were driving the horses up ahead of Tunstall, while Bonney and John Middleton were about five hundred yards behind chasing a flock of wild turkeys. Brewer and Widenmann had gone some fifty or one hundred yards off the trail when a party of about eighteen men started shooting at them. They sought cover, for against such odds they could do little else. It was later established from the testimony of eyewitnesses that Tunstall did not fire a shot. Widenmann made a written statement five days after the shooting as follows:

"We started from Tunstall's ranch about 8 o'clock A. M., and traveled slowly. About 5 o'clock P. M. (Feb. 18th) while Tunstall, Brewer and I were driving the horses, Middleton and Bonney were about 500 yards in the rear, a flock of wild turkeys rose near the trail. Brewer and I had gone some 50 or 100 yards off the trail, when we heard a noise in our rear. Turning in our saddles we saw a body of horsemen coming over the hill at a gallop. No sooner did these men see us than they turned in our direction and commenced firing at us. There were 18 men in the party. We saw at once that we had no chance against such odds on the ground we were on and therefore made for the opposite hill which was covered with rocks and timber. On our way there we were met with Middleton and Bonney and we took our stand on top of the hill. Middleton at once said that Tunstall had been murdered, that he had tried to induce him to come our way, but Tunstall evidently excited, did not understand him and rode up to the attacking party. It was afterwards ascertained that Tunstall rode up to the party, that Morton commenced cursing him and ordered him off his horse, and when on the ground, Jesse Evans shot him through the chest, which shot felled him to the ground. Morton then jumped from his horse, drew Tunstall's pistol from its scabbard, shot Tunstall through the head, shot Tunstall's horse in the head with the same pistol, returned the pistol to its scabbard, and then mashed Tunstall's skull with his (Morton's) gun."

In his account of this incident, Upson continues: "This murder occurred on the 18th day of February, 1878. Before night the Kid was apprised of his friend's death. His rage was fearful. Breathing vengeance, he quitted his herd, mounted his horse, and from that day to the hour of his death his track was blazed with rapine and blood." It was common knowledge, even in Upson's day, that the Kid was with Tunstall when he was murdered.

Morton thought he was establishing a plea of self-defense when he fired the two chambers of Tunstall's gun, and then claimed that he was shot at first. When John Newcomb and several of his native neighbors found Tunstall's body, his pistol was near by, with two chambers empty, and a search revealed no empty shells anywhere. The body was brought to Lincoln and prepared for burial by Dr. Ealy, a newly arrived medical missionary. "Tunstall's body was in bad shape," writes Dr. Ealy, "as he had been shot and then beaten until his forehead was battered very badly.

There are some discrepancies in the statements of Frazier Hunt and Dr. Ealy. Hunt says that Post Surgeon D. M. Appel performed the post-mortem and reported that only two wounds were found, with no other marks on the head or body; that Dr. Appel embalmed the body, and it was buried in a wooden coffin. Dr. Ealy, on the other hand, noted in his diary that he did the embalming, that he found the body in bad shape from a beating on the forehead, and that Tunstall was buried in a metal casket.

In Chapter X of Garrett's *Authentic Life*, Upson tells of the killing of Buckshot Roberts, and, as in many other places in the book, there are discrepancies between his account and the probable facts. He says that when the Kid and his party were out hunting Roberts, as they approached the building at Blazer's Mill from the east, "Roberts came galloping up from the west. The Kid espied him, and bringing his Winchester to rest on his thigh, he spurred directly

toward him as Bruer [*sic*] demanded a surrender. Roberts'
only reply was to the Kid's movements. Like lightning his
Winchester was *at his shoulder* and a bullet sang past the
Kid's ear."

I put those three words in italics because it was well-
known that because of a crippled arm acquired by being
hit with a load of buckshot, from which Roberts acquired
his nickname, he was unable to raise a gun to his shoulder
and always shot from the hip. In spite of this handicap,
however, he was an excellent shot.

"Quick as his foe," Upson continues, "the Kid's aim was
more accurate, and the ball went crashing through Roberts'
body, inflicting a mortal wound."

Here he was again mistaken, for it was Bowdre who
gave Roberts his mortal wound in the stomach. David M.
Easton, clerk and bookkeeper for Blazer, Dr. Blazer, Andrew Wilson, Frederick G. Godfrey, superintendent of the
Mescalero Indian Agency, and all other eyewitnesses stated
that it was Bowdre. Upson says that Bowdre was severely
wounded in the side, but the truth is that the bullet struck
Bowdre's cartridge belt and glanced off to wound George
Coe in the hand. Dr. Ealy recorded in his diary, "As the
result of that accident, I took off a thumb and finger for
him [Coe]."

The Kid was charged with this killing on government
property, but his attorney, Judge Leonard, proved that
Blazer's Mill was not on the Mescalero Indian reservation
and Judge Bristol sustained the plea and freed all the
defendants.

It was during this fight that Brewer was killed, and afterward the Kid seemed to assume leadership of his crowd.

In this same chapter Upson tells of the killing of Brady
and Hindman: "Sheriff Brady held warrants for the Kid

and his associates, charged them with the murders of Morton, Baker and Roberts. The Kid and his accomplices had evaded arrest by dodging Brady on the plaza and standing guard in the field. They resolved to end this necessity of vigilance, and by a crime which would disgrace the record of an Apache. The Kid was a monomaniac on the subject of revenge for the death of Tunstall. No deed so dark and damning but he would achieve it to sweep obstacles from the path which led to its accomplishment. Brady with his writs barred the way, and his fate was sealed.

"On the 1st day of April, 1878, Sheriff Brady, accompanied by George Hindman and J. B. Matthews, started from the Murphy & Dolan's store, Lincoln, to go to the court house, and there announce that no court would be held at the stated April term. In those days of anarchy a man was seldom seen in the plaza or streets of Lincoln without a gun on his shoulder. The sheriff and his attendants each bore a rifle. Tunstall & McSween's store stood about halfway between the two above named points. In the rear of the Tunstall & McSween building is a corral, the east side of which projects beyond the house and commands a view of the street, where the sheriff must pass. The Kid and his companions *had cut grooves in the top of the adobe wall in which to rest their guns.* As the sheriff came in sight a volley of bullets were poured upon them from the corral, and Brady and Hindman fell, whilst Matthews took shelter behind some old houses on the south side of the street. Brady was killed outright, being riddled with balls. Hindman was mortally wounded, but lived a few minutes."

Most writers since Upson have repeated that the shooting was done from behind an adobe wall, but Dr. Ealy, who afterwards lived in the house adjoining this place, said it was from behind a "wide door into the corral which swung open," and Frazier Hunt declares that it was from behind a plank gate.

Dr. Ealy's diary and notes read: "I saw some men pass our house, and just opposite the house Sheriff Brady stopped to talk to a woman; I took it to be Mrs. Ham Mills. He was laughing and then he hurried up to overtake the posse. At the eastern end of the large house, which then was unoccupied—the house with the bank, law office, store, and drug room—but where we afterwards lived, a wide door into the corral swung open, a shot rang out, and the sheriff fell mortally wounded. I did not hear him groaning but the women said he did. At the same time Geo. Hindman fell. He called for water and someone helped him up and as he was being helped toward Stockton's Saloon, he received another wound and fell dead. One of the men in the corral, who ran out to pick up Hindman's or Brady's gun was shot as he stooped over, likely by Matthews. The report was that he was shot through the bowels but this was a mistake, as I dressed the wound when he came walking in our back door. The ball passed through his left thigh. I drew a silk handkerchief through the wound and bound it up. He was taken in charge by Sam Corbett. The Murphy-Dolan men were soon hunting for the wounded man. They searched the house, for they said they tracked him by the blood. I learned later that Sam Corbett had sawed a hole through the floor under a bed, and as there was no cellar, had laid the wounded man under the bed on a blanket with a revolver in his hands."

Practically all who have written about the affair state that the Kid was the one who went out to get the sheriff's gun and was wounded. Dr. Ealy knew the Kid, and I believe that if it had been he, the doctor would have said so.

Regarding the "adobe wall," I again quote from Frazier Hunt's *The Tragic Days Of Billy the Kid:*

"Billy and the five men with him slipped out of the Mc-Sween house that Monday morning. They took positions behind the *plank gate* just east of the rear end of the Tunstall store. It led to the corral on behind. This wooden gate was hung in line with the back, or north end, of the building.

"Men lounging behind this plank gate could not be seen by anyone coming down the dirt road from the right or west until they had actually passed the store. It was long accepted that there existed a high adobe wall at this spot where the plank gate actually hung and that this adobe wall offered secure rampart for anyone behind it. This is incorrect, for both Dr. Ealy, the medical missionary, and others familiar with the settings made positive statements that there was no adobe wall but only an ordinary swinging gate on hinges, with a wooden fence running at right angles to the rear."

On the subject of Brady's death Dr. Ealy had this to say: "Being on the ground, I got but one story on the death of Brady. I will tell it as I heard it. Sheriff Brady went after A. A. McSween 80 miles east of Lincoln, with a large posse of soldiers to bring him to court. [This was for the charge of embezzlement of the Fritz insurance money.] McSween had heard that Sheriff Brady had made threats that he was going to put McSween into the jail, which was a hole in the ground with a watch-tower over it, and that he was going to run water into the jail and drown him. So Mc-Sween promised before the men that he would be in town at sunup in plenty of time for court, and according to his promise he came. The sheriff had everything timed so well that had not Brady been killed he would have met Mc-

Sween just in front of the jail, which was a few feet from the place Brady fell mortally wounded. A man who helped carry Brady past the house to the Murphy and Reilly [Riley] headquarters told me that the sheriff had hand-cuffs in his pocket. It looks as if he were ready to carry out his threat to put McSween handcuffed into jail. Three men did not believe Brady when he promised on the Pecos River not to put McSween into jail and so had stationed themselves in the corral to enact vengeance on Brady."

There have been many estimates of the number of men behind the gate, varying from three to twelve.

Upson's account of the battle and the burning of the McSween home is short, but not far from the truth, and he did try to correct the report concerning Mrs. McSween and her piano, which had gained popularity in one of the early dime novels. On this subject he said: "A magnificent piano in one of the front rooms was hit several times by these marksmen on the hillsides, and at each impact sent forth discordant sounds. This circumstance elicited from a Lamy, New Mexico, correspondent of the *New York Sun* the following: " 'During the fight Mrs. McSween encouraged her wild garrison by playing inspiring airs on her piano and singing rousing battle songs until the besieging party, getting the range of the piano from the sound, shot it to pieces with their heavy rifles.' " Unquestionably this is the genesis of the tale, which has since been repeated over and over.

It seems likely that Pat Garrett really wrote or dictated the latter part of the book, for the narrative of events after he was elected sheriff and took a personal hand in the Kid's affairs is written in the first person and is much closer to the truth than the preceding portion. In addition, the flavor of the professional reporter disappears.

Garrett says that in April (1878) the Kid and his gang returned to Fort Sumner and "resumed depredations on loose stock, and followed the business industriously throughout the summer and fall." Yet the records show that the Kid was in the custody of the Lincoln County sheriff from March until July of that year.

In 1879, John J. Webb was in jail at Las Vegas, sentenced to be hanged for the murder of a man named Kelleher. In helping Webb escape, Dave Rudabaugh killed Antonio Lino, the jailer, and the citizens of Las Vegas were incensed against Rudabaugh. Pat Garrett captured Webb for the second time, along with a horse thief named Davis. He took his prisoners to Fort Sumner, then proceeded to continue his chase after members of the Kid's gang. His narrative continues with his return to Fort Sumner:

"On my arrival at Fort Sumner I dismissed the posse, except Mason, and they returned to Roswell. I hired C. B. Hoadley to convey the prisoners to Las Vegas. On my arrival at Sumner with them from below, I had written to Desiderio Romero, sheriff of San Miguel County, advising him that I had them under guard at Fort Sumner and requesting him to come after them. I had heard nothing from him, and concluded to take them to Las Vegas myself, and get them off my hands. The day we were to start, Juan Roibal and two other Mexicans came into Sumner from Puerto de Luna to inquire about the horses of Grzelachowski stolen by the Kid. They returned as far as Gayheart's ranch with us, assisting Mason and myself to guard the prisoners. At Gayheart's they took the direct route to Puerto de Luna, and, after some delay, we started by the right-hand road. We were only three or four miles on our way when a messenger from Roibal intercepted us with information that a sheriff's posse, from Las Vegas, were at

Puerto de Luna on their way to Fort Sumner after the prisoners.

"This changed my route and I took the other road. We met the Las Vegas posse about eight miles from Puerto de Luna. They were led by two deputy sheriffs, Francisco Romero and a Dutchman—and he *was* a Dutchman. They had arrived at Puerto de Luna with three men, in a spring wagon, and had there swelled the party of five to twenty or twenty-five, all Mexicans, except the irrepressible Dutchman. Discarding the wagon, they were all mounted, and came down upon my little party like a whirlwind of lunatics—their steeds prancing and curveting—with loud boasts and swaggering airs—one would have thought they had taken a contract to fight the battle of Valverde over again, and that an army of ten thousand rebels opposed them instead of two manacled prisoners.

"At Puerto de Luna the deputies receipted to me for the prisoners, and, as I was turning them over, Webb accosted me and said he had but $10 in the world, but would give me that if I would accompany him to Las Vegas; that he thought it was my duty to do so, as I had arrested him, and he never would have surrendered to such a mob as this. I replied that if he looked at it in that light, and feared for his safety—I would go on, but, of course, refused his money.

"The deputies took the prisoners to have them ironed. I was sitting in the store of A. Grzelachowski, when Juanito Maes, a noted desperado, thief, and murderer, approached me, threw up his hands and said he had heard I wanted him and had come in to surrender. I replied that I did not know him, had no warrant for him, and did not want him. As Maes left me a Mexican named Mariano Leiva, the big bully of the town, entered, his hand on a pistol in his pocket, walked up to me, and said he would like to see any d——d

Gringo arrest him. I told him to go away and not annoy me. He went out on the porch, where he continued his tirade of abuse, all directed against me. I finally went out and told him that I had no papers for him and no business with him, that whenever I did have he would not be put to the trouble of hunting me, that I would be sure to find him. With an oath, he raised his left arm in a threatening manner, his right hand still on his pistol. I slapped him off the porch. He landed on his feet and fired without effect. My pistol went off prematurely, the ball striking at his feet—the second shot went through his shoulder, when he turned and ran, firing back as he went, way wide of the mark.

"I entered the store and got my Winchester. In a few moments Deputy Romero came in and informed me that I was his prisoner. I brushed him aside and told him I did not propose to submit, asking him the cause of my arrest. He said it was for shooting at Leiva, and reached for my gun. I told him I had no intention of evading the law, but he could not disarm me; that I did not know what sort of mob I had struck; that one man had already deliberately shot at me, and I proposed to keep my arms to protect myself. Mason had come in, and now picked up his rifle and said: 'Shall I cut the son-of-a-b—— in two, Pat?' I told him not to shoot, that I did not mind the barking of these curs. My friend, Grzelachowski, interfered in my defense and the bold deputy retired. I went to an alcalde the next morning, had an examination, and was discharged.

"Deputy Romero had written the sheriff at Las Vegas that he had arrested the two prisoners, and was on his way up with them, and, also, had Barney Mason, one of the Kid's gang, in charge. The sheriff immediately started his brother, with five or six men, to meet us at Major Hay's ranch.

They came in all the paraphernalia of war; if possible, a more ludicrously bombastic mob than the one inaugurated at Puerto de Luna. Threats and oaths and shouts made a pandemonium there. The Romero who had just joined us swore that he had once arrested the Kid at Anton Chico (which was a lie, notwithstanding he proved it by his posse), that he wanted no weapons to arrest the Kid—all he wanted was to get his eyes on him. And yet it is pretty sure that this poodle would have ridden all night to avoid sleeping within ten miles of an old camp of the Kid's. Ruda-baugh once remarked that it only required lightning-bugs and corn-cobs to stampede officers of Las Vegas or Puerto de Luna. . . .

"A few miles from Las Vegas, this delectable posse stopped at a wayside *tendejon* to hoist in a cargo of *aguar-diente;* I seized the opportunity to escape their objection-able society, and rode on, alone, into town. I was ashamed to be seen with the noisy, gabbling, boasting, senseless, undignified mob, whose deportment would have disgusted the Kid and his band of thieves."

This statement has never been challenged, to my knowl-edge, by any critic of Garrett's book until now. I have in my possession an affidavit, originally in the papers of Jim East, made by Deputy Sheriff Francisco Romero himself:

"STATEMENT OF FRANCISCO ROMERO AS TO CORRECT FACTS OF REFERENCES TO HIM IN THE BOOK 'THE AUTHENTIC LIFE OF BILLY THE KID.'

"Historical narrative of what happened during five days when I was deputized by Don Deciderio Romero, Sheriff of San Miguel County, in regard to Webb's second arrest and other prisoners who escaped from the San Miguel

County jail about the year 1880; the exact date I do not recall.

"These prisoners, after having been held in San Miguel County jail for some crimes they had committed, escaped in daylight, killing one of the guards by the name of Lino. They left in a two horse carriage which was in the surroundings, and at that time it was suspected that some one helped them to leave. They left towards the east from the plaza, and the guards or deputies who followed them delayed for quite a while getting horses ready for the search, yet caught up with them at the foot of the Mesa where they had a struggle and exchanged shots without any effect. The prisoners finally escaped once more, and having met two men on horseback took their horses away from them and kept on their escape. Later on (I do not know how long afterwards) Pat Garrett wrote a letter to Don Deciderio Romero, who was then Sheriff of San Miguel County, telling him that he, as a Sheriff from Lincoln County, had captured and was holding the fugitive prisoners from San Miguel County who were Webb and another, and were being brought by him and to send some one to meet him at Puerto de Luna. Don Deciderio Romero took action at once to have some one go after them. It was late in the evening, and while getting an ambulance ready for the purpose, he sent for me. After I got to the place where he was, he told me that Webb and Rudabaugh [an error; it was Davis], the fugitives, had been captured by Pat Garrett, Sheriff of Lincoln County, and that I should go after them, telling me that he was going to let me have four men to go with me. I said I had to go home and get ready and would return in a few minutes and go. When I came back they were almost ready and Don Deciderio Romero handed me my credentials, and also to Baker, as deputies. This man Baker was one of the men going along with me, he was well known and considered as an American. I knew him very well. The other three men were Vidal Ortiz, Doroteo Sandoval and Martin Vigil. These were natives of New Mexico. We left Las Vegas about 12 o'clock noon and arrived next day at Puerto de Luna but did not meet Pat; he had not yet arrived. The following day, after we had breakfast, we went out to meet him. We had driven about a mile when four men caught up with us on horseback. They seemed very happy, singing and talking, but showed no signs of liquor. They carried no weapons, although I felt suspicious and kept on riding behind them and warned Baker about my suspicions and inquired of him if he knew them. He said he did not, so I told him to go and ask Sandoval and Ortiz in a dissembling way about them, for I had fears that perhaps they might be members of some desperate gang. I kept riding behind and told Baker about what I had in mind, and when they were notified they stayed behind the strangers under the pretext they were going to tighten the saddles on their horses. After the strangers left, I asked Ortiz and Sandoval the same questions I had put to Baker, and Ortiz told me that he had known them for quite a while and that they belonged to respectable families; and he, Sandoval, also told me that he knew them, and that they were related to him and that there was nothing to fear from them. So we kept on in company of these men, but they were in a way connected with our errand. We had ridden about six or eight miles when we met Pat with the prisoners, five in all; Pat, Mason, the two fugitives and the man who was driving. I am positive that one of the prisoners was Webb, but the other one I do not remember if he was Davis or Rudabaugh. From the place we met them we drove back and when we arrived at Puerto de Luna we met a group of people who were trying to find out what was going on. When we got to A. Grzelachowski's store we still found a larger group. There I presented my credentials to Pat and he delivered the prisoners to me, getting a receipt for them, and from there I took them to a room which I already had arranged for them. I did not know or had ever met before Juan Roybal or Juanito Maez, but I did know Marino Leyba, who was from Puerto de Luna and I knew him quite well; also his family who were very respectable. He was a desperado and mean, participating continually with thieving gangs. I say he belonged to a good family because two of his uncles were always endeavoring to guide him right and dissuade him from his lawless career, but always failed. They were men of means and well liked throughout the county; so it was that he [Marino] was watched by the authorities who were after him when he ran into the officers from Lincoln County. From the place where I was keeping the prisoners, I left with Ortiz and Sandoval, taking Webb along with us to a blacksmith shop nearby to get some fetters and put them on his ankles, and leaving the other two men right there taking care of the other prisoner. Pat and Mason remained at Mr. Alejandro Grzelachowski's store. And when we were in the blacksmith shop I heard shots in succession, whereupon I left the place, leaving Ortiz and Sandoval in charge of Webb. I went towards where I thought the shots had been fired and at the same time seeing many people that were going in a hurry toward Mr. Grzelachowski's store. But since the people had already been excited by what had been going on since the arrival of the prisoners, I thought they were more aroused in vain than what in reality had happened. While going towards Mr. Grzelachowski's place, I met Marino on horseback cursing and very furious, without a coat on and his shirt unbuttoned. I supposed he had weapons on him but I did not see them. I inquired of him what was the matter, what happened, and he answered me that such and such (using profane language and cursing them) have wounded him. With his right hand he opened his shirt and found a wound in his left shoulder, and kept going on his horse, galloping. When I arrived at Grzelachowski's store, I saw a lot of people gathered there in a group trying to get into the store, and many other people running towards the same direction. Having arrived at the store I made my way in and told the people not to come in. Within about eight or ten feet from the door Pat was sitting upon the counter with his gun in his hand but he was not in a position to use it, and Mason was within about four feet from Pat, also with his gun in hand aiming towards the door. He was standing on the floor near the counter. I passed Pat to where Mason was and before I got to him he discharged the gun without hurting anyone; at that time and up to the present I never did think that he shot at me, for the shot hit under the counter. I got to him, took the rifle away from him and told him that he was under arrest, to which he inquired by what authority I was arresting him, and without losing hold of the rifle with my right hand I took out my credentials from my pocket and showed them to him, he giving up his weapons which I handed to Mr. Grzelachowski. As soon as they handed over their weapons, the people all in a group wanted to come into the store, but at once I raised up my gun and aimed it toward the door saying that no one should enter, whereupon all kept back. All the people were alarmed and it seemed as though they wanted recourse to violence. I told Mr. Grzelachowski to close the door and I remained with the two officers and Mr. Grzela-

chowski, when I was informed how and why the shots had
been fired upon Marino. The officers did not demonstrate
any excitement, yet the people were very alarmed at what
had happened. I told Pat and Mason to remain in the house
until next day to have a preliminary hearing before a Justice
of the Peace so they would be discharged without any
further responsibility. Next day I took them over to a
Justice of the Peace and after a hearing he set them free.
After that we got ready to leave for Las Vegas, it was already late in the evening when we left. We had traveled
about six or eight miles when we got to a place and there
was an abandoned stone house where we slept that night.
Next day we left towards Las Vegas, and after we had
driven for about six miles from the place we were caught
up with by a party of men who were coming from Puerto
de Luna and who also were going to Las Vegas. These were
four men on horseback and three in a small carriage. They
were men I had seen at Puerto de Luna the day before. They
kept on riding with us until we arrived at Juan Paiz at one
o'clock in the afternoon, where we got our dinner, but these
men did not remain with us. On the other side of a river
nearby there was a herd of sheep and the man who was
herding them sold me one, as we were out of meat. I paid
him $2.00 for it. After our dinner we began our journey once
more to Las Vegas, but late in the evening we arrived at
Hay's Ranch where we slept that night. Next day we left
and met two men who were coming from Las Vegas; these
men met us after having been sent by Deciderio Romero.
One of them was the regular deputy sheriff, who was a
brother of Don Deciderio Romero, by the name of Dolores
Romero. The men who left us at Juan Paiz had told them we
were close to Las Vegas and Don Deciderio Romero of his
own accord had sent them out. I never asked him to send

more men; that I requested of him to send more men is false. When I arrived at Las Vegas the people gathered in groups trying to find out what was going on. I delivered the prisoners to the sheriff and thereby my deputy credentials ceased, and I left for home and did not know any more about the prisoners. Within about a day or two afterwards, Barney Mason arrived in town and came to see me at my home and told me that he was in need of money, saying, 'Let me have some and I will pay it back tomorrow. I want seventeen dollars.' I made him the loan and I have never seen him or the seventeen dollars since. I am not related to Don Deciderio Romero in any way. The regular deputy at that time was his brother, Don Dolores Romero. It is a falsehood that we were twenty-five in number when I met them on the other side of Puerto de Luna: it is a falsehood that they did not give up their weapons when I arrested them for the shots upon Marino, for they gave them up without any opposition; it is a falsehood that I wrote to Don Deciderio Romero telling him that I had with me two prisoners belonging to Billy the Kid's gang; it is a falsehood that I requested of him, through a letter, demanding more men; it is a falsehood that I ever did say that I was able to get hold of Billy the Kid as he relates, or in any other way. I never did say that, or anything connected with him. I never went after him, with or without an order; I never did know Billy the Kid; it is a falsehood that I went to Puerto de Luna with liquor or drank it at any other place; it is a falsehood that I ever had any difficulty with Lincoln County officers, or they with me. In regard to the exploits which he claims he played against Billy the Kid, I do not know. It may be true and it may not. I have no way of telling that, but the book 'Authentic Life of Billy the Kid' lies in that part connecting my name with it."

There is a trace of braggadocio throughout Garrett's account, and no doubt this is the case here. I see no reason to doubt the sworn affidavit of Mr. Romero. True, this incident is not important in the larger context, but I feel that it is only just to get the facts straight and to examine all sides, if opportunity affords, even of the trivial or incidental phases of history.

Because of their popularity and frequent reprintings, Charlie Siringo's books have been a prime factor in publicizing Billy the Kid and spreading the legends about him. Siringo's *A Texas Cowboy; or, Fifteen Years on the Hurricane Deck of a Spanish Pony* (1885) was probably the first cowboy autobiography ever published. It was kept in print for years, and it is estimated that over a million copies were sold.

In telling of the murder of Tunstall in this book, Siringo says: "The Kid *hearing* of his employer's foul murder, rode into Lincoln from the Tunstall ranch to learn the full particulars concerning the killing." As we know, the Kid was among the party with Tunstall on his way to town, but with Middleton had given chase to some turkeys when the killing took place. Therefore, although not present at the actual killing, the two were on the ground immediately after it took place.

Siringo also claims that while the McSween home was burning, the Kid played Mrs. McSween's piano "during the whole time 'just to amuse the crowd outside' he said." This is rather far-fetched in view of the fact that the Kid was supposed to be the leader of the fighters and should have had more to do than entertain their enemies outside. One wonders also where and when the Kid got his musical education. Every writer seems to be determined to have the

McSween home burn to music, differing only in identification of the performer. Siringo goes on to say that "finally everything was wrapped in flames but the little kitchen which stood adjoining the main building on the north, but still the coarse music continued to sail forth onto the night air." A dramatic touch indeed!

In this book it is said that Bell was reading a newspaper when the Kid started to escape and when he saw the Kid making a leap for him, he "almost fainted on looking up from his paper. He broke for the door after receiving a stunning lick over the head with the hand-cuff. But the 'Kid' was right at his heels; and when he got to the door and started down stairs the 'Kid' reached forward and jerked the frightened man's pistol which still hung at his side, he having never made an effort to pull it. Bell fell dead out in the back yard, near the foot of the stairs, with a bullet hole through his body."

It is hard to believe that a man chosen as an officer of the law, especially one selected to guard so desperate a prisoner, would be so cowardly that he would run from an unarmed man without pulling his own gun.

In 1920, Siringo's *The History of Billy the Kid*, now quite scarce, appeared to strengthen further some of the legends by this time well established. He starts this little book off just as Upson did by having the Kid born in New York, November 23, 1859, and moving to Coffeyville in 1862. He follows Upson's book, too, in having the Kid's father die in Coffeyville and the mother move to Colorado and marry Antrim. Then he has the family move to Santa Fe, to run a restaurant for three years before moving again, to Silver City. Thus he continues to perpetuate misinformation.

Siringo says that "at the tender age of twelve, young Bonney made a trip to Fort Union, New Mexico, and there gambled with the negro soldiers. One 'black nigger' cheated Billy, who shot him dead. *This story I got from the lips of 'Billy the Kid' in 1878"* He goes on with the story of the killing of the blacksmith who insulted the Kid's mother, saying that the Kid escaped into the night on foot, and "for three days and nights Billy wandered through the cactus covered hills, without seeing a human being." He follows Upson's account of the Kid's robbing Indians, going to Mexico, and throwing in with Segura to rob monte dealers, rescuing a wagon train from the Indians, liberating Segura from a Texas prison, and so on.

Siringo joins the other writers who relate that the Lincoln County War was between John Chisum and the smaller ranchmen. "Chisum," he declares, "claimed all the range in the Pecos valley, from Fort Sumner to the Texas line, a distance of over two hundred miles."

He also states that the Kid first joined the Murphy faction, but didn't want to fight John Tunstall, whom he had met and liked. Therefore, he talked with Tunstall, who gave him a job on his ranch, and then he rode back and told Morton, Baker, and the others of his new deal. According to this version, Morton rode out with a posse to one of Tunstall's cow-camps to attach some horses.

"Tunstall," he writes, "was at the camp with some of his employes who 'hid out' on the approach of Morton and the posse.

"It was claimed by Morton that Tunstall fired the first shot, but that story was not believed by the opposition.

"In the fight, Tunstall, who never carried a gun, was simply shot in cold blood. Before sunset a runner carried the news to 'Billy the Kid,' on the Rio Feliz." In all other accounts Tunstall had a gun, and it was well known that he did carry arms. In a letter to his parents written in 1877,

Tunstall tells of an occasion when Sheriff Brady came into his store and started a quarrel with him. He writes: "Then Brady commenced making some insinuation, which I took up & told him what I thought of. I was leaning my back against a counter at the time; he called me 'a fool' [and] I affixed a couple of adjectives & raised my voice one note louder than his & returned his compliment. He reached round to his left hip for his Colt's revolver, but did not get his hand on it, for I had him covered with my pocket pistol that carried a half-inch ball & I should have turned loose had his hand once touched the butt of his pistol."

Throughout his account Siringo follows the Upson-Garrett book very closely, even to the spelling of proper names —Bruer for Brewer and Skurlock for Scurlock for example, although Tom O'Folliard is Tom O'Philliard instead of Tom O. Folliard, as Upson had it.

He tells that when Roberts and the Kid saw each other at Blazer's Mill, "both had pulled their Winchester rifles from the scabbards. Both men fired at the same time, Roberts' bullet went whizzing past the 'Kid's' ear, while the one from Billy the Kid's rifle found lodgement in Roberts' body. It was a death wound, but gave Roberts time to prove his bravery, and fine marksmanship." These are practically the same words as in Garrett's *Authentic Life*. He says that Roberts soon expired from the wound the Kid had given him, and thus he credits the Kid with killing another man for whom he was not entitled to carve a notch.

His account of the killing of Sheriff Brady and George Hindman is also exactly the same as Upson's, even to the notches cut in the adobe wall by the Kid's henchmen as a rest for their guns. He differs somewhat, however, in his story of the battle at the McSween home, by saying: "Mrs. McSween and her lady friends had left the building before the fight started. She made one trip back to see her husband. The firing ceased while she was in the house." Like Upson, he does not have Mrs. McSween play her piano, but he does have the boys move it from room to room to keep it from being burned, and "the crowd made merry around the piano, singing and 'pawing the ivory,' as the Kid expressed it to the writer a few months later."

His account of the Bernstein killing is all wrong, for he says Bernstein rode up to the Kid's gang when he thought they were "stealing their band of gentle saddle horses . . . and told them to 'vamoose.' . . . The 'Kid' drew his rifle and shot the poor Jew dead. This was the 'Kid's' most cowardly act. His excuse was that he 'didn't like a Jew, nohow.' " We know that the Kid did not even see Bernstein or know that he was dead until after the fight was over. Some of the Mexican members of his crowd did the killing, as I have related previously.

All the rest of Mr. Siringo's book, including the killing of Carlyle and the Kid's own death, is much the same as in the Garrett saga.

But he declares: "On one of his trips to Fort Sumner, 'Billy the Kid' fell desperately in love with a pretty little seventeen-year-old half-breed girl, whom we will call Miss Dulcinea del Toboso. She was a daughter of a once famous man, and sister to a man who once owned sheep on a thousand hills." Anyone familiar with the area at that time could identify the young lady as Paulita Maxwell.

Most writers say that Olinger was across the street at the Wortley Hotel for his noon meal when Bell was killed, but Siringo says he went to the Ellis Hotel at five o'clock in the afternoon. In addition, he tells a third version, like the one in his first book, about how the Kid was able to get Bell's gun. Most accounts have him drop a card, then snatch the gun from its holster, and a number of others have him kill Bell when returning from the outhouse in the back yard. Siringo tells it this way: "J. W. Bell sat on a chair, facing the 'Kid' several paces away. He was reading a newspaper. The 'Kid' slipped his left hand out of the cuff and made a spring for the guard, striking him over the head with the steel cuff. Bell threw up both hands to shield his head from another blow. Then the 'Kid' jerked Bell's pistol out of its scabbard. Now Bell ran out of the door and received a bullet from his own pistol. The body of Bell tumbled down the back stairs, falling on the jailer, a German by the name of Giess [Gauss], who was sitting at the foot of the stairs." As has been pointed out, Gauss was the jail cook, not the jailer. Siringo also makes Poe a deputy United States marshal, when in fact he was only a deputy sheriff under Garrett.

In the revised edition of his *Riata and Spurs* (1927), Siringo says that soon after the Antrims moved to Silver City, the Kid "went on a trip to Fort Union, and killed his first man, a Negro soldier. On the LX Ranch in the fall of '78, the Kid told me that his first killing was a Negro soldier in Fort Union. On returning to Silver City he killed a blacksmith in a personal encounter." He repeats the version of the killing of Bell given in his earlier books and adds that Charlie Wall was one of the prisoners taken across the street by Olinger. This is no doubt what prompted the statement made later that Wall was one of the guards at the jail. Siringo also states that "Billy the Kid [after he had killed Olinger] called to a Mexican, whom he knew, telling him to throw up a file. This was done, and the shackle chain was filed apart in the center, leaving a shackle and piece of chain on each leg."

This time he comes right out and says that the Kid was

in love with Pete Maxwell's sister instead of giving her a fictitious name. Of course, each writer thinks his account of the Kid's death is the true one, and Siringo is no exception: "Many stories have been circulated about the underhanded manner in which Garrett murdered the Kid. Therefore I will here give you the true account of it," and he proceeds to repeat Garrett's version.

Walter Noble Burns, in *The Saga of Billy the Kid* (1926), probably did more than any other man to give the legends of the Kid a new and lasting impetus. I believe he made an honest effort to follow the Kid's trail and interview the old-timers of his country, but he had difficulty separating fact from fiction and so decided to include both. Such an able writer of romance could hardly fail to write an interesting book. When he reached the Billy the Kid country, most of the acquaintances of the Kid were dead, and the few still living had told and retold the story to so many eastern writers that they were growing weary of it and thus turned more or less to tall tales to satisfy the inquiries directed to them.

Burns was honest enough to call his work a "saga," and I doubt that he expected his readers to take it as history. I hardly believe he would have included such a quantity of imaginative dialog if he had. He gives few dates and cites no sources, and although the book is highly entertaining, it reads more like folklore than biography. It became so popular that it has been kept in print both in this country and abroad for the past thirty-odd years. Yet it is to be regretted that it has been accepted by some as truth.

The author agrees that the legend of the Kid seems destined to take its place beside the tales of the Robin Hoods and Claude Duvals of earlier days, and he has certainly done his part to perpetuate the legend. He admits that "the history of Billy the Kid has been clouded by legend. Less than fifty years after his death, it is not always easy to differentiate fact from myth. Historians have been afraid of him, as if this boy of six-shooter deadliness might fatally injure their reputation if they set themselves seriously to write of a career of such dime-novel luridness. As a consequence, history has neglected him. Fantastic details have been added as the tales have been told and retold. He is already in process of evolving into the hero of a Southwestern *Niebelungenlied*. Such a mass of stories has grown about him that it seems safe to predict that in spite of anything history can do to rescue the facts of his life, he is destined eventually to be transformed by popular legend into the Robin Hood of New Mexico—a heroic outlaw endowed with every noble quality fighting the battle of the common people against the tyranny of wealth and power."

Burns opens his fifth chapter with, "Billy the Kid's legend in New Mexico seems destined to a mellow and genial immortality like that which gilds the misdeeds and exaggerates the virtues of such ancient rogues as Robin Hood, Claude Duval, Dick Turpin, and Fra Diavolo. From the tales you hear of him everywhere, you might be tempted to fancy him the best-loved hero in the state's history. His crimes are forgotten, or condoned, while his loyalty, his gay courage, his superman adventures are treasured in affectionate memory. Men speak of him with admiration; women extol his gallantry and lament his fate. . . . A halo has been clapped upon his scapegrace brow. The boy who never grew old has become a sort of symbol of frontier knight-errantry, a figure of eternal youth riding for ever through a purple glamour of romance." Mr. Burns, with such writing, helps to perpetuate the legends which make this young outlaw a hero.

He admits that "though it is possible that the record of twenty-one killings attributed to Billy the Kid is exaggerated, there is strong reason to believe it is true." Again he says, "He is supposed to have killed twelve men before he appeared in Lincoln County. . . . It is impossible now to name twenty-one men that he killed, though, if Indians be included, it is not difficult to cast up the ghastly total."

In another place he says about the Kid: "He died when he was twenty-one years old and was credited with having killed twenty-one men—a man for every year of his life." All writers concerned with the Kid emphasize this point, but Burns did not take the trouble to verify the statement— he merely followed the legends of earlier years. He admits that the Kid "would fare badly under the microscope of Psychoanalysis."

Farther along he writes: "The Kid himself claimed to have killed twenty-one. He made this statement unequivocably a number of times to a number of men and he was never regarded as a braggart or a liar.

" 'I have killed twenty-one men and I want to make it twenty-three before I die,' he said a little before his death to Pete Maxwell at Fort Sumner. 'If I live long enough to kill Pat Garrett and Barney Mason, I'll be satisfied.' "

This is the only account I have seen that the Kid claimed to have killed any certain number of men. I'm sure this is all a piece of imaginative fiction.

To prove his point, Mr. Burns quotes a letter he says John Poe wrote him shortly before his death in 1923: "Billy the Kid had killed more men than any man I ever knew or heard of during my fifty years in the Southwest. I cannot name the twenty-one men he killed; nor can any man alive today. I doubt if there ever was a man who could name them all except the Kid himself. He was the only man who knew exactly. He said he had killed twenty-one and I believed him."

"If Poe," writes Mr. Burns, "with his first-hand knowledge of the Kid, had faith in the Kid's own statement, it would seem fair grounds for presumption that the statement is true."

Poe really did not have much first-hand knowledge of the Kid. He did not enter the picture until toward the end of the Kid's life, and by his own admission had never seen him until the night he was killed.

"Innumerable stories in which Billy the Kid figure as a semi-mythical hero are to be picked up throughout New Mexico," writes Burns. "They are told at every camp fire on the range; they enliven the winter evenings in every Mexican home. There is doubtless a grain of truth in every one, but the troubadour touch is upon them all. You will not find them in books, and their chief interest perhaps lies in the fact that they are examples of oral legend kept alive in memory and passed on by the story-tellers of one generation to story-tellers of the next Homeric succession. They are folklore in the making. As each narrative adds a bit of drama here and a picturesque detail there, one wonders what form these legends will assume as time goes by, and in what heroic proportions Billy the Kid will appear in fireside fairy tales a hundred years or so from now."

There are many legends printed in books about the Kid, and Mr. Burns seems to have done his best to further their life by handing them down in his "saga."

Burns repeats the legend of the Kid's birth and of his parents' moving to Coffeyville in 1862, with Billy "and a baby brother named *Edward*." He states that the father, William H. Bonney, died there and the widow moved to Colorado. Here he is merely following Upson.

"How Mrs. Bonney made the trip across the plains, or in what town in Colorado she located, is not of record; but in whatever town it was, she married a man named Antrim and soon set out for Santa Fe."

Again, it is clear that he is merely following the accounts which had been in print for many years. He further states that after *three years* in Santa Fe, "the Antrims moved in 1868 to Silver City in southwestern New Mexico, a silver camp in its raw boom days." Remember, silver was not discovered there until 1870 and no town existed there in 1868.

Burns also repeats that old legend about the Kid killing his first man in Silver City for insulting his mother. With his rich imagination he even describes how the mother was dressed, "in her plaid gingham and sunbonnet."

He follows Upson in having the Kid waylay and kill a bunch of Indians with robbery as a motive. He tells that the Kid lived in Tucson, Arizona, "for an undetermined period," making his living gambling, and here the Kid killed another man over a card game. "Nothing is known about it," he writes, "neither the name of the man nor any single circumstance." If the Kid had killed such a man, surely there would have been some sort of record of it. Burns, during his travels through New Mexico, was listening to too many tall tales.

The next man Burns credits the Kid with killing is a Negro soldier, although he is highly indefinite about it: "But no more is known of this murder than the other in Tucson; not even where it occurred."

Still following the Upson account, he places the Kid in Mexico with Segura robbing people on the streets, and later riding eighty-one miles to San Elizario, Texas, to release Segura from jail. There is no proof that any of these episodes actually took place. Of them Burns writes: "The foregoing tales may be regarded, as you please, as the apochryphal cantos of the saga of Billy the Kid. They are not thoroughly authenticated, though possibly they are, in the main, true." If there was so much doubt about their authenticity in his mind, why did he repeat them in a biography?

"Most of these," he continues, "are perhaps too ugly to have been inventions. If you are skeptical, your doubt may be tempered by the fact that they have at least always gone with the legend and have such authority as long-established currency may confer." As I have said before, repeating false information does not make it history. That there was much doubt about the truth in the author's mind is all the more reason he should be criticized for furthering these legends as fact.

Of Tunstall's death he writes: "While riding across the divide between the Feliz and the Ruidoso on their way to Lincoln, the three [Brewer, the Kid, and Tunstall] ran upon a flock of wild turkeys which scurried off among the chaparral thickets in the hills. With visions of a fat tom roasted to a turn and served with dressing and savoury sauce for their dinner that evening at the McSween home, Brewer and Billy the Kid set off into the hills after the turkeys. Tunstall rode on alone, his horse at a walk, expecting the other two to join him farther along the trail." We know that Billy the Kid and Brewer were not the only riders with Tunstall; Widenmann and Middleton were there, too.

Mr. Burns has the Murphy posse ride up to Tunstall at this time. When Tunstall asked these men, many of whom he recognized, " 'What's up?' " the answer was a shot "which tumbled him from the saddle."

"Some say, Billy Morton fired the shot," continues Burns; "some say, on what seems better evidence, Tom Hill. At least after Tunstall had fallen to the ground, Hill leaped from his horse and sticking a rifle to the back of Tunstall's head blew out his brains." In this account, the posse first rode to Tunstall's ranch, and finding it deserted [which it was not], they overtook Tunstall five miles from home. The truth of the matter is that Tunstall and his party had left his ranch at eight o'clock in the morning and it was five o'clock in the afternoon when he was overtaken by his murderers. Surely the party could have traveled more than five miles in this time.

Of the killing of Morton and Baker, Burns writes that when the Kid heard the shot which took the life of Mc-Closkey, he "turned to see Morton and Baker spurring their ponies in a breakneck dash for liberty. He made no attempt to pursue but, sitting still on his horse, fired twice. Morton and Baker threw up their hands and, toppling over backward, plunged lifeless to the ground." If this is what actually happened, then the Kid certainly should get credit for these killings; but according to more reliable accounts, the whole posse was shooting at these two.

In telling of the killing of Sheriff Brady, Burns has the sheriff and his companions carry on quite a lengthy conversation as they walked up the Lincoln street. "They did not see six heads lift furtively and six pairs of eyes peep dangerously above the top of a low adobe wall that came out flush with the street at the east end of the McSween store, forming a corner of the side and the back yard."

There was a volley of rifle bullets fired by Billy the Kid, Charlie Bowdre, Tom O'Folliard, Jim French, Frank Mc-Nab, and Fred Waite; yet with all this fusillade, the Kid alone is credited with the death of Brady.

In writing of Mrs. McSween and her piano during the time her home was burning, Burns says: ". . . she sat at the instrument and let her fingers wander over the keys. Snatches of old tunes took form beneath her touch like fugitive ghosts. Before she knew it she was playing 'Home Sweet Home.' She sang a bar or two softly—'There's no place like home.' The music seemed to voice her tragedy. Her home was burning. In a little while, with all its associations of love and happiness, it would be a mere heap of ashes and blackened timbers. As the last note trembled into silence, she bowed her head upon the piano and her tears dropped upon the keys."

He told this incident far more romantically and dramatically than anyone before him because he was an artist at using words. Yet, in spite of all this fine writing, the fact remains that Mrs. McSween emphatically denied she had played her piano while her precious home was burning.

Mr. Burns has an ever fresh sense of the dramatic. When Mrs. McSween left to go to Colonel Dudley for help, he has her walk out of the door while "a cloud of smoke swooped down around her. Out of it she passed into the sunlight. Rifles began to crack from windows in the Murphy store. Bullets struck all about her. She paid no heed. She did not turn her head. A rifle ball struck so close it scattered dust over her skirt. She paused for a moment, stooped and brushed off the dust. Then she marched on down the road." With short, crisp sentences he builds up dramatic suspense; yet if he had told the plain truth, he would have had to admit that when Mrs. McSween appeared, all shooting in her direction ceased. It was the code of the West that no man would shoot at a woman or endanger her life.

After a couple of fruitless visits to Colonel Dudley, Mrs. McSween returned to her twelve-room house, of which only three rooms remained, and "threw herself upon the stool at the keyboard," and with the hope that "a war-song might inspire them to still more heroic courage," she played and sang *The Star Spangled Banner* until the "music died in the crash of a flaming fragment of the roof."

According to Burns, Mrs. Juanita Mills walked all the way to Fort Stanton to seek aid from Colonel Dudley, asking him to go to Lincoln and stop the fighting. The author then makes it appear to be a mystery to the Murphy crowd just who the horsemen were who were now entering the town. The Murphy men knew, have no fear, for Sheriff Peppin had sent word for them to come since the McSween faction, they claimed, had fired upon one of the Colonel's soldiers who had come to town with a message. When Dudley called to Mr. McSween and the besieged attorney came out to see what the Colonel wanted, Mr. Burns has Dolan seize the opportunity to gather a few men and materials to set the McSween residence on fire. After the victory of the Murphy faction over the McSween crowd, Burns has them dancing in the street to celebrate their victory.

His account of the killing of Bernstein follows that of Upson. He says that the Kid's crowd was on a horse-stealing expedition and when Bernstein saw them rounding up some of the agency's horses, he rode out to stop them. "His blunder cost him his life," writes Burns. "Without stopping to argue the matter, Billy the Kid shot him." And he has the Kid say, ". . . it takes a bullet to teach some people to keep their noses out of other men's business. He was only a Jew anyhow."

Burns definitely pins the murder of Carlyle on the Kid when he writes: "The Kid jerked his revolver, and while Carlyle was in midair, sent a bullet through him. Badly wounded, Carlyle struck the ground on his hands and knees and began to crawl away. The Kid's second shot stretched him out dead in the snow." This, of course, was after Carlyle had jumped through the window.

In writing of the killing of Bell, Burns goes into detail about which cards were played, how much was bet on them, and even names the card the Kid knocked off on the floor. This is all surmise; Bell did not live to tell and the Kid kept it to himself—that is, if they really played cards, which I doubt. Burns even records Bell's thoughts. All these touches are tools to create the readers' interest, fine for romantic fiction but out of place in a factual biography. One moment the Kid was so handicapped with leg irons that he moved with difficulty, yet immediately after he killed Bell, without pausing to get rid of the leg irons, "he *sped* through the hall with strange swiftness," and "like a flitting shadow, he curved into the court-room, glided across the floor, and halted against the wall by the east window." Yes, Mr. Burns did a great deal to strengthen the legends about the Kid, when he should have made some attempt to seek the real truth and lay these legends.

Ten years later Miguel Antonio Otero, a former governor of New Mexico, wrote a biography of the Kid entitled *The Real Billy the Kid* (1936). Like many other New Mexicans, he is very much in sympathy with the Kid. He holds Pat Garrett to be a cold-blooded killer and quotes many other contemporaries to the effect that Garrett was a horse thief and a coward who shot without giving his victim a chance.

In his foreword Otero states that Charlie Siringo's book on Billy the Kid "was largely copied from Garrett's book" and declares that the same might be said of Walter Noble Burns's *The Saga of Billy the Kid*. He says that "each of these authors add many tales originating solely in their rather vivid imaginations"; and he claims that these tales are "pure fiction, wholly devoid of fact." He further states that when Garrett presented him with an autographed copy of his book, he accompanied the gift with the words, "Much of it was gathered from hearsay and 'made out of whole cloth.'"

Notwithstanding these statements, Otero begins, like the others before him, by giving the Kid's name as William H. Bonney, Jr., born November 23, 1859, in New York City, with a brother named "Edward" born two years later. The family moved to Coffeyville in 1862, the father soon dying; the mother remarried in Colorado, then moved to Santa Fe, where the family lived for *five years* before going to Silver City.

He says the Kid "acquired the habit" of dealing monte when he was only eight years old. He soon became as skillful at dealing as any of the professional gamblers, and this led him to the saloons. He continues with the information that although Billy loved his mother above everyone else on earth, his home life was unhappy on account of his stepfather's cruelty.

Mr. Otero, having been governor of the Territory, certainly should have had access to the early newspapers, and if he had read them, he would have known the Kid had been born a McCarty and that his mother did not die in 1878 as he says, but in 1874.

He repeats that old tale about the killing of the blacksmith for insulting the Kid's mother. When the Kid and a companion were on the way to Fort Bowie, Arizona, they met three Indians with a band of horses, and when the Indians refused to part with any of them, the Kid killed all three Indians, writes Otero. He also tells of the killing of an unarmed soldier blacksmith at Camp Bowie. "The record is not clear concerning this event," he writes. "Bonney never liked to refer to it, and all that could be gathered was hearsay."

He then follows Upson in having the Kid go to Mexico, where he formed a partnership with Segura and robbed monte dealers. Although in the latter part of his account he criticizes Garrett's book, he follows it very closely in telling of the Kid's first escapades, his fights with the Apaches, his riding eighty-one miles to rescue Segura, and so on.

Otero tells a different story from that of other writers about the death of Tunstall. He says that when the Morton-Baker group overtook Tunstall, he was accompanied by four natives, Ramon Montoya, Hijinio Salazar, and two others whose names were never revealed. All other accounts say that he was with his foreman Brewer, Billy the Kid, Middleton, and Widenmann.

He pictures the Kid standing beside the open grave of Tunstall swearing vengeance, although the Kid was in jail at the time and could not attend the funeral. Even before Tunstall's body had been brought to town, papers were sworn out for the arrest of Dolan and his crowd. These were given to the local constable Antonio Martínez, and he chose the Kid and Fred Waite to accompany him. But when they reached the Murphy store, Sheriff Brady put them under arrest and herded them into a back room, where they were kept under guard. Tunstall was buried at three o'clock on Friday afternoon, and the Kid and his companions were not released until two days later. Thus, in spite of the fact that many writers claim the Kid stood by the open grave and swore vengeance, we find that he did not even attend the funeral.

In relating that the Kid killed Morton and Baker, Otero declares this was the way the Kid himself claimed it happened. He tells of the killing of Buckshot Roberts, of Roberts shooting Middleton and shooting the belt off Bowdre, and adds that another shot "took off a finger of George Coe's hand." Coe's hand was injured by the same bullet which glanced off Bowdre's belt. This author also has twelve men behind the adobe wall shooting at Brady and Hindman. In other accounts the number varies from three to twelve, with six the most popular number.

He quotes Mrs. McSween as saying that the Kid told her he tried to get Billy Matthews and didn't even aim at Brady. She claimed his trial for killing Brady was unjust. He further states that Mrs. McSween told him that the killing of Bernstein was blamed on the Kid simply to get a United States warrant against him.

Otero very plainly reveals throughout his book that he had little use for Pat Garrett and takes every opportunity to discredit him, frequently citing the opinions of others. For example, he quotes Mrs. McSween as saying: "Billy often told me that Pat Garrett was a cattle rustler and had stolen many a herd of cattle from the Canadian while he was living at Fort Sumner. . . . Pat Garrett was much overrated as to bravery; he was a coward at heart and only shot when he had the advantage, or as they used to say, 'had the drop' on his opponent. It was said of Garrett that every man he ever killed was shot without warning, and I can well believe that this was the case."

He has Hijinio Salazar, the survivor of the big fight who saved himself by playing dead, declare: "Pat Garrett, who took up the pursuit of the Kid for them, was a cow thief himself, as everybody in Fort Sumner knew. He went back on Billy the Kid for money and for the promise of office. He was not the brave man many think he was. He was smart and cunning and above all, careful. He would never give the man he was looking for the slightest possible chance to defend himself."

Then he quotes Frank Coe: "Pat Garrett was an overrated man. He was a cowthief and everybody knew it. At Fort Sumner he stole many bull teams and sold them to butchers at Las Vegas. His killing of Charlie Bowdre, Tom O'Folliard and Billy the Kid were little short of deliberate, premeditated murders. He acted the part of traitor to his best friends, turning against them for money and office. Pat's conscience must have worried him a lot; he never succeeded in anything, even with the assistance of the President of the United States and the favors of several governors of New Mexico."

It is significant that Otero quotes only former members of the McSween faction, who were naturally enemies of the man who had killed their chief warrior and idol.

He relates that the Kid and his followers were captured at Stinking Springs by Frank Stewart, and that it was the Kid the mob at Las Vegas wanted. The account of this capture is word for word that which appears in Buffum's *Smith of Bear City* (1906). In truth, it was Garrett who made the capture, and the mob was after Dave Rudabaugh because he had killed jailer Antonio Lino while attempting to help John J. Webb escape from jail in Las Vegas.

Concerning the piano-playing legend, he says that Mrs. McSween told him: "I would like to say one more thing. I wish to correct the statement made in Walter Noble Burns' book, *The Saga of Billy the Kid*, about my playing patriotic airs and other melodies on my piano while the fighting was going on about my house. I certainly would not have been so inhuman as to do such a thing while my home was burning and there was no knowing when a bullet might take our lives. We were all too nervous and serious to think of playing the piano! Our only thought was—How are we to be saved."

In an interview, George Coe told Otero: "The first man he [the Kid] killed was a blacksmith in Silver City, for whom his step-father forced him to work. He domineered the Kid intolerably, forcing him to do all the disagreeable labor, and in turn refused to pay him for his services, very frequently beating him. Billy stood all this until the blacksmith one day insulted his mother, whom he adored. That was more than Billy could stand. He immediately secured a pistol and sought an encounter, to which there was a hasty conclusion, resulting in the shooting and killing of the blacksmith." Here is the making of another legend.

The author quotes from another interview, with Martin Chavez, which tells an entirely different story than any other about the killing of Bell.

"A line," says Chavez, "had been drawn down the center of the Kid's room, and he had been ordered to stay on one side of it. The reason was that his jailers did not want him to come too near the weapons. His penalty was to have been immediate death. The Kid deliberately stepped a foot across the line, for which he was severely reprimanded by Bell. Bell started toward the Kid. Billy waited until he was within two feet of him and started to walk away again, Bell followed him slowly, still avoiding him for the risk he was taking. The Kid slackened his pace as if to hear better what Bell was saying, and detected the fact that Bell was off his guard. Turning quickly on one heel, he brought himself face to face with Bell, jerking Bell's pistol from its scabbard." He also says the Kid had large wrists and small hands so that "it was a simple matter to remove the handcuffs whenever he felt so inclined."

Before writing this book, Otero toured the Billy the Kid

country and interviewed the remaining participants in the war, but they were all on the Kid's side and had nothing but praise for him and condemnation for Pat Garrett. All readily said that the sheriff was a cow thief and a coward and that he shot only when he had the advantage. It is too bad that Otero did not gather material for his book earlier, when there were more witnesses living. He was governor of the Territory and could have obtained information denied to others.

Although George Coe's book, *Frontier Fighter* (1934), is an autobiography, it contains so much about Billy the Kid, with whom he was very friendly, that I feel it has a place in this chapter. Coe declares in the first sentence of his preface, "My chief reason for publishing my experiences is to correct some of the false rumors that have misled an ever-critical public. It is unbelievable, the number of misleading statements there are afloat; clever tales to catch the curious, whereas the truth is entirely sufficient."

He says the Kid's own account of his first act of violence was defending his mother from the abuse of his stepfather, whom he knocked out by hitting him over the head with a chair. Thinking he had killed him, the boy fled, never to return. He says the killing of the blacksmith took place after this.

Coe declares the tale about Mrs. McSween's playing her piano is "wholly absurd," but the Kid and Tom O'Folliard did "play the piano occasionally between battles, and with their irrepressible high spirits tried to dispel the gloom settling around the survivors." He also says the Kid shot Bob Beckwith down as he entered the door, "and faithful to the last, called to McSween to follow him. With a six-shooter in each hand, firing as he went, he strode over Beckwith's lifeless body and McSween followed him." It hap-

pens that McSween had been killed before this and the
Kid and Tom O'Folliard were the last to leave the burning
building. Since Coe was not in the McSween home during
this battle, but some distance away in the McSween-Tunstall warehouse, he did not know at first hand what was
taking place in the burning home.

He tells that Colonel Dudley was arrested for his part
in this fight, taken to Las Vegas, and tried, and that the
cost of this trial to the government was between forty and
fifty thousand dollars. He claims that on the strength of
the evidence found against him, the Colonel was court-
martialed and thrown out of the United States Army. The
Colonel was tried, but found not guilty, and so was not
dishonorably discharged. Coe also makes the common mistake of having the Kid taken to Las Vegas to be tried for
killing Sheriff Brady. This trial, was held at Mesilla.

Like many old-timers, Coe misspells a great many proper
names, and although it may be a typographical error, he
says that Pat Garrett died in 1904 instead of 1908. Strange
to say, nineteen years later Glenn Shirley, in his *Toughest
of Them All* (1953), repeats the same mistake in quoting
Coe, and in the 1951 reprint of Coe's book by the University of New Mexico Press this error is not corrected.

Many histories—as distinguished from biographies and
memoirs—include material on Billy the Kid, and, sad to say,
many are unreliable. George B. Anderson, in his *History
Of New Mexico* (1907), misspells many proper names,
founds his account on the unreliable writings of Emerson
Hough, and quotes him freely. The volume entitled *A History of New Mexico* (1925), by Charles F. Coan, likewise
contains careless spelling such as "Chisom" for Chisum,
"McSwain" for McSween, "Tunstel" for Tunstall, etc. Ralph
Emerson Twitchell, an able historian, makes like errors in

proper names in his *The Leading Facts of New Mexico* (4 vols., 1911–17). He quotes Hough liberally and follows Upson's account closely.

Just about the most absurd account found in a recognized state history is in the chapter on criminals in the three-volume work by Frank Hall entitled *The History of the State of Colorado* (1889–95). ". . . the people of the Territory, especially the inhabitants of Lincoln County," he writes, "were kept in constant turmoil by the acts of large bands of thieves, cut-throats and outlaws, chief of whom was a remarkable character known all over the border as 'Billy the Kid.' In the broad annals of frontier life, filled as they are with the outrages of lawless men perpetrated in Colorado, and elsewhere, there was not one whose deeds of blood and successful evasions of punishment attracted so much interest and horror as the short, but marvelous career of the mere youth who forms the subject of this sketch."

Hall's excuse for including information on Billy the Kid in a history of Colorado is that the Kid was alleged to have been at one time a resident of Denver. "Although a part of the annals of New Mexico," he continues, "I am persuaded to attach an outline here because it was said at the time that the 'Kid' had been a resident of Denver, and for the further reason which is well established, that one of the prominent criminal lawyers of that city was engaged as his counsel.

"Billy the Kid was born in New York City, bred in the streets of that metropolis as a newsboy, bootblack and irreclaimable young desperado from the time he could *range its busy avenues. . . .*

"Shortly after his birth his father died, and a few years later his widowed mother settled in Kansas where she at length married a man named Antrim. In due course they moved to Lincoln County, New Mexico, where Billy took employment as a cowboy herder for one of the large owners of range cattle. When he had reached maturity his step-father died when the mother, widowed the second time, went back to her old home in Kansas, leaving Billy, who had become one of the rough and tough wild riders of the cattle ranges."

According to this historian a certain criminal lawyer had defended the Kid several times. When Billy was captured at Stinking Springs and taken to Santa Fe, this lawyer, according to Hall, heard that a mob was forming to lynch his client. (The author must have read about the mob at the railroad station in Las Vegas.) When the authorities refused to post a guard around the jail, the attorney organized his own guard to protect his client. This guard would stay only until midnight, leaving the lawyer at his post alone. Soon afterwards the mob attacked, but the faithful lawyer got behind a wall and exchanged shots with members of the mob until daylight, when they retreated.

Hall has the Kid rush into the jail yard after the killing of Bell and Olinger, seize Olinger's *Winchester*, and break it over the dead officer's head. Again, when the Kid rode away from Lincoln, he killed four of Chisum's cowboys and sent a message back to the cattleman by the fifth. He has Garrett follow him *with a large posse* and surround Maxwell's house. Garrett entered Maxwell's bedroom through a window, and when the Kid *rushed in with a rifle,* Garrett cut him down, ending the Kid's life at the age of *twenty-six.*

It is indeed unfortunate that we find such irresponsible statements in a recognized history, and this one certainly takes the grand prize for unreliability containing not one truthful statement.

7. *Among the Paper-Backs*

SINCE ALL THE DIME NOVELS and many of the small outlaw books were issued with wrappers, a number of paper-backs have already received mention, but there are others. Among the extremely scarce paper-backs is the little booklet by John Milton Scanland, entitled *The Life of Pat Garrett and the Taming of the Border Outlaw,* published in 1908. It adheres to the rule of inaccuracy and legend. The Lincoln County War is described as being between John Chisum and the small ranchers. The Kid is said to have killed Sheriff Brady, and to have been accompanied by Jesse Evans and Segura at the time.

Scanland uses the version that the Kid killed Bell when the latter took his prisoner downstairs to the prison outhouse. He employs Pat Garrett's wording in his description of the death of the Kid, but says he was in his twenty-second year and had "killed twenty-seven men—perhaps more." He claims that at the tender age of five Billy "began to show his viciousness among his companions—his inherent criminal nature was asserting its mastery, and developing him for a career of crime." Like many others, Scanland says the Kid went to Maxwell's on that fatal night "to see his lady love." Like many others, too, he misspells proper names frequently, calling O'Folliard "O'Fallin" in one line and "Folliard" two lines farther on.

In the late 1880's when the daring deeds of Billy the Kid

were still on everyone's lips, a French nobleman, Baron E. de Mandat-Grancey, came to the United States for a visit, and on his return to his homeland, he wrote two books about his American experiences. One of them, published in 1889 and as far as I know never translated into English, is *La Brêche aux Buffles,* in which he attempts to tell his French readers something about this American outlaw by giving a brief account of his participation in the Lincoln County War and especially of his escape from the Lincoln jail. The Baron seems to have relied upon Siringo's account in his then recently published *A Texas Cowboy,* but obviously became somewhat confused in the translation, for he names "Mr. William *Bonny*" as one of the guards killed by the Kid.

One of the most ridiculous paper-backs it has been my privilege to examine is *Oklahoma Charlie* (plus a subtitle as long as my arm), by Marion Hughes (1910). The author relates, among other drivel, a preposterous tale about Billy the Kid. He tells that the Kid was born in Illinois and named Billy LeRoy—evidently he was a *Police Gazette* reader. In the course of his narrative he has the Kid hold up a stagecoach with a corncob on a stick to prove his bravery to a gang of road agents hanging out in the mountains of Colorado, a gang he wanted to join but who would not admit him until he had proved his courage. The whole account shows a strong influence of the *Police Gazette's Billy LeRoy.* The corncob incident no doubt was suggested by an episode in this novel: when Billy LeRoy's guards wondered at his using a gun as small as a .38, LeRoy explained, "A corncob is just as good as a pistol to hold up a coach with."

In that rare little booklet *Famous in the West,* by Eugene Cunningham (1926), there is a chapter devoted to Billy the Kid. In it Cunningham has the Kid born William H. Bonney and follows the common legends concerning the move to Coffeyville, Mrs. Bonney's moving to Colorado and marrying Antrim, the killing of the blacksmith by the Kid with a pocketknife at the age of twelve, and other generally repeated tales.

"When he needed money," Cunningham writes, "it was easy to either win it by gambling with the Mexicans, or by 'sticking them up.' When in the mood, he was apt to shoot down a Mexican 'just to see him kick.' "

He has Tom Hill kill Tunstall, and says the Kid killed Morton and Baker while they were on their knees begging for mercy. He deals briefly with the fight at the McSween home, but does say the Kid had sixty men on his side while Dad Peppin had only "thirty or forty."

Of the Kid's escape at Lincoln he writes: "April 28th came, and the day drew near its close. Ollinger, in charge of some cowboys who were also prisoners, went across the street to supper. Bell took the Kid outside. As they returned, Bell turned to speak to one Goss [*sic*], jailer and cook. The Kid ran upstairs ahead of his guard, got into a room where arms were kept and snatched a Colt. He leaped back to the stairhead and as Bell started up, fired on him. The bullet missed Bell, but glanced from the wall—according to the story—and passed clear through the deputy's body. He reeled into the yard and fell dead."

Of the killing of the Kid, he relates: "Garrett had gone inside and now sat in the darkness *beside* Maxwell's bed. He was questioning Maxwell about the Kid and receiving evasive answers." Then the Kid came in bootless, "with a .41 double-action in one hand, a butcherknife in the other." When he asked "*Quien es?*" Garrett shot him. "Garrett's bullet struck the Kid just over the heart and he reeled back.

His gun pointed at Garrett, went off, but the bullet ranged high. Garrett leaped up and fired again, missing. But the Kid was already dead, without knowing who had killed him." Ah, me, every man seems to have his own version of the Kid's death as well as of many incidents in his life.

Anthony Gish wrote a little pamphlet entitled *American Bandits* (1938), which adds nothing new. Although he deals largely with modern outlaws such as Dillinger and "Pretty Boy" Floyd, he admits that Billy the Kid was one of the worst desperadoes of the Southwest, but "does not properly belong in a history of bandits. So he will be mentioned but briefly. He was a killer, who rustled cattle and went in for *petty thievery* as a sideline." Only four short paragraphs are allotted to this best-known and most popular outlaw, who "early became a blacksmith's apprentice" and later became angry and "shot the blacksmith."

G. G. Price's *Death Comes to Billy the Kid* (1940), is a wildly imaginative and fantastic tale. The Governor of New Mexico sent a trusted messenger to find the Kid and bring the outlaw before him so that he might receive a pardon. The Kid and the messenger made their way back in spite of the fact that they were both suffering from mountain fever. The messenger was a very religious young man, and by the time they reached the Pecos River, he had succeeded in converting the Kid to God and baptized him in the river.

During this journey they were shadowed by representatives of the big cattlemen, one of whom, though no names are mentioned, can readily be identified as Garrett—"tall and angular with a hawklike face and a beak of a nose. His shaggy brows shading deepset eyes, bony hands hanging almost to his knees."

When the Kid and the messenger arrived at Fort Sumner, they were both delirious with fever. First they went to the home of a friendly Mexican woman, and after she had sent for the Kid's sweetheart to come nurse him, the Kid went across the street to Maxwell's house. When the women heard the shots at Maxwell's, they knew what had happened.

The morning after the Kid was killed "officers came taking messages. As they passed from the house, a lean, lank, hawk-faced man was backed against the adobe wall of the building. His clutching, sinewed fingers reached far down on the barrel of the gun in his hand. He never spoke. He did not open his mouth. He did not belong there, nor was he one of them. He was the gunman of the cattle kings, who stood accused of ruthlessly murdering homeseekers without cause, secreting their bodies, so no one would know their fate."

Billy the Kid, according to this writer, had been loved by the Spanish people because he had helped to fight the big cattlemen in their ruthless attempts to steal the homesteads of the settlers and the land grants of the people of Spanish descent. Now "Billy the Kid lay dead *in the street* below, martyr for the oppressed. A shot had stifled a life, wanted, misled, loved—whose memory would be forever loved. But the bullet killing him, also pierced the vitals of the all powerful cattle association. It could never rise again. It was dead, shot by the backfire of its own six-gun."

I might mention in passing the little book, *Taylor's Thrilling Tales of Texas* (1926), by D. K. Taylor. He claims to have known the Kid personally, but says Billy was twenty-three when he died and continues the tradition of approximately one man for each year by having him kill twenty-two men.

Roscoe Logue, in his *Under Texas Skies* (1935), says the Kid's father died on the trail to Kansas and that when the

family finally landed in Silver City, New Mexico, the widowed mother was insulted by a "rum-soaked bum" whom
the Kid killed with a pocket-knife. He adds that in those
days "men shot each other down to acquire prestige and
to inspire awe and envy among the lesser ilk," and hints
that the Lincoln County War was between the Murphy
faction and Tunstall, the Kid's boss.

Again, he says that after the Kid was captured at Stinking Springs, "as they went through Santa Fe, New Mexico,
a mob assembled to take the Kid"—more of those recurring half-truths. This mob, as we know, was at Las Vegas
when Garrett was loading his prisoners on the train to take
them *to* Santa Fe, and the man they were after was Dave
Rudabaugh, not the Kid.

Logue relates that the young outlaw went to Maxwell's
to see his girl friend, who was a servant in the Maxwell
household, and when the "boyish figure soon came *tripping*
across the yard toward the front door" to his death, his girl
"came on the run and her noisy grief broke the fatal news."

William Yancey Shackleford, in his *Gun-Fighters of the
Old West* (1934), says, "Alexander McSween, a *Presbyterian preacher*, appeared in the town of Lincoln. There
was no opening for a minister in the vicinity, but McSween
had once studied law, so he set up as an attorney."

He states that the first man the Kid killed was a cowpuncher who slapped him in a barroom fight, whereupon
Billy "cut the man's belly open with a jack-knife." The
author also says that the first authentic account of the Lincoln County War was written by Emerson Hough and that
he himself has followed Hough's account closely. He reports that after he got away from the McSween house in
Lincoln County, the Kid claimed that the 'murdering
preacher' owed him some money, and many people thought

that he collected this at the point of a pistol from John Chisum, who had backed McSween in his fight against the Murphy faction."

In Walter Pannell's little pamphlet, *Civil War on the Range* (1943), it is said that "as a legal basis for the coming campaign against the Kid, it was necessary to have him charged with a definite crime. That charge was ready made and his enemies lost no time in making use of it. During the hostilities of the Lincoln County War, a *stray bullet* had killed Sheriff Brady of Lincoln County, who had aligned his forces with those of the Murphy-Dolan Cattle Company. It was thought that Billy the Kid had fired the shot, but it was not definitely known. Brady was killed on the streets of Lincoln during a gun battle when almost anything could have happened. Armed with a warrant for Billy the Kid, charging him with the murder of Sheriff Brady, and backed by a formidable army of deputies 'armed to the teeth' and with orders to 'shoot on sight,' Pat Garrett commenced his campaign of warfare against the border outlaw—Billy the Kid."

This author makes Olinger a United States marshal; and of the Kid's escape from the Lincoln jail, he says: "What really happened in the second story jail room, which enabled the Kid to get possession of the marshal's gun, no one but the Kid and Bell knew. The lips of Bell were too soon sealed by death, and the Kid never told. As is usually the case, widely divergent stories compete for acceptance, any one of which might be true or false." He then proceeds to give the three conjectures which have been the most popular.

Pannell further relates that the Kid was a hired gunman who killed from a list of victims given him by Chisum. His first killing had been that of a blacksmith when the Kid was sixteen. Maxwell's home was the Kid's hideout, and, "as a matter of fact, Garrett had accidentally stumbled into the Kid's hide-out at the home of a leading citizen and supposed friend of the law; and the outlaw was at that identical moment in another room of the same house in which Garrett sat at the foot of a bed in a darkened room. According to information that afterwards became available, the Kid had just come in and had taken off his boots preparatory to going to bed, himself. In a fateful moment he decided to get himself something to eat before retiring. There was a small stove in the room and he, ostensibly, thought he would awaken his friend, Maxwell, and get the key to the smoke house where the usual quarter of beef hung and get him a steak. In his sock feet, making no noise, he went softly upon the porch toward Maxwell's room, where the sheriff sat in the dark trying to obtain information of the very man that was walking toward him with noiseless tread. It was an eventful moment—spelling disaster for the Kid in large capital letters."

In an appendix the author quotes in full an account of the Kid's escape at Lincoln taken from the *White Oaks Leader* of 1890. Written by G. Gauss, the jail cook who had saddled the horse for the Kid to ride away, this article is an excellent example of how old-timers forget dates and events, even after a very short time. He begins his story thus: "Once upon a time, it was, if I mistake not, in the month of April, 1880, 1881, or perhaps 1882 . . . ." He then proceeds to tell how Bell died in his arms and Olinger fell dead at his feet.

A typical example of careless reporting is that done by William Alexander Miller in his *Early Days of the Wild West* (1943), in which he says he had heard the story that "a sheriff and his deputies traced him [the Kid] to a deserted cabin. As they stepped inside they found him lying on his back asleep on an old couch with his hands in his overcoat pockets. Each of the men drew two guns and commanded him to throw up his hands. Without moving he fired two guns and killed both men."

"Billy the Kid," he says later, "was killed by Sheriff Pat Garrett *before he reached the plaza in Santa Fe*. Billy's love for a Mexican girl was the lure that cost him his life."

Harry H. Bailey, in his *When New Mexico Was Young* (1948), makes a statement I have never seen elsewhere when he says, "The Kid was really married to Maxwell's daughter, and they had two children. That was the real incentive for the Kid's visit to the Maxwell house the night he was killed."

The little book, *The Story of Billy the Kid* (1948), by J. W. Hendron, is quite different from any other account of the Kid. He declares that "Billy the Kid knew not his kin, but no doubt they knew of him and dropped a few words which helped to piece together a more human and less illusory account. William Bonney's mother was born in New Orleans. She was of French extraction and it is said that she was beautiful. Her grandfather was born in Haiti of French parentage who had gone to this island after the fall of Napoleon. Gene, as she was called, was the oldest of nineteen children, her father having married three times. The family moved to Mississippi from New Orleans where her father practiced medicine and ran a store. Billy's mother ran away from home and went to New York with a man who never married her but who was the father of William Bonney Her family rarely ever spoke of her because of her irregular conduct and lost personal contact with her after she went to New York."

The author admits that details of the Kid's early life are

"vague and indefinite," and has him tell a bunch of cow-boys in the stockyards of Kansas City that he "ran away from home in New York in 1871 because I was tired of going to school." This would make him twelve years old when he left New York. In this version the Kid persuaded Chisum's foreman, who was in Kansas City to market Chisum's cattle, to let him go to New Mexico with him. Yet, when he got there, the author has him working for Maxwell, not Chisum, and "since that time Fort Sumner has always been known as the home of Billy the Kid." Later he went to work for Chisum, and at seventeen, "despite his age was given a free range with the hiring and firing."

This writer has Beckwith kill McSween while the latter was sitting in the corner of the burning house; his account of the killing of Grant and Carlyle is also different from other recorded accounts.

He tells that while the Kid was a prisoner at Lincoln, "prisoners at the Courthouse took their meals across the road at the hotel, that is, all except the Kid. He ate his meals in jail. On this particular evening he was presented with a meal of *chili, tortillas* and beef. On the plate was a *tortita,* a little sweet cake about the size of a biscuit. Inside the *tortita* was a tiny pocket knife and a small piece of *algerita,* or yellow wood. At the first opportunity, the Kid cut a slit in the facing of his trousers at the waistband in which to conceal that flat piece of wood. He placed the slender knife in his rectum."

Thereafter at every opportunity he whittled on a key to fit his handcuffs. The day finally came when he freed himself after Bell had taken him down to an outside toilet. When they got back upstairs, he hit Bell in the head and knocked him out, then jerked Bell's gun and fired it at him, but missed because "it was the first time he had handled a gun in four months." Olinger, hearing the shot, came running over, and the Kid killed him with his own shotgun. He then ran back and killed Bell with a Winchester, before dashing out to empty the second load from the shotgun into Olinger. Need I say that all this running about and exchanging guns is ridiculous?

When Brewer's posse rounded up Morton, Baker, and the others in the crowd which had killed Tunstall, Hendron has Morton snatch a gun and shoot one of the possemen in the head; and then when Morton and Baker made a run for it, the Kid shot twice, and their bodies were "left for the buzzards to pick." All through the book there are different versions of the incidents appearing in other accounts, and especially of the killing of Joe Grant.

Just before he was killed in Maxwell's room, "the Kid came close to the bed and almost touched Garrett's knee which was crossed. At that minute the Kid threw his pistol down on Garrett." But Garrett "fired at the white shirt which was easy to see in the dark," and the Kid was no more.

Mrs. Mary Hudson Brothers' *Billy the Kid* (1949) is taken from her earlier cloth-bound book, *A Pecos Pioneer*, which will be discussed in the next chapter.

In a recent little volume entitled *One Hundred Years Ago* (n. d.), author Larry Kane says Mrs. Bonney took Billy to Santa Fe, New Mexico, after her husband died, and there married Mr. Antrim. Kane's account of Billy's death is told thus: "One evening Pat Garrett lay in wait for Billy in Pete Maxwell's room, where Billy was later expected to come. He did, and as he walked into the darkened room Pat could see him from the time he came in the door because his eyes had grown used to the darkness. When at last Billy caught a glimpse of Garrett, *he threw his gun at him*—however one second too late. Pat Garrett had shot and killed Billy the Kid."

To go into all the mistakes these little paper-backs made would make this work far too long; therefore, I will point out only enough of them to demonstrate their universal unreliability.

In 1954 two little paper-backs made their appearance, both filled with unreliable information, as is characteristic of this type of publication. William Waters, in his *A Gallery of Western Badmen,* says that after the Kid's killing of the blacksmith, "Billy's mother packed him a lunch and kissed him goodbye. The boy was on the run, and as far as is known, he never saw his mother again."

He also states that McSween was a former preacher and that during the siege of the McSween home Mrs. McSween "ran twelve miles to Fort Stanton and summoned the cavalry." Even though Fort Stanton was only nine miles from Lincoln, it would have made quite a run for a frail woman. The author further declares that before the Kid went into the Maxwell house, and to his death, he was in a little house in the rear where "Garrett's sister-in-law, Celsa Gutierrez, was fixing dinner for him." He also tells that when Garrett recognized him, "he leaped to the floor *firing three shots on the way down.*"

The other book published during this year is *Howard's Original Texas Guide Book,* in which the author says the Kid "lived and commuted between old Tascosa (Texas), Lincoln, and Las Vegas, New Mexico." The compiler also tells that the Kid "was captured, escaped, and finally killed by Pat Garrett, *sheriff of Oldham County, Texas, who lived at Tascosa.*"

Famous Western Outlaw Sheriff Battles (1954), by Hank

Sterling, is one of those pocket-book publications written strictly for entertainment, filled with conversation which never took place and repeating the many legends that have grown with the years, such as the judge's sentence at Mesilla and the Kid's saucy answer.

The author introduces a girl he calls Pabalita to warn the Kid when John Poe went to Fort Sumner looking for him. Whether the writer seized upon the false report that the Kid's sweetheart at this time was Paulita Maxwell, I do not know. It is common practice for romanticists to introduce a love affair into their writings as a means of creating interest. But a real historian would not know that "the Kid took her in his arms, brought his lips down on her soft eager mouth. His two protruding upper teeth dug into her lip and she knew the bruises would be visible for days, but she did not care. He raised her off the floor and she surrendered willingly as he carried her to a blanket covered spot in the room." All this tender romance might raise one's blood pressure, but where were the witnesses who reported this private love scene?

This author is another who repeats Judge Bristol's sentence and the Kid's answer. He also states that the Kid was "chained down to an iron ring in the floor" in Lincoln. Regarding the killing of Olinger, he writes: "The Kid walked out on the balcony overlooking the street, waited for Ollinger to come out of Sam Wortley's hotel where he was having his dinner, and when the man *started across the street,* shot him dead."

There are many other errors in details in this story, such as calling John Poe the sheriff of Tascosa, Texas, describing the Maxwell house as a one-story building, and relating that Garrett "seated himself *in a chair* at the head of Maxwell's bed on the fatal night of the Kid's death." In regard to the last bit of information, Garrett himself says, "I walked to the head of the bed and sat down on it, beside him, near the pillow." Incidentally Sterling spells Brewer's name "Bruer" and in one place calls Billy Wilson, "Dave."

In 1957 there was published a little book entitled *Great Western Heroes*, edited by Rafe Brent. One chapter, by Clair Huffaker, is devoted to Pat Garrett. This is the same article which appeared in *Saga* magazine, previously mentioned. It is a repetition of Garrett's own account with the addition of quite a lot of dialog which never took place. O'Folliard's name is spelled "Foliard," and in writing of Garrett's posse cooking breakfast and tempting the Kid's gang by its smell at Stinking Springs, the author says: "Over a *roaring* fire, Pat's men *roasted several sides of prime beef.*" That is a lot of meat to feed thirteen men, and anyhow, who would roast meat over a "roaring" fire?

Huffaker says that when Garrett reached Las Vegas with his prisoners, he dropped Pickett off and then took the other three on to Santa Fe. He does not mention the mob at Las Vegas, but does say that "at several points, mobs of hostile citizens had the idea they would like to string Billy up personally." He further states that at Mesilla the Kid was tried before Judge Ira Leonard for the murder of Sheriff Brady, when in fact Judge Leonard was the Kid's attorney and Judge Bristol was on the bench.

He tells that when Pat went to see Pete Maxwell, he "made his way into Pete's large, *one-room* house." And as the Kid approached the bed upon which Garrett was sitting, the knife in the Kid's hand "brushed Pat's knee." He says Pat fired twice and the Kid once. "Every man present heard three shots fired," he writes, "but no one could find where the Kid's slug went. All other writers say there were two shots fired, both from Garrett's gun.

A Fitting Death for Billy the Kid

As a last example, let me cite another publication, *Famous Guns from Famous Collections*, (1957), by Hank Wieand Bowman. In a chapter entitled "Outlaw Guns," the author tells about the guns of various outlaws of the West. Referring to Billy the Kid, he has this to say: "Conflict again arises concerning the firearms used by Billy Bonney, better known as Billy the Kid. Billy was one of the most cold blooded of all the western killers. But what firearms did Billy use? That's a tough one to answer. Pictured in this chapter is a .41-caliber short-barreled double-action Colt which unquestionably was one of Billy's guns. However, there are other reports to claim that Billy used a .38-caliber Colt Lightning; others insist he swore by a single-action Colt .44 and still others are adamant that Remington won Billy's endorsement. Concerning one fact there is no argument. By the time he was 21, of his own admission, Billy had knocked off 21 men, beginning with his first at the age of 12, though that first one was a knife job. Numbered among his conquests were two sheriffs. What Billy's ultimate score might have been is hard to estimate, for in 1881 he was shot down by Pat Garrett."

Thus it becomes apparent that writers still believe all the legends which Upson and a few others created, and continue to palm them off on us as fact.

To return to Garrett's *Authentic Life* briefly, in a four page addendum he complains that some of the early writers have him "shooting the Kid from behind a bed, from under a bed, and from other places of concealment. . . . I was not behind the bed, because, in the first place, I could not get there. I'm not 'as wide as a door' but the bed was so close to the wall that a lath could scarce have been introduced between. I was not under the bed, and this fact will require a little more complicated explanation. I *could* have gotten under the bed; but, you see, I did not know the Kid was coming."

Why complain about one relatively inconsequential error in one incident? My reply is that the whole history of Billy the Kid's life, as it has come down through the years, has been false. It has been made up of misstatements of fact, some more consequential than others, but all contributing to the tissue of lies.

8. *All That Glitters*

THERE REMAIN a number of books which should be examined before bringing this work to a close. These will be taken up chronologically by year rather than in order of importance so as to show how through the years would-be historians and biographers have copied, one after the other, the legends of the past, content to take the other fellow's word concerning the Kid. Each writer seems to have had a smattering of information about the important events in the Kid's life or a hazy sort of knowledge, but when he put it on paper, the result was something far from what actually happened.

One of the earliest cloth-bound books to deal with Billy the Kid was Forbes Heerman's *Thirteen Stories of the Far West*, published in 1887. In his foreword the author states that these stories "are reports of actual experiences, written up from his note-book, with such changes in names, places, and minor incidents as his personal safety seems to require." No doubt he was here using a device to make his readers think he was recording actual happenings, but judging from Chapter VII, which concerns the Kid and is entitled "The Wedding at Puerto de Luna," his stories are wild fiction.

The author's fertile imagination has Billy the Kid staging a holdup at a dance, killing his own father because the father recognized him, and then losing his own life when he became bogged in the quicksands of the Pecos River while trying to escape from his holdup victims.

It is claimed that four men are primarily responsible for the preservation of the numerous Billy the Kid legends: Ash Upson (for Pat Garrett), Charlie Siringo, Emerson Hough, and Walter Noble Burns. Upson created many of them, and Siringo repeated them in his widely read books. Because of his extensive magazine writing and his very popular books, Hough became a favorite with American readers, and although he made free with facts, his readers believed what he wrote. More recently, Burns revived a smoldering interest in the Kid, and with his ability to tell a fascinating, romantic story, he is now perhaps the most widely quoted "authority" on Billy the Kid.

Hough was a lawyer and well educated; and since he was schooled in the legal field, I cannot understand why he was not more careful of events and dates. Evidently he wrote his *The Story of the Cowboy,* or at least the chapter on the Kid, from hearsay. This book was published in 1897 and was among his earliest writings.

"Billy the Kid," he writes, "died at the ripe age of *twenty-three,* and at that time had killed *twenty-three* men, committing his first murder when he was but fourteen years of age. He and his men inaugurated a reign of terror, which made his name a dread from one end of the country to the other. They lived on their earnings as robbers, and glad enough were the Mexicans of the remote *placitas* to give them anything they asked in return for life. This young fiend and his gang at one time shot down in cold blood a party of seven Mexicans whom they found encamped at a waterhole, declaring later that they did this 'just to see them kick.' "

It is rather disappointing to find such an able journalist

writing a paragraph of this length without one true statement in it. From the age at which he was killed and the number of men he had slain to the killing of the Mexicans "just to see them kick" and the robberies in the country, all are untrue. The Mexican people were the Kid's friends and did more for him than anyone else. They fed him, hid him, spied for him, and loved him. Mr. Hough created that incident of the killing of the seven Mexicans out of whole cloth, and the sad part about creating such a legend is that many writers after him repeated it as a fact, though most of them did cut down the number of victims.

Hough must have had in mind the Jimmy Carlyle incident when he wrote: "A band of pursuers was made up, and the Kid was besieged at a ranch house some miles north of White Oaks. The self-appointed leader of the pursuers went into the house with a flag of truce and was detained there. Later he tried to escape from the house and was shot down by the Kid as he ran, thus breaking up the siege with Billy still in possession of his fortifications."

On the next page he continues: "If a man was suspected by the Kid as apt to convey undesirable news to undesirable parties, the Kid never made any accusations, asked any questions, or waited for any denials. He simply shot the man, laughed about it, and rode on." He makes the Kid a cold-blooded killer indeed.

He intimates that the Lincoln County War was between the Kid's gang and Chisum, who was trying to protect his ranch and cattle. "Some of them," he writes about the outlaws, "knew all about the Chisholm [sic] outfit, and it seems to have been agreed among them that it would be a desirable thing to kill the owners of the ranch, take possession of the property, and settle down to being cattle kings themselves."

All That Glitters

He says that every man was forced to take sides in this contest, and "the wayfarer who saw a body of men approaching was obliged to guess, and guess very quickly, which side he favored. If he guessed wrong, the coyotes had another meal. The victim was left lying where he fell."

To the siege of the McSween home, though it was perhaps the most important conflict of the Lincoln County War, he devotes only a few sentences: "At one time there was a sort of pitched battle waged at the county seat in Lincoln County, and some of the Kid's men 'holed up' in a 'dobe house until driven out by fire, meantime making deadly rifle practice upon any of the enemy who chanced to show a head anywhere along the street of the tiny 'dobe town. Upon the hillside back of the courthouse one of the opposing force attempted to run to the cover of a big rock, from which he could command the windows of the 'dobe fortress of the Kid's men. As he ran there spoke a heavy buffalo gun from the window, and he fell shot through the back at four hundred yards. He was not killed at once, and lay upon the hillside all the rest of the afternoon waving his hand for help, but no one dared go near him; and there he died, one of the cowboy victims of this war—a death inglorious enough, but met in pursuance of what the poor fellow thought was his duty."

Of the killing of the Kid, he writes: "It was reported that Billy was to call at night at a certain ranch and say goodbye to his sweetheart, a Mexican *señorita*, and Pat Garrett went to the house and secreted himself *behind* the bed of the ranch owner in the room nearest the entrance." And when Billy came backing in the room *"with his boots in one hand* Garrett shot and killed him."

In 1898 there was published in London a now scarce book written by an English lady, Miss Edith M. Nicholl

(Mrs. Bowyer), who had come to the United States to live on a New Mexico ranch. Her experiences are recorded in a book she entitled *Observations of a Ranch Woman in New Mexico*. Like most writers of that day who treated western subjects, especially New Mexico, she had to include Billy the Kid.

She starts out by telling how the Englishman Tunstall, whom she calls "Morton," established his ranch in Lincoln County. "Just about this time," she relates, "an incident occurred in one of the cities of the Territory which, slight as it appears, was nevertheless destined to affect very materially the lives of several hundred human beings. A young *dish-washer*, ill-used by a big and burly man-cook, drew his pistol and wounded his assailant. The boy then took refuge in flight, and days after turned up, weary and half starved, at the ranch occupied by Morton [Tunstall]. The wanderer was none other than he who was soon to become notorious under the pseudonym of Billy the Kid." Of course this is far from the truth.

Rival cattlemen caused the arrest of Tunstall, and when they were bringing him back to town, "he was fired upon by the men in his rear and his body abandoned to the crows and buzzards." The news of this tragedy, she says "turned the Kid into an avenging demon."

She calls McSween "Mackintosh," and in telling of the burning of his home, she says, "In this house dwelt Mackintosh with wife and children [the McSweens had no children], and at the moment several other persons, Billy the Kid amongst them—fifteen in all."

Farther along she states: "Under cover of darkness the attacking force sent across to the hotel on the other bank of the river. There they procured a quantity of kerosene oil, which one of their number proceeded to pour through the holes in the door, soaking the wood within, his comrades firing over his head the while in order to distract the attention of the besieged. A few lighted matches finished the business. While the flames, fanned by the draught, gathered strength and volume, shots continued to rain like hail into the hall-way, rendering it impossible for those inside the house to extinguish the blaze.

"Although adobe bricks are practically fireproof, the woodwork of the dwelling offered no resistance to the flames, and the wretched inhabitants, driven from room to room by the smoke, finally made a dash for their lives, and were all, with *one exception, helpless women and children included, brutally murdered.*"

The one exception, of course, was Billy the Kid, and after this he became more vengeful than ever: "Banned now as an outlaw, the sheriffs sought him untiringly, and at last ran him to earth in a lonely house, where, without food or fuel, he was in the end obliged to surrender." This was evidently his capture at Stinking Springs. Of his escape from the Lincoln jail, she writes: "True, he was in irons, but that was a mere circumstance to Billy the Kid. Unobserved by his goalers, he had long ere this succeeded in filing—though how he obtained his tools no one knew—the fetters confining his hands and feet. *Both* jailers went out to dinner one day, *leaving him alone,* and it was only a matter of a few minutes before he was free." Then she tells of the killing of Bell and Olinger, though she does not name them.

"But," she continues, "the career of even Billy the Kid has to close at last, and the present sheriff of this county was the man to close it. Hearing that the youthful desperado took up his quarters at the ranch of a certain cattleman, he rode thither one night prepared to 'take chances.'

"The house, after the manner of adobe houses, was one-storied, and finding an open window, the sheriff quietly entered, to find himself in the room of the owner, who challenged the intruder from his bed. The sheriff explained his errand in whispers, and, taking a seat on the bed, continued the conversation in the same tone.

"Now, it happened that the redoubtable Billy was actually in the house at the time, and finding himself attacked with the pangs of hunger, arose from his couch, and, taking a knife, was proceeding to the store-room to cut himself some meat. Hearing voices in the room of his host, he opened the door and demanded to know who was there.

"Of course the sheriff made no reply, but *while the other man was explaining,* he took careful aim at the young outlaw, as he stood in the door *with a lighted lamp in his hand,* and shot him through the heart. And that was the end of Billy the Kid. His career had lasted for five years, and in that space of time *three hundred persons* had met death by violence. History does not relate the number that fell by the hand of the Kid alone." Even the ladies can spin 'em tall!

In that rare book much sought by collectors, *Prose and Poetry of the Live Stock Industry* (1905), there is a chapter entitled "The Range Rustler," in which there is mention of Billy the Kid. The author calls him an "infamous cutthroat" and says he died a violent death at the ripe age of "twenty-three" and at that time had killed *"twenty-three* men—one for each year of his horrible life—having committed his first murder when he was about fourteen years old."

Here we see Hough's influence in the verbatim repetition of his statement, thus demonstrating once again the irresponsibility of writers who neglect to check the authenticity of information before repeating it.

Governor Lew Wallace, in his *Autobiography* (1906), claimed that the New Mexicans had been living in peace

Drawing from Garrett's *The Authentic Life of Billy, the Kid.*

Capture of the Kid, Wilson, Pickett, and Rudabaugh at
Stinking Springs by Sheriff Garrett and posse.

Drawing from Garrett's *The Authentic Life of Billy, the Kid.*

The Kid killed by Sheriff Garrett at Fort Sumner.

with each other until "a rich stock-raiser from Texas came up to New Mexico, and in a short time had three hundred thousand dollars worth of cattle. He settled on the Pecos River, and in a little while had succeeded in driving away almost all the small grazers. To retaliate, they began stealing from him. Now, they do not steal in that country as they do farther east, but drive off large herds of cattle, sometimes 500 at a time. To protect himself, the Texan went down into his native state and recruited about 70 men—murderers, thieves and dangerous men of all classes, together with a number of sharp-shooters and buffalo-hunters."

This is practically the only mention of the Lincoln County troubles in his two-volume autobiography, although his wife does mention the Kid by name in a quoted letter. From the above statement by the Governor it is obvious that, although he was on the ground and should have known the facts, even he got the wrong story. Perhaps it was because he was a novelist, not a historian.

In 1906 another unreliable account of the Kid made its appearance. This is a beautifully printed and bound little volume by George T. Buffum entitled *Smith of Bear City and Other Frontier Sketches.*

"Whether he [the Kid] was ambitious to have the deaths at his hands keep pace with his years," writes Buffum, "we do not know, but at the age of *twenty-six* he had killed *twenty-seven* men. He seems not to have known the 'honour among thieves,' for when he was pursued after having killed his jailer he displayed the white flag, and when the posse came near to receive his surrender *he shot the entire band.*

"At that time there lived in Las Vegas a man by the name of Stewart; he was employed by some large cattle company to prevent the stealing of the animals and their shipment out of the country. Stewart was a fine shot and fearless, and had been mainly instrumental in the extirpation of the Stockton gang of 'cattle rustlers.' He was deputized to capture Billy the Kid, and took with him Webb, Mysterious Dave Mathews [*sic*], Ruddebaugh[*sic*] and Bill Goodlet—each one of them a man-hunter with a death record established. When the Kid was surrounded, and learned who were his captors, he offered to surrender provided that Stewart would promise not to turn him over to the authorities at Las Vegas, but agreed to place him safely in the Santa Fe jail. Stewart accepted the terms. When the news was *telegraphed* that Billy was captured and that he was to be taken to Santa Fe, the sheriff at Las Vegas determined to gain possession of him and see that he was punished for the cruel murders of the citizens of San Miguel County. When the train arrived at Las Vegas the sheriff and his deputies demanded the Kid. For an hour the train was delayed while the sheriff's demand was repeatedly refused. Finally Stewart announced that he had given his word of honour to Billy, and he proposed to keep it. 'Billy surrendered on one condition,' he added, 'and if you propose to make that condition null and void, all I can do is give Billy back his gun and turn him loose, you can come and take him.' The ghostly array of Billy's numerous victims rose before the sheriff, who had a decided repugnance to becoming a 'has-been,' and he immediately decided he did not want Billy after all. So Stewart delivered his prisoner to the keeper of the jail in Santa Fe."

Here is a confused account indeed. As we know, Garrett was the captor of the Kid, and they arrived at Las Vegas by wagon from Stinking Springs. The mob did not form until the next morning when the prisoners were put on the train after a night in the Las Vegas jail. Dave Rudabaugh was the man the mob was after, not a member of the posse as Mr. Buffum has him.

After writing his first book, Emerson Hough moved East, returning to Lincoln County in 1904 to gather material for his *Story of the Outlaw*. At this time he must have interviewed some of the more reliable citizens and talked with Garrett. Ten years after the publication of *The Story of the Cowboy*, his *Story of the Outlaw* (1907) was issued, in which he followed Garrett's account more closely, correcting some of his former misstatements and improving his account of the war as a whole. However, he still has the *Bonneys* moving to Coffeyville in 1862 and the mother marrying in Colorado. He says that Tunstall was killed by Tom Hill and that this incident marked the actual beginning of the Lincoln County War.

Morton and Baker, he writes, "surrendered under promise of safekeeping, and were held for a time at Roswell. On the trail from Roswell to Lincoln, at a point near the Agua Negra, both these men, while kneeling and pleading for their lives, were deliberately shot and killed by Billy the Kid."

He declares that Brady was killed by Billy the Kid and "at least five others of his gang," Brady having been "struck by five balls." All of which would indicate that the Kid did not do the killing alone, although he was convicted for it.

He makes the statement that Andy Boyle, Jack Long, and two other men set the McSween home on fire, and charges the Kid with killing Beckwith. In speaking of the aftermath of the war, he writes: "The only man ever actually indicted and brought to trial for a killing during the Lincoln County War was Billy the Kid, and there is many a resident of Lincoln today who declares that the

Kid was made a scapegoat; and many a man even today charges Governor Wallace with bad faith."

In another chapter on Billy the Kid he follows Upson very closely in saying: "The true name of Billy the Kid was William H. Bonney, and he was born in New York City, November 23, 1859. His father removed to Coffeyville, on the border of the Indian Nations in 1862, where soon he died, leaving a widow and two sons. Mrs. Bonney again moved, this time to Colorado, where she married again, her second husband being named Antrim."

He has the Antrims move to Silver City in 1868 and says they lived there until 1871, Mrs. Antrim dying in 1870. We know that she died in 1874. Hough continues to follow Upson closely in writing of the Kid's early life. He passes over the killing of Bernstein with only a mention that he was killed by the Kid on a horse-stealing expedition. He says the Kid's killing of Carlyle "was a nail in the Kid's coffin, for Carlyle was well liked at White Oaks."

He further states that the story of the Kid's slipping his hands from his handcuffs, striking Bell over the head, and then shooting him with his own gun is all wrong. "The truth is," he writes, "that Bell took the Kid, at his request, into the back yard of the jail; returning, the Kid sprang quickly up the stairs to the guard-room door, as Bell turned to say something to old man Goss [*sic*], a cook, who was standing in the yard. The Kid pushed open the door, caught up a revolver from a table, and sprang to the head of the stairs just as Bell turned the angle and started up. He fired at Bell and missed him, the ball striking the left-hand side of the staircase. It glanced, however, and passed through Bell's body, lodging in the wall at the angle of the stair. Bell staggered out into the yard and fell dead."

Mr. Hough claims that this story was corroborated by

both the Kid and Gauss and that he, himself, was very familiar with the place as he had had a law office in this same building.

Although Pat Garrett said in his own book that he was sitting on Pete Maxwell's bed, at the head, Hough claims that Garrett told him, "I was sitting in a chair and leaning over toward him [Maxwell] as I talked in a low tone."

The Great Plains, by Randall Parrish (1907) barely mentions the Kid, but even this scant notice is wrong. "Billy the Kid," he writes, "a mere boy of twenty-two when he fell, had killed in cold blood more than one man for each year of his miserable life." This legend remains common to the present time.

Another good example of the many books containing these half-truths about Billy the Kid and filled with misstatements is *Seven Years on the Pacific Slope,* by Mr. and Mrs. Hugh Fraser, published in 1914. This book, or at least the chapter on Billy the Kid, does no credit to the scholarship of those who, because of inadequate research, have again perpetuated legend as history or myth as truth.

Although the authors call no names, one cannot mistake the fact that they are writing about Billy the Kid and Pat Garrett. The story about the Kid is told by a visiting cowboy, who starts his tale with another version of that old legend of the Kid killing Chisum's cowboys.

"Well," he says, "as I was saying, we stood there, talking among ourselves when we heard a man get off his horse and come toward us. We didn't move, thinking it was one of the others, but he was close beside us before we turned round and got a look at him. He was a kid like me, an openfaced kid with a big mouth and laughing eyes. He looked from one to the other as if he expected to recognize us.

" 'Howdy, boys,' he said.

" 'Howdy,' says we.

" 'Who are you riding for?' he asks.

" '——,' says we.

" 'Oh, are you?' says he in a gentle, surprised sort of voice. 'Well, then,' before we could lift a finger, he's got his gun out and us covered. 'Then there's your pay,' he says, and shoots the fellow beside me through the head. 'And you,' he says to me as the fellow's body straightened out under my feet, 'You tell —— that I'll shoot a man of his for every five dollars that he owes me until the account is settled—see?'

"All the time he was talking he was backing off, still smiling, just like he was asking me to have a drink, but the muzzle of his gun was looking at me between the eyes and his left hand was hanging over the hammer, *all ready to start fanning.* Back he went, creeping like a cat, and I just stood with my tongue out, staring at him."

A bit farther on the cowboy continues "The fellow that did it? He had a heap of names. The Southwest was lousy with bad men, but he was the worst of them. He wasn't twenty that night—he wasn't much more than nineteen, and he'd killed fifteen or sixteen men then. He was the only man I ever heard of who owned up that he killed because he liked killing—he liked seeing them wriggle—that's what he said—wriggle!"

This character admits that he never saw the Kid again, though he "heard a heap about him. He rampaged around for two years after that—but they got him in the end all right, all right—and the man that got him was got himself a year ago. He was a quarrelsome son of a she wolf, too. I worked for him at one time."

In further comment about the Kid, he says: "Things got so at last that the Governor—(I think, of Arizona, but I can't swear to it—I heard he took to writing books)—sent out after the kid. I don't know who it was he sent—but he had him visit him somehow or other, alone, at midnight, to try and get him clear out of that part of the country. Did you ever hear of anything like that? Yes, sir, he talked to him—and the kid got away afterwards! Oh, that Governor acted like a perfect gentleman! But he didn't get the kid to see the error of his ways at all, and a few weeks later he got his skin full of booze, the kid did, and shot three perfectly harmless greasers, riding out of town one afternoon, just because he felt good."

And later: "It wasn't long after that that a man was found —I don't know whether he was imported or not, but anyway he was found—who allowed that he was ready to go after the kid, if he was provided with a man-sized posse. Once a leader was on the spot, it didn't take long to get a posse together—young fellows who could light out if things went wrong and who hadn't any family cares to get between their eyes and their foresights, or houses to be burnt or stock to run off.

"They started in the dark of the moon, just such a night as this and, for once, the kid's human telegraph system didn't work, so that he was run into before he knew anything about it, and rounded up and corralled in a cabin. He was game, was the kid, and they had to shut him up for a whole day before he called it off. One of his men got hit when he was *standing by the window* and the kid pulled him over towards the door. 'He ain't dead yet,' he said to the others. 'Push him outside and maybe he can get a shot at the ——!' But the man got shot as soon as the door was opened, and when the kid ran out of cartridges, he came out and put his hands up.

"He laughed when they took him, and called them every

fighting name he could think of just to see if he could get 'em mad—but the men with him didn't laugh. They were the meanest collection of human coyotes that ever crawled —which they did. They fought and they screamed and they carried on something fierce; which made the posse feel considerably better, and they got some of their own back by telling them what was going to happen to 'em just as soon as they hit a gaol and a gallows."

We can see that the narrator had a smattering of the truth, but got most of the circumstances wrong. He continues in the same way: "Well, they took 'em in, the kid and his outfit, and locked 'em up. They had to take 'em by rail, though, and they nearly got 'em lynched at the depot —by the very men who let 'em run loose all these years, for fear of getting themselves hurt. . . . The kid and the fellow that got him were the only two men in the crowd, barring the posse. The kid jeered at the mob out of the window, while his pals were trying to crawl through the floor, and the sheriff threatened to give his prisoners guns and let 'em defend themselves if the crowd got gay with him. . . .

"The trial," the narrator continues, "didn't take long, as you may imagine. The kid, who was just twenty, had eighteen or nineteen proved killings to his name and the others had each five or six. It was just a matter of identifying them and handing 'em over to the County Sheriff for what was coming to 'em; but the Judge reckoned that this was a pretty good time to explain to the savages of the place what was meant by the law of the land and he spread himself good and thick over the farewells.

"The kid let him get through, just blinking and grinning at him, never offering to cut in till it was all over. Then the Judge mopped his face and sat back.

" 'And,' he said, 'now that you know what I think of you,' or words to that effect, 'if you've got anything to say, get shut of it.'

" 'Oh, you go to hell,' drawls the kid, and they removed him, but not until he'd had time to make a few parting remarks about the Judge's birth and parents."

In telling of the Kid's escape from the Lincoln jail, he says: "I don't know how long they'd had him in the *pen* [!] when it happened, nor I don't know whether they had bumped the others off, but one morning his keeper, who couldn't have been very strong in the head, unlocked his handcuffs so as to let him get his food to his mouth. The kid thanked him nicely and asked him if he wouldn't mind opening the window a piece, which the fool did. I must explain that the gaol, for that was the best they had, wasn't much of a strong box, and that, *in the room below,* there was an assortment of guns and Winchesters and ammunition belonging to the gaolers. Also there was only two men in charge. You'd say the whole thing had been arranged wouldn't you? Number two had gone across the street to dinner, and when the other had his back turned, and his hands on the window, the kid made a leap at him and smashed his head in with the handcuffs. The next thing that anybody saw was when the other warder came out of the eating house across the street and heard the kid hail him from a lower window.

" 'Hallo, you —— son of a ——!' he calls to him. 'Here's yours!' and he lets drive at him with a load of buckshot. He waits with the other barrel to see if he moves after he's dropped, and then helps himself to two guns and a Winchester, breaks up the artillery he can't take with him, and walks calm and secure out of the front door."

He says that after the Kid's escape, "the champion Sheriff of the Southwest was sent for again. He was mad clear through this time, and he swore to stay out until he'd fixed him—he didn't propose to give the State another chance to bungle the job. But the kid had been near enough to smell the smoke once, and that was plenty. He didn't let them get within hailing distance this trip, and, one way or another, *they rode over a good part of several States.* But they didn't lose his trail once they'd picked it up. Sometimes he might be a week ahead of them, but they stayed with it and kept after him, until, one evening when they were just about all in, they came to a ranch house, *way off by itself,* and asked after news of him.

"The man they found there shook his head, and when they said they'd like to stop for the night, he said he'd be pleased to have them, but that he was shy on bedding and horse feed. They told him they'd chance that, because they were shyer on sleep and rest than he was on the other things. It was dark when they got there, the Sheriff said, and when his posse had cooked what they could find for supper, the man told them that he could sleep on another bed in his room if he liked but that the others would have to make themselves at home where they found themselves. He told me that he was just about gone, then, but he braced up and went inside, thinking what a dandy sleep he'd get in a real bed.

"It was pretty black in the room when he got there, but there was a bit of a moon and he could just see the pillars of the porch out of the window.

"You know how oily quiet the desert can get at night— it's just like some one had given the air a dose of sleeping mixture—and he was good and ready for sleep. But no sooner was he in the room than he woke up! Yes, sir, he told me it was just as though he'd been stuck full of pins, and he sat down on the side of the bed, and hung up his gun beside him on his right hand.

"He sat like that for a quarter of an hour or so, not thinking of anything at all, least of all the job he was at, when he heard some one moving on the porch and a voice whispering something to somebody at the other end. But he still did not move, because although his mind was wide awake it was too blame worn out to think very much.

"Then the fellow outside came nearer and he spoke again —this time he did not whisper.

" 'Hallo, boys,' he said. 'Where are you from?'

"They told him they were hunting strays, which was a fool sort of an answer, because men don't go after strays in packs, and he passed by them and stopped at the door of the bedroom. Then the Sheriff came to himself. He could see the man standing in the doorway—and he'd heard that voice before; but he didn't dare move because he didn't know whether the other could see him. He was *carrying a steak of raw meat,* the other one was, and he stood there peering in, one hand on his belt, and called to the ranch owner, but he didn't get any answer, so he came in a step nearer. Then he saw that there was some one on the bed and he jumped back, pulling at his gun.

" '*Quien es?*' he asked, just loud enough to be heard.

"The Sheriff had sense enough to turn sideways when the other jumped, and crouched himself over the bed as he reached for his gun that was *hanging up beside him.* He must have crouched and drawn and pulled all in one piece, for he got the first shot, shooting upwards; then, he said, he dropped to the floor ready to let go another. For a second he thought he was going to have to, because the kid—for that's who it was—stood still, there, *just outside the door,* staring at him; but as the Sheriff was holding up the ham-

225

mer with his thumb, the gun dropped onto the floor, and the kid clapped his hands up to his stomach and spun round, and came down in a heap.

"The Sheriff told me that he felt like the whole damn thing was something he'd read out of a book—said he didn't feel as though he was in it himself at all, till he got outside and found the boys on their feet.

" 'I got him,' he says. 'It was the kid fellows—I got him!' "

Such distortions of reality scarcely deserve comment. By now it should be obvious that through the years the tall tales of garrulous old-timers and the lively imaginations of colorful writers have nourished the myths of the Kid until they have grown to formidable proportions.

In 1920 the first volume of *The Trail Drivers of Texas,* edited by J. Marvin Hunter, was published. In it there appeared a supposedly personal experience of Fred Sutton, whose writings were always unreliable. In this account, he gives the date of the Kid's birth as *July* 9, 1859, and states that at the age of twelve [still in New York] he killed a boy companion with a pocket-knife and escaped, going to Kansas, where he worked on a farm for a year and a half.

"In the latter [part] of 1880," writes Sutton, "a then noted frontier officer by the name of Pat Garrett was detailed to bring 'the Kid' in, dead or alive, and as he knew our boys had been bothered a great deal, and had lost several cattle, he came to our place for help. I was detailed as one of the posse to go with Garrett, and we finally located the outlaw in a ranch house about forty miles from White Oaks. After surrounding them a halt was called for a parley, during which 'Billy the Kid' sent out word by a Mexican outlaw, by the name of Jose Martinez, one of his leaders, that if Garrett would send the writer . . . and Jimmy Carlyle, a young cowboy, to the house he would try and come to some kind of agreement. Garrett readily consented to this, as he knew his men and those of 'the Kid,' and he knew a battle meant death to many. Leaving our guns behind, Jimmy and I went to the house where we found as tough a bunch of out-laws, gun-fighters, and cattle thieves as ever infested a country, or were ever congregated in a space of that size. After an hour spent in propositions, and counter-propositions, we agreed to disagree, and started back to our own crowd with the promise of not being fired on until we reached them. But we had only traveled about three-fourths of the distance when there was an avalanche of lead sent in our direction, and poor Jimmy, Sheriff William Bradley [i.e., Brady, killed long before this in Lincoln], and a ranchman by the name of George Hindman were instantly killed."

Hindman was Brady's deputy and was killed with him on the streets of Lincoln. Garrett was not present when Carlyle was killed; neither was Sutton, for that matter, in spite of what he claims. Sutton also says the Kid was killed in 1882 instead of 1881. At the close of his story he makes the statement that he and his crowd were "on our way to Dodge City by way of the Chisholm Trail with thirty thousand head of cattle." Driving a herd of this magnitude would never be attempted by a real cattleman.

All of this is a bit of romancing by Mr. Sutton. There is no evidence that he ever took part in the Lincoln County troubles. Personally, I sometimes wonder whether he was ever in New Mexico. Judging from his other writings, it seems that he is one of those fellows who knew every western outlaw personally and participated in events in which they were concerned—or was he simply spinning tall yarns?

The following year (1921) there appeared a book by Francis Rolt-Wheeler, entitled *The Book of Cowboys,* and since no western book seemed complete without a mention of Billy the Kid, this author wrote: "One of the worst of all these cattle-stealing outfits was 'Billy the Kid's' gang, famous as having held the whole of Lincoln County, *Texas*, in a state of guerilla warfare, for years. A side-light is thrown on the character of the gang when it is remembered that they were currently called the 'man-killing fence-haters.'"

I have never heard the Kid's gang labeled thus before, and, of course, the author meant Lincoln County, New Mexico, not Texas. He contends that the Kid's first killing was of a Negro soldier when he was fifteen years old, the blacksmith being killed later. He declares that Tunstall had enemies, "mainly the leader of a gang headed by 'Noddy' Morton. This gang, in the *spring* of 1878, killed Tunstall." He has the Kid kill every man in the Morton gang and "with Tom O'Phalliard [*sic*] and ten others, he started open warfare throughout the county. It was not long until the list of killings became so outrageous that the Kid and his followers became hunted outlaws." The rest of his account is quoted verbatim from Charlie Siringo's *A Texas Cowboy*.

The rare 1920 edition of O. S. Clark's *Clay Allison of the Washita* does not mention the Kid at all, but the revised and enlarged 1922 edition makes the statement that Billy the Kid "had killed his two guards while a prisoner at Cimmaron [*sic*], New Mexico, and was again on the rampage." More carelessness.

Pike's Peak or Bust, by John O'Bryne (1922), is another example of how an old-timer spells names by ear "I had heard and read of Rincon," he writes, evidently meaning Lincoln, "ever since I was a child. This is the place where Billie the Kid was jailed and sentenced to be hanged away back in the *seventies* [!]. However, *on the morning set for his execution* Billie cheated the gallows once more; he asked his keeper, who brought him his *breakfast* to please unlock one of the handcuffs so he could use his hands to *eat his last meal*. The keeper complied with his wishes, but as soon as the Kid's hand was free he knocked the jailer silly, took his gun, the keys to the jail, locked the jailer in, walked down the street, if it could be called a street, stole a pony, rode over to the judge's house who sentenced him, shot him through the window, got on his pony and rode away.

"I looked for the old jail but could not locate it, but it must be there still as the place doesn't look as if there has been any change in the past fifty years."

Small wonder he failed to find the Lincoln jail if he was in Rincon! And this is merely a sample of the confusion of events that pervades his whole account.

In Frederick R. Bechdolt's book, *Tales of the Old-Timers* (1924), there is a different version of the Kid's escape from the Lincoln jail. He says the Kid had been starving himself since his confinement so that he could slip his hands out of his handcuffs, and that on the day of his escape he asked Bell to secure a paper for him which had come that day—a Las Vegas paper. When Bell brought it to him he asked him to find an article in it about a shooting "down Three Rivers way." While Bell was giving this his attention, the Kid slipped a hand from his cuffs, jerked Bell's gun from its holster and when Bell got to the head of the stairs toward which he immediately started running, the Kid shot him. Bell tumbled down the stairs and "old Geiss [Gauss], the regular jailer [he was the *cook*, remember?], was sitting on the lowest step. The body struck him. He ran into the street shouting the alarm." This brought Olinger to his well-known death.

This author also has a different tale to tell about why

the Kid went to Maxwell's that fatal night. It seems he had heard some tales about strangers in town that day, and as he listened to one, "he was drawing on his clothes; he buckled his belt, slipped the revolver in its holster, picked up his Winchester, and hurried out unshod to the sheepman's room." The author also misspells many names, such as "McSwain" for McSween, "O'Phalliard" for O'Folliard, and "Geiss" for Gauss.

Owen P. White, nearly always unreliable when it came to writing about outlaws, had his book *Trigger Fingers* published in 1926. His chapters on the Kid are virtually the same as those which appeared in his two-part serial in *Collier's Weekly* the year before.

"At the tender age of twelve," he writes of Billy the Kid, "he shot and killed a 'black nigger' who was endeavoring to 'put something over on him' in a card game. This initial killing, which was the first one of '*twenty-six, not counting Indians,*' occurred at Fort Union, and, according to Billy, he kept the story of it a secret from his mother because he did not want her to worry about the conduct of her wayward son."

Like so many writers, Mr. White was just bound to have the use of Mrs. McSween's piano, so he had some of the boys "picking out 'Turkey In the Straw' with two fingers, the balance of the gang indulged in an old-fashioned breakdown." He also had the Kid shooting Beckwith before the latter had killed McSween, this event happening as Beckwith fell.

Mr. White says the Kid's guards at Lincoln were Olinger and Dave Wall. He is mistaken in this, since the second guard, as we know, was J. W. Bell. He also calls Gauss "an old German named Geiss."

He writes further that "in the first week of July Garrett

Pete Maxwell (seated), with Henry Leis

Pat Garrett (left), John W. Poe, (right), and James Brent (standing), three peace officers of Lincoln County.

received a letter from a man named Brazil telling him that the Kid was visiting his sweetheart with lover-like regularity, and he could be located nearly any night."

The three officers went to Maxwell's home, where Garrett woke Pete Maxwell. In the meantime, "having finished his courting for the evening Billy the Kid had come up the back way to the room he occupied at the rear of the Maxwell home, and slipping off his *shoes* [I'm sure he wore boots] and stockings, he read a paper for a while and then asked a Mexican servant to prepare him some supper. Upon being told there was no meat in the house, the Kid picked up a butcher knife, with which to cut off a piece, and went around to Maxwell's room after it," and to his death. We wonder if he expected to find meat in Maxwell's bedroom.

The year 1928 found Lorenzo D. Walter's *Tombstone's Yesterdays* in circulation, and in it there are chapters on Billy the Kid and Pat Garrett which really do not belong there, for the Kid and Garrett had nothing to do with the history of Tombstone. Authors writing of the West just seem to be unable to resist bringing these two popular characters into their works.

The author's discussion of Billy the Kid is filled with misstatements from the very beginning, where he suggests that the Kid was a bootblack in New York City. "This has been denied by many," he writes, "but as such denials have never been backed up by proofs to the contrary, we are forced to believe that, in accordance with the preponderance of testimony in the case under consideration, Billy the Kid started his business career as a manicurist of footwear at an early age." I do not know the source of his "preponderance of testimony," but it has generally been agreed that the Kid left New York when he was three.

He relates that Billy's father died when he was a mere

baby, then says it fell upon him to help support his mother. "After struggling with adverse circumstances for a few years," he continues, "Billy's mother managed to save enough money to pay their way to some point in *Texas* [!], where she and Billy tarried for some time. During her hesitation in said Texas town she annexed another husband whose name was given as Antrim in that locality."

He has the Kid kill his first man with a borrowed six-shooter, not a knife, as in most accounts. He continues with the legend that Chisum owed the Kid $5,000 for a split in mavericks, and says, "Billy threw in with the Murphy-Dolan faction, and soon after, at the age of nineteen years he found himself the leader of one faction in the greatest cattlemen's war ever known in the United States."

Baker and Morton, he declares, "deliberately killed Turnstall [*sic*] just because he was a cattleman." He has Garrett imported from Louisiana by Chisum for the express purpose of killing the Kid. His account of the circumstances of Bowdre's killing at Stinking Springs is wrong; he is careless with the spelling of proper names and with geography and places the Kid's trial at Las Vegas instead of Mesilla. He uses the Siringo and Burns version of Bell's killing and praises the latter's book as being "the most complete history of Billy the Kid that has ever been published."

There is the usual repetition of the judge's sentence being flippantly answered by the Kid. The author admits that Garrett had never been in Tombstone, but uses as an excuse for including him in this book the fact that he had killed Billy the Kid.

During this same year there was published in Santa Fe, New Mexico, a book by Kyle S. Crichton entitled *Law and Order, Ltd.*, which tells of the boyhood friendship between Elfego Baca, the subject of this book, and Billy the Kid. The author says the Kid had barely reached the age of twenty when he was killed. He also writes, "At the time the two rode from Socorro to Albuquerque, Elfego was sixteen and Billy the Kid seventeen. They put up their horses at Isleta, the Pueblo Indian village thirteen miles from Albuquerque, and walked into town. There was cheap stabling at Isleta with the Indians and your horse was safe—which it was not in Albuquerque or elsewhere."

I rather doubt this statement, for I cannot picture a cowboy walking thirteen miles in high-heeled boots when he had a horse to ride. Most cowboys would not walk a city block if they could help it. I think also that Mr. Crichton is mistaken in the ages of the two men; that is, one was not sixteen at the same time the other was seventeen. According to Crichton himself, Baca was born in 1864, and if the Kid was born in 1859, he would have been five years older than Baca.

The author also claims that the Kid was an accomplished pianist, that his marvelous playing wrung the heart of many a lady, and "it is almost enough to excuse him for the *few* cattle he stole, for the few men he killed in the course of his rambles."

He also errs in placing the Kid's trial for killing Sheriff Brady in Lincoln instead of Mesilla. He repeats that old fable about the judge's sentence and the Kid's answer, but he does give a slightly different version of it. When the judge said, "I thereby sentence you to be hanged by the neck until you are dead—dead—dead!" the Kid in most accounts answered that his wish is for the judge to "go to hell —hell—hell!" Mr. Crichton creates a new version by having the Kid say, "Before they ever hang *me* in Lincoln County, the top of your head will be red—red—red!" Neither is true.

William M. Breakenridge, in his *Helldorado* (1928),

does not devote much space to Billy the Kid because he is writing mostly about Tombstone, Arizona, but the little he does say about the Lincoln County War is all wrong. He states that Major Murphy was mustered out of the California Column and soon became a "powerful politician and controlled all the offices in that county. He then undertook to break in on the business that Chisholm [*sic*] was doing with the Government, and to establish a stock ranch on the range that was covered with Chisholm's cattle. He hired an army of cowboys as fighting men to rebrand these cattle in his brand. As Chisholm had fallen out with the cowboys, Murphy had no trouble to get them to work for him. This was the beginning of the Lincoln County War."

He further states that Chisum then had to send to Texas for a lot of fighting men, paying them big wages to protect his cattle and to steal from Murphy. He says that Murphy controlled all the peace officers, who were nearly all outlaws. "Wallace was hired on one side," he writes, and "Billy the Kid on the other." Except for Governor Lew Wallace, I have not seen the name of Wallace mentioned in any other account.

The following year (1929) William Kent wrote a book called *Reminiscences of Outdoor Life*. He thought he knew something about the Kid, but his book quickly proved otherwise. In writing of New Mexico, he said: "It was in this country that the most homicidal of our old-time outlaws Billy the Kid, served his apprenticeship. There were sheep and cattle wars and feuds going on continually. A great cattle owner named Chisholm [*sic*] had employed a number of men to clean up the sheep and sheep owners. These gunmen were supposed to be paid 'fighting wages,' namely, eight dollars a day, and I have met more than one who complained about human injustice in failure to obtain the due reward for his hazardous services. Billy the Kid was one of these victims of misplaced confidence. Chisholm the boss, refused to come through, whereupon Billy the Kid swore a solemn oath that he would make it his business to kill Chisholm and any of his cowboys he might encounter. This threat he carried out as far as the unfortunate cowboys were concerned, but Chisholm took pains to evaporate.

"After being arrested and escaping, he was finally hunted down and shot by Sheriff Pat Garrett, who *crawled in his stocking feet* into the room where he was sleeping and walked around in the dark feeling for the bed, with a drawn six-shooter. Billy heard the noise and got out of bed with his gun, and the two men were crawling around in the dark looking for each other. Finally the strain was too great and Billy spoke up and queried '*Quien es?*' (Who is it?), whereupon Garrett shot, and Billy's objectionable career was at an end." Such careless reporting scarcely deserves comment.

In Edwin L. Sabin's *Wild Men of the Wild West* (1929), there is a section devoted to Billy the Kid. "It was the forepart of 1877," he begins, "when this Billy the Kid entered upon his renowned career in New Mexico. He then was seventeen, and had *drifted up from Old Mexico and the Arizona and Rio Grande border.*" He goes on to say that the Kid was twelve when he killed his first man, a Negro soldier "with whom he was gambling at Fort Union." A little later he has the Kid stab a blacksmith to death in Silver City, and says his mother "*was a widow* . . . but there is no record of his having seen her again."

He follows Upson's account of the Kid's killing Indians and gambling in Mexico and says, "Consequently when he returned into southeastern New Mexico in 1877 he was an accomplished desperado." According to him the Lincoln County War was a struggle between Chisum and the smaller cattle owners, whom Chisum was trying to squeeze out to gain control of the range. He also says the Kid first worked for Murphy but changed over to the McSween faction because they *"paid him better wages."* When Murphy's posse went to seize some stock from Tunstall, *"they found Tunstall alone,* and when he came to meet them they murdered him with a shot."

Of the killing of Morton and Baker, who are not named, he writes: "A McSween squad, including Billy the Kid, gave chase to a squad of Murphy riders, unhorsed two of them, and took them prisoners under the promise not to harm them but to deliver them into custody of the law. Billy the Kid did not subscribe to this promise.

"Forthwith, upon a side trail the two prisoners were shot down by the Kid after a fellow rider who had declared that he would protect them with his life had been pistoled by another member of the squad." He has two other men shot along with Sheriff Brady, but he does not give their names. His account of the killing of Bernstein is similar to Upson's. He states that the Kid and his party rode up to the Mescalero Indian reservation in broad daylight and were "rounding up a bunch of government horses when Joe Bernstein, one of the agency clerks, hurried out to tell them that those horses belonged upon the government range. Billy promptly shot and killed him, in order to teach him not to stick his nose into other folks' business; furthermore, as the Kid remarked, he was only a Jew and 'I don't like a Jew nohow.'"

His account of the killing of Carlyle is very close to Upson's, as is the rest of the chapter. He follows Emerson Hough, whom he calls "a reliable gentleman," in his account of the Kid's escape from Lincoln after killing Bell and Olinger. He says Garrett was sitting in a chair at the head of Maxwell's bed when he killed the Kid, and declares that the Kid "had been intending to make off for Old Mexico. He had delayed in order to see his girl here in Sumner, and by that bravado to cover his tracks."

The more we read the books and articles on the Kid, the clearer it becomes that most writers are content to follow Upson unquestioningly or to pick and choose what appeals to them from the legends already published.

A year after Sabin's book there appeared the *History of Mesilla Valley* (1930), by George Griggs. This author credits the Kid with killing twenty-seven men, and his account differs from the others in stating that the Kid's first victim was a miner who had run off with the Kid's fifteen-year-old sister. When the Kid followed them and demanded that the miner marry the girl, he learned that the miner was already married. The Kid then bought a six-shooter and killed him. Like various other authors, he repeats the fable about the Kid's killing four of Chisum's riders and sparing the fifth to send back to Chisum the now widely accepted message. He also states that Garrett killed the Kid with a rifle when he was twenty-six, and that Billy's father, *Frank Bonney,* was killed by the Apaches in Arizona. He is mistaken about the circumstances of Bell's death, and about the weapon Billy used to kill Olinger, identifying it as a Winchester instead of a shotgun.

Robert E. Riegel's *America Moves West,* published this same year, does not devote much space to Billy the Kid, but he does say: "His exploits during the 'Lincoln County War,' including his escape from prison, need a volume for their adequate portrayal. When he died in the early '8o's at the age of twenty-one it was his boast that he had killed twenty one men, not counting Mexicans and Indians. This count may have been wrong—*possibly he killed more.*"

A Fitting Death for Billy the Kid

Mr. Charles J. Finger, a writer of some note, took a trip throughout the Southwest and wrote a book about what he saw and what he thought he knew. It was published in 1931 under the title *Under Sapphire Skies*. Naturally no book about this section of our country would be complete without some mention of Billy the Kid. Mr. Finger makes quite a hero of Martin [Marion] Turner during the siege of the McSween home. In telling of this fight, he writes: "After three days of such work [fighting], fire broke out in the building occupied by the outlaws and the defenders were driven to the kitchen in the back of the house. Next came treachery. Someone called out from the house that the besieged would surrender if firing ceased, and a cattleman named Beckwith, with John Jones, went towards the open kitchen door. *There are the facts*. The firing on the part of the besiegers did cease. Beckwith and Jones did go into the danger zone, and Beckwith called on McSween. Then two shots were fired at the cattlemen, one took Beckwith in the hand, the other, fired by Billy the Kid, entered his head. And out of the house poured the outlaws, making for the valley and cover. McSween, trying to escape, was shot, but the leader and his followers got away."

Mr. Finger's sympathies are plainly with the Murphy faction. Beckwith did not approach the door of the McSween house under any truce, but because he thought he could get a good shot at one of the enemy. It is recorded that Beckwith did kill McSween, but that was like shooting a sitting duck. He closes his chapter by telling of the Kid's death at the hands of Pat Garrett, but he places the Maxwell house in *Fort Stanton* instead of Fort Sumner.

Also in 1931, Ruth Laughlin Barker's *Caballeros* was published, and although Billy the Kid is mentioned only in one short sentence, the same old story crops up. "The boy bandit, Billy the Kid," she writes, "who killed twenty-one men before he was twenty-one, terrorized the country."

Seldom did a year pass without the publication of at least one book concerned more or less with Billy the Kid. In 1932, Sister Blandina Segale's book, *At the End of the Santa Fe Trail*, made its appearance. It is a journal kept by this nun detailing her experiences in a new, raw country. In it she makes several mentions of Billy the Kid, whom she encountered more than once, and for whom she had once done a favor. She says the Kid and his gang stopped a stage en route from Trinidad to Santa Fe, but when he saw that she was a passenger, the Kid let the stage go on.

Sister Blandina confuses her dates when she claims she went to see the Kid on May 16, 1882, when he was in jail chained hand and foot. On this date the Kid had been dead for nearly a year, but she mentions his death in her entry of September 8, 1882, as if it had just happened.

In this same year Dane Coolidge, a prolific though not always accurate writer, published his *Fighting Men of the West*. In it he states that just after the Kid escaped from the Lincoln jail, he made a bet with a drunken cowboy about which one of them would kill a man first, and the Kid "killed the bettor himself and collected the fifty dollars from the barkeep." Such yarns were to feed the tenderfoot, for no such thing actually happened.

"Then," he writes, "John Chisum came driving into town, just back from St. Louis, where he had had troubles of his own, and Billy the Kid leapt in front of him. Pointing his double-action .41 caliber pistol full in his face he fell to cursing, demanding five dollars a day for himself and his men for every day they had served in the just-ended Lincoln County War." He then has Chisum talk the Kid out of killing him.

Mr. Coolidge declares that the proper spelling of Chisum's name was Chisholm, but in order to collect a pension the cattleman had to accept the change to Chisum. He also spells Tunstall "Tungstall." Of Morton and Baker, he says, "the Kid killed them both, and another man for luck."

Jesse Evans, says Coolidge, was foreman of the Chisum ranch, and after a winter of running up bar bills he quit and took ten men with him, including the Kid. "On their way to Arizona," he relates, "they robbed stores and saloons and held up Government paymasters." As I have said repeatedly, Billy the Kid could never truthfully be accused of highway robbery. This author makes Lincoln the scene of the Kid's trial for killing Sheriff Brady. He says that after the Kid had killed Bell and Olinger, "Garrett lost his fighting nerve and John Poe was put on the job." We know this to be untrue, as Garrett stayed on the job until the Kid was killed.

He says further that "the Kid had a weakness never mentioned by his biographers—and one that brought him his death. He was not satisfied to have 'a woman in every *placita*,' but cast his ruthless eyes on one of a different class, who met his advances with scorn. It was to save her that Billy the Kid was killed. And, to protect her good name, John Poe himself built up a fictitious account of the event."

Garrett, Poe, and McKinney went to Maxwell's house, and Garrett went inside to talk with Maxwell. Thus Coolidge makes Garrett the leader, in spite of the fact that he has just said that Poe had been put on the job in Garrett's place. "He [Garrett] had just started to talk," he writes, leaving Poe and McKinney outside, when the Kid, greatly excited and in a hurry to leave town, came scurrying down the walk with a butcher-knife. Having the run of the house, for Maxwell was afraid to antagonize him, he had come to cut off a *slab of bacon*, to take with him to the sheep ranch where he hid."

Mr. Coolidge also has Poe and McKinney waiting near the gate instead of on the porch. In fact, he says that McKinney was sitting on the edge of the board sidewalk because one of his spurs was hung under a plank and he couldn't move. Of the Brady murder he writes: "Sheriff Brady was walking down the street when he was shot six times in the back by Billy the Kid and five of his followers. A deputy sheriff was also killed, and as Billy the Kid was robbing their bodies, he himself was shot in the rump but stayed till he finished the job."

After the battle at the McSween home, "The Kinney Gang from Doña Ana County rode a hundred miles, leading their pack animals, to rob McSween's store after his death." Later he continues, "It was a regular recognized war, in which everybody quit but the woman. Mrs. McSween held the fort, though her store was looted, until General Lew Wallace *rode in with the soldiers* and endeavored to establish a government."

Like many others, Eugene Cunningham, in his *Triggernometry, a Gallery of Gunfighters* (1934), follows Upson's account of the Kid's birth as William H. Bonney in New York, the family's move to Coffeyville in 1862, and Mrs. Bonney's removal to Colorado after the death of her husband and her marriage there to Mr. Antrim. He continues with the Kid's killing of the blacksmith when the latter was attacking a friend named Moulton with a chair, and states that "there was more motive to the boy's attack than friendship—this blacksmith had once insulted his mother and Moulton had whipped him at the time." Cunningham also repeats the story of the Kid's killings of Indians in Arizona, the soldier-blacksmith of that Territory, and various others in Mexico.

He describes at some length the Kid's eighty-one-mile ride to rescue his friend Segura. When the Kid received the message from Segura, " 'Six o'clock, now,' he said, looking at the evening sun. 'By midnight I will be starting back from San Elizario with Segura.' " He has Billy Matthews at the head of the posse which went to Tunstall's ranch to seize his horses, but when it was found that Tunstall had already left, "he sent Murphy's foreman, Billy Morton, with Jesse Evans and other hard cases, enemies to Tunstall, to overtake the young Englishman." He tells a pretty straight tale about the actual killing of Tunstall.

Mr. Cunningham's account of the shooting at Blazer's Mill is somewhat confused. He has Roberts first shoot Jack [John] Middleton, then shoot a finger off George Coe. He then "jammed rifle-muzzle into the midriff of the Kid and only a misfire beat Pat Garrett out of the job he did three years later." Charlie Bowdre then shot Roberts through the body, and Roberts staggered back into the house.

While he gives no name, he evidently meant Walter Noble Burns when he wrote, "Four or five years ago, a literary stranger came wandering through the Lincoln country, hunting material for a book on Billy the Kid. He was not among us long, but after he went away he produced a very detailed and thrilling and factual (and most readable) 'biography.' The only draw-back we who live here find, about this saga, is its inaccuracy in most details. Dramatic writing does not relieve a historian of all necessity for facts." Toward the close of his chapter he speaks of Burns's book again when he says, "Perhaps it is good literary technique to cover absence of fact by 'vivid writing' but this particular story falls very quickly flat before a brief official document."

In *Sky Determines,* by Ross Calvin (1934), it is stated that "Sheriff Turner, bringing warrants and accompanied by a posse of about forty men laid siege to the McSween house in Lincoln." Turner was not the sheriff, though he was in the sheriff's department.

In 1936, there was published a collection of stories by Jack Weadock entitled *Dust In the Desert,* in Chapter XI of which is an account of the Kid's killing of Carlyle. This story is evidently founded upon that wild tale Fred Sutton told in *The Trail Drivers of Texas,* for all the circumstances are just as he told it, and therefore all incorrect.

In his *Chisholm Trail* (1936), Sam P. Ridings states that Morton and Baker were "shot down by this boy of the frontier," and that McClasky [*sic*] met his death "by a bullet from an unknown source when he tried to protect the prisoners." He writes that the Kid's gang "took their quarters in the store and home of their leader, Alexander McSwain [*sic*]" and that they were "set upon by about seventy-five or more of the Murphy men." He says that in this battle many men were killed, that McSween was deeply religious, and was "forced into this war by the patent justice of his cause, and who never fired a shot in this battle or in the war, and who died fleeing from his burning house and clutching his Bible to his breast." He misspells many proper names and has the Kid kill twenty-one men by the time he was twenty-one.

Two books published in 1938 contain only slight errors concerning the Kid, but then they have only slight mention of him also. *Southwest Heritage,* by Mabel Majors, Rebecca W. West, and T. M. Pearce, gives the date of the Kid's death as 1880. We must hold this against them, however, for as compilers of several other books on western literature and history, they should have known better, especially since one of them lives in New Mexico. Wilson Rockwell, in *New Frontiers* (1938), says that after Billy's escape from Lincoln, Garrett and "thirteen men" chased him down at Fort Sumner. Garrett took only John Poe and Kip McKinney with him.

During this same year there appeared a book entitled *Wagon Yard,* in which the author, Mrs. Grover C. Johnson, says Billy the Kid was visiting the Cattle Exchange Saloon in Tascosa every hour or so to have a cocktail, very nervous because the sheriff was after him. Let us look into this statement a little. We find that the Kid left Tascosa in late 1878, and there was no sheriff in that county until 1880. Furthermore, rarely did the early western saloonkeeper even know what a cocktail was, and few men wanted their whiskey any way except straight. Dr. Hoyt, who knew the Kid well when he was in Tascosa, said he never saw the Kid take a drink while there.

In his *Trampling Herd* (1939), Paul I. Wellman says that when Tunstall was murdered, "on a distant hill a boy sat his horse and watched with a wild glare the men leaving after the atrocious murder. Billy the Kid had idolized Tunstall. They were opposites in the social scale—the ignorant, undersized border waif, and the cultured, handsome and wealthy English gentleman."

He follows the Upson account of the early life of the Kid when he writes: "He was born in New York's Bowery, christened William Bonney, and was taken at an early age by his parents to Coffeyville, Kansas, a tough border town where later the Dalton bandit gang was wiped out in a street fight. [He repeats this same statement later in his *Glory, God, and Gold.*] After his father's death, his mother took him to the mountains where, in Colorado, she married a man named Antrim. . . . He is said to have killed his first man at twelve—a blacksmith in Silver City, New Mexico, who spoke slightingly of the boy's mother. After the killing, Billy bade his mother good-bye and fled from the country. Forever afterward he was an Ishmaelite; mother and son never met again."

These legends have been repeated so often and over such a long span of time that it will be difficult to convince many people that they are merely legends.

Wellman continues with the statement that "In the lurid gallery of super-killers in the West, Billy the Kid stands out in sharp relief, eclipsing all, with the possible exception of Wild Bill Hickok." He admits that Hickok and one or two others had a longer notch list than the Kid, but "considering the Kid's age and the brief era of his fighting days, Wild Bill's fame as an executive of the six-shooter pales before that of this young genius of annihilation."

In recounting the killing of Morton and Baker, he says that when these two spurred their horses toward freedom, the Kid "whipped out a revolver and fired, *rather negligently*, twice." Like many others, he had Brady and Hindman killed from "behind the adobe wall that surrounded the patio of the McSween home," and has the Kid "clambering over the wall to get Brady's guns then taking them back with him over the wall." Of the fight with Buckshot Roberts, he writes, "Just why Brewer wished to eliminate Roberts is not clear; it has been said the real object of the expedition was someone else but Roberts came in the way." Brewer's band knew that Roberts was in the posse that murdered Tunstall. He says "the attackers retreated, carrying their dead and wounded," but they did not. Brewer was left behind where he fell because Roberts was still alive and shooting. He also makes the old mistake of saying that Frank and George Coe were brothers.

Garrett now comes into the picture, and Mr. Wellman says that "for months he failed to corner the Kid, and the Kid killed and killed until his death total was nineteen." During the fight prior to his capture at Stinking Springs, his closest friends, Charlie Bowdre and Tom O'Folliard, were killed," but O'Folliard, as we know, was killed earlier.

Of the Kid's escape from Lincoln he writes: ". . . the Kid asked J. W. Bell, one of the deputies guarding him, to play a game of cards. Ollinger yawned and presently went across the street to eat lunch. It was an old trick the Kid played. Dropping one of his cards on the floor, he stooped as if to pick it up, then quick as a striking adder dove for the guard's pistol holster. Out came the six-shooter in the outlaw's manacled hands. Bell, knowing his fate was upon him, leaped in frantic fear for a window, but fell clattering full length on the floor as the Kid shot him in the back." Then when Olinger heard the shot, he came back to be "almost cut in two." Then, he says, "Billy, obtained a Winchester from the arms rack inside, *ordered the citizens* of Lincoln to remove his leg-irons and handcuffs and bring him a horse."

After this episode the Kid's friends advised him to leave the country, but the Kid "elected to pay a visit to a woman who fascinated him. She lived at Fort Sumner and it was there, through chance and the treachery of a derelict friend of the outlaw's, that Garrett found him."

Later, he continues: "Greatly daring, Garrett left his men to watch outside and entered the house alone. Into Maxwell's bedroom he *crept* and *lurked* there in the darkness," and when the Kid came in and inquired who the men on the porch were, there was a flash from Garrett's gun, "and Billy the Kid curled up lifeless on the floor. He was twenty-one years old, and he had killed twenty-one men." This legend simply refuses to die.

In her *Our Southwest* (1940), Erna Fergusson mentions the Kid briefly in a few places, the greatest space being devoted to the old tale about his being killed when he went to Pete Maxwell's house to "visit his sweetheart."

In 1941, *The Bad Man of the West,* by George Hendricks, was published. This book deals with many different phases of the bad man, and Mr. Hendricks seems to have read many books on the subject, but I am afraid he took too many of the unreliable ones literally.

Of Billy's start in outlawry he writes: "Billy the Kid blamed cruel treatment by his step-father Antrim for his always wanting to 'get even' with just anybody who trod upon his small toes. At the age of twelve, the Kid began his career of lawlessness. Most boys at that age or earlier have some 'hero' whom they positively worship. He had one, a fine young man. The Kid's folks had just moved into a small western town from back East. . . . Some mashers had bothered his mother and his 'hero,' a perfect stranger, stepped up and intervened in her behalf, thus dispersing the villains. Billy followed his 'hero' around town admiring his every move. A drunk bumped into the 'hero' and began fighting him, whereupon twelve-year-old Billy the Kid jumped astride the drunk and stabbed him to death. . . . He ran home to his mother after the affray; she hid him for a time but advised him to run away when some officers approached the place."

In another place he says: "Murphy dispatched about a dozen ruffians to murder Tunstall because he was interfering with his plans. They caught him *alone* riding horseback from his ranch to town and *brutally beat him up, lit-*

erally stomped him to death. Billy the Kid was the first to discover the body. He swore right then and there to get vengeance on each and every foul murderer of his beloved and kind boss. He found out who they were and one by one picked them off."

And still farther on: "It has been asserted and denied that on the spur of the moment Billy the Kid killed a stranger cowboy just because he was working for his enemy land baron John Chisum, that he killed four Mexicans just to see them kick, and that he said when questioned why he *killed a keeper of an Overland Stage station* named Bernstein, 'Well, I needed horses; and besides, he was a Jew.'"

In a chapter entitled "Technique of the Bad Man," he writes: "Out at Lincoln, New Mexico, Billy the Kid literally turned the cards and the tables on his jailer Bell and ordered him to precede Billy down the stairs, keeping the jailer covered with the jailer's own gun, which the Kid had taken by a clever trick we'll describe later. Bell took a long chance, hoping he could beat Billy's bullet around a corner of the stairs. Before Billy shot him he yelled a warning for Bell to halt, but it was too late. Of course, in the race of Bell and the bullet around the corner, Bell came out second. But the Kid had observed the code of the West in shouting the halt signal, even if there wasn't much use in it." He also contends that the Kid upheld the code when he shouted, "Hello, Bob," just as he pulled the trigger of the shotgun which sent the deputy to eternity.

"One of the best examples of a heroic mortal gun battle was that at Blazer's Mill," he writes, "in northern New Mexico. The Murphy-Riley-Dolan faction in the Lincoln County war had offered 'Buckshot' Roberts a *hundred dollars for each dead McSween follower to his credit*; and Billy the Kid, the leader, of the McSween faction had heard about it."

248

The Kid was not the leader at this time, for the posse here was under the leadership of Dick Brewer until he was killed in this same battle. Hendricks also says that Roberts holed up in a small house and, though shot through the middle, stood off "single-handed, the whole gang of Billy the Kid, killing Dick Brewer and wounding others before he finally expired."

In writing of the battle at the McSween home, he says that McSween was a "preacher of the gospel," and he gives Colonel Dudley the title of "Major."

"Enraged over the outlandish death of their beloved leader [McSween], and scorched by the heat of the flames," he writes, "McSween's men *filed out* firing rapidly and running for a high fence. Some of them made an escape in this manner, but some were killed en route to the fence. Billy the Kid calmly lighted a cigarette from a burning beam, enjoyed a few good puffs while the other men left, and was the last to leave the edifice. He emptied his guns while side-stepping dead bodies, killing one enemy and wounding two others, and finally hurdling the fence untouched."

He admits that there are several versions of the Kid's escape from the Lincoln jail. "But the most interesting yet plausible one is that while keeper Bob Ollinger was at dinner across the street," he writes (though he had previously said that Olinger had gone for a cup of coffee), keeper Bell and the Kid were in a pleasant, casual game of seven-up. The Kid, of course, was shackled and unarmed, *sitting on the table*. Bell, seated in a chair, wore pistols on his hips. The Kid, sensing his opportunity, purposely dropped a card. Bell stooped to get it and Billy grabbed Bell's six-shooter, covering the astonished *sheriff*. When the two started down the stairs of the temporary jail, Bell took a long chance, leaping for the corner. Billy shouted for him to stop and, seeing Bell wouldn't, shot him." Then, after killing Olinger, "Billy made the cook chop away his shackles and danced a jig while his horse was saddled."

In another place the author says that "Billy the Kid would have been safe in Mexico had he not gone to see a girl in Fort Sumner, where Pat Garrett found him." He also makes the mistake of saying that the mob at Las Vegas was "threatening to lynch Billy the Kid."

We meet old stories with new twists, this, for example: "Billy the Kid at twenty-one years of age said that he had killed twenty-one men and that all he wanted then in the world was just to make it two more before he, himself, met death. The two men he wanted were Pat Garrett, who he knew was gunning for him, and Lew Wallace. Lew Wallace was the Territorial Governor of New Mexico, who had promised to pardon the Kid if he ever got in jail and who failed to keep that promise."

Of the Kid's death, he writes: "Pat knew that Pete might give him information of the Kid's whereabouts, so on the very ordinary night of July 13, 1881, Pat left deputies Poe and McKinney on Pete's doorstep while he slipped into Pete's dark bedroom to wake him up—western friends were very informal in those days.

"Just then who should step up on the porch outside but the Kid himself! He was barefooted, supposedly after a long ride, and he was returning from Pete's smokehouse *with a strip of ham* his *mamacita* was to cook for him." Ignoring the deputies on the porch, he walked into Pete's room to be shot by Garrett.

Of course, the date of the Kid's killing is wrong, and the whole account shows carelessness, even in reporting the legends of the day.

In 1941, also, there was published a book entitled *Belle*

Starr, by Burton Rascoe, probably the most complete biography of this notorious female outlaw even written. In this book the author criticizes other works, some of them dealing with Billy the Kid, such as the *Saga* by Burns. He says the Burns book was mostly legends and "the facts he was able to obtain about Billy the Kid could be stated in a paragraph." He says the Kid "appeared out of nowhere in Lincoln County, New Mexico, in the fall of 1887, when he was eighteen years old." Unless this is a typographical error, he has the Kid "appearing" six years after his death, when he would have been twenty-eight years old. Farther along, he says the Kid "was shot to death by *Marshal* Pat Garrett at Pete Maxwell's house near Fort Sumner, *Texas,* and that the body was buried in a little cemetery in that now deserted spot."

In this same year, too, a beautiful little privately printed book appeared under the title, *These High Plains,* written by Mrs. Avery Turner. Here is another example of carelessness in regard to historical facts. The author states that the Kid was born "July, 1881, in New York City." She has him born in the same month and year in which he was killed. At the close of the paragraph, she writes, "He was *shot in the back* in the dark by Sheriff Pat Garrett in Fort Sumner, New Mexico."

An Englishman named Escott North, who came to the United States and worked a few years as a cowboy, later wrote a book about his experiences entitled *The Saga of the Cowboy* (1942), in which he included some popular outlaw legends. His account of Billy the Kid is all from hearsay, as is obvious from this statement: "This Bonney was an orphan lad from the purlieus of New York City, *who had somehow got out West,* secured a job with John Chisum while 'only a kid.'" The author further states that the

Kid "had ridden up the long miles of the Chisholm Trail, from its southern beginning to its northern terminus."

"Morton and Baker," he writes, "were arrested by the posse, but on the way from Roswell to Lincoln, so it is said, Billy the Kid demanded to know if either of them fired at Tunstall. He threatened that if they did not give him the names of the men who actually killed Tunstall he would assume that they were the murderers themselves, and save the hangman a job by executing them himself. Anyway, he added, they were equally guilty and would be better out of the way.

"Covered by his guns, both men pleaded desperately for their lives, and while so pleading were told, 'Oh, well, if you *will* have it—!' and they were coolly shot dead by the Kid."

He shows the influence of Hough when he says: "It soon happened that if a man were riding the range, and saw a group of heavily-armed men approaching—he was in a quandary. They would be sure to ask him which side *he* was on. . . . Upon his guess his life depended! Lucky indeed was he if he guessed right."

He also intimates that only the Kid and one other escaped from the burning McSween home. As for the death of the Kid, he says Pat Garrett "shot him dead at Pete Maxwell's ranch near Whiteoaks [*sic*]. When Billy the Kid *fell on the porch* of the Maxwell ranch there died one of the most desperate gunmen the West has ever known."

Owen P. White, in his *Autobiography of a Durable Sinner* (1942), does not seem to have a very high regard for Pat Garrett. In writing of a certain saloon in El Paso, Texas, where bad characters "hung out," he says, "Noteworthy among these bad characters was Pat Garrett, whose only claim to fame was that from a hiding place behind a bed he had murdered Billy the Kid."

In *A Pecos Pioneer* (1943), Mrs. Mary Hudson Brothers deals mostly with the life of her father, who was in Lincoln County during the Billy the Kid days. Most of her information on the young outlaw is reliable, but I do question her version of the Kid's killing of Bell, who, by the way, she calls "George," though his initials were J. W. She says the Kid asked Bell to take him downstairs to the toilet after Olinger had gone to dinner.

"On their return," she writes, "he [Billy] was ahead of the guard when they reached the steps. In jumping from step to step, the farther he got the faster he went. George Bell called to him to stop, but the prisoner pretended not to hear, expecting every moment to get a bullet. He reached the top well in the lead, and instead of unlocking the guard-room door, he threw his entire weight against the arsenal door next to it." How did he manage to run so fast in leg irons. What would he have had to unlock the door with?

"The cheap pot metal lock gave way," she continues, "and the door flew open. Billy almost landed on his head because the lock broke so easily. In easy reach lay two .45s ready for instant use. Billy grabbed one and fired just as George Bell fired. Bell's shot went wild and he crumpled as a second bullet crashed through his body, rolling down the stairs, dead." This is the first report I have seen that Bell shot at all.

Of Garrett's visit to Pete Maxwell's bedroom on that fateful night that ended the Kid's career, she says, "The sheriff was *squatted,* cowboy style, against the far wall of the bedroom where he could not be seen."

In Frank King's *Pioneer Western Empire Builders* (1946),

it is said: "It was not long after this [the battle at Chisum's ranch] till the battle of the McSween house in Lincoln occurred, with the soldiers from Fort Stanton under *Colonel Buttler* [Dudley], and the Dolan gang fighting about twenty cowboys under Billy the Kid. This was the stubbornest and bloodiest battle of the whole war, and the Dolan outfit would have lost, had not the soldiers appeared on the scene without authority. Buttler [*sic*] lost his commission because of his actions later."

He says Coe told him that "it was almost uncanny to hear the Kid and Tom O'Folliard playing Mrs. McSween's piano between battles, trying to keep up the spirits of the survivors." King has the Kid escape first and Mr. McSween follow, "unarmed, with a Bible in his hand, and saying 'I am McSween.'"

In one paragraph he says that George and Frank Coe were brothers, and in the next, cousins. He is also mistaken in saying that the Kid's trial for killing Brady was held in Las Cruces. His version of the killing of Brady is different from the others I have found. It seems that Brady had arrested George Coe and tied him on a horse "in such a way that George nearly died before he got to Lincoln, after an all night ride. . . . when Billy the Kid and some others of the gang met George and heard his story of the treatment of their friend and saw the rope marks on his body, they said Brady would pay for it. So that same evening the Kid, accompanied by Hendry Brown, Fred Waite, John Middleton and Jim French rode into Lincoln in order to get Sheriff Brady, Deputy Sheriff Hindman and Circuit Court Clerk Billy Matthews. As they were passing the Tunstall store a round of shots roared out and Brady fell from his horse dead. The Kid and his four companions rose up from behind the adobe wall and showered the remainder of the sheriff's posse with lead, killing Hindman and wounding Bill Matthews." My understanding is that they were afoot when they were shot.

Of the Blazer's Mill fight he writes: "The Dolan outfit was getting anxious to clean up on the Kid and his followers, and was picking up all the gun fighters he could find, that would use their abilities in his cause. They had secured the services of one Buckshot Roberts, who posed as a bad gun man and ex-Texas ranger. He turned out to be a tough hombre. Buckshot was offered $1000 a head for all of these young farmer boys he could kill.

"Frank Coe had an overnight guest, this Buckshot Roberts, and next day they rode toward Lincoln, but Roberts went on to Lincoln while Frank rode on to see his cousin George. The Kid's gang was assembled at George's ranch. The boys started out to try to capture a hoss thief named George Davis. They were captained on this trip by Dick Brewer to start with. They stopped at Blazer's Mill and while there Buckshot Roberts rode up. Frank Coe took him around the house for a talk to see could he prevent a fight. While they talked, Billy the Kid, Charlie Bowdre and George Coe stepped up to Roberts and ordered 'Hands up!' Roberts raised his Winchester and fired just as Bowdre let go with a bullet through Roberts' middle. Roberts' bullet glanced off Bowdre's cartridge belt and then hit George Coe in the right hand, takin' off his trigger finger and knocking his gun out of his hand.

"Roberts pulled himself into the house where he fell on the bed, but while he was dying he shot and killed Dick Brewer."

In an earlier volume, *Wranglin' the Past* (1925), King writes: "There have been hundreds of stories written about Billy the Kid, but most of them so highly colored that they seem to be devoid of facts." He also says that Kip McKinney, one of Garrett's deputies, who was with him at the killing of the Kid, was a cousin of Tom O'Folliard's.

Also in 1946, Boyce House's *Cowtown Columnist* made its appearance. One short chapter is devoted to the Kid. On the killing of Olinger, House writes: "He, the Kid, could have shot Ollinger down without ceremony but he wanted his foe to know who was sending him into eternity," so he called down to him and shot him as he looked up. "Then," he continues, "there was a roar, as Billy the Kid killed his last man: No. 21 not counting Mexicans and Indians."

In 1946, too, John L. McCarty, in his *Maverick Town: The Story of Old Tascosa*, devotes a chapter to Billy the Kid, mostly relative to his trips to Tascosa and to the chase and capture of him at Stinking Springs with Tascosa men in the posse—Jim East, Cal Polk, Lon Chambers, Charlie Siringo, and Lee Hall. He does, however, continue the legend that the Kid was born William H. Bonney in Brooklyn and that the first man he killed had insulted his mother.

In the *Brand Book* of the Los Angeles Westerners (1947), there is an article entitled "Billy, the Kid," by E. A. Brininstool. The author says the Kid's *real name* was William H. Bonney and that he was born in the slums of New York. He has the mother move to Colorado "with Billy and a baby brother named Edward," and says "of this younger child history leaves no further trace."

He continues to follow the well-worn pattern of the mother's marrying Mr. Antrim in Colorado, then moving to Santa Fe where she operated a boardinghouse, thence in 1868 to Silver City, where Billy killed the blacksmith for insulting her when he was only twelve years old. Billy then went to Arizona, where "he developed into an expert cowboy," and killed several more men, including a Negro soldier at Fort Union, before going to Mexico.

There is nothing new in the entire article, merely the listings of the ageing legends—the killing of Morton and Baker, Brady, Hindman, and all the others, even to repeating the judge's sentence and the Kid's flippant answer. Brininstool gives two versions of the killing of Bell and relates the old story about the Kid's death at the hands of Garrett.

"By far," he writes, "the most truthful account of the Kid's activities before the killing, is in the splendidly-written volume by Walter Noble Burns of Chicago. I urge every *Westerner* to get that book if interested in the history of the Lincoln County War and Billy the Kid's many murders and activities."

If Mr. Brininstool considers Burns's book history, it is no wonder he sticks to the false tales about the Kid.

Lloyd Lewis in 1947 published a collection of his newspaper and magazine articles, which he entitled *It Takes All Kinds*. And indeed it did seem to take all kinds, for he relates some very wild tales told about Billy the Kid by an old man who called himself Tom Blevins and claimed to be a friend of the Kid. Many old-timers have great talent for telling them tall, but for the wildest tall tales on Billy the Kid, I vote this one the medal.

"This Billy the Kid," says Tom Blevins, "was twenty-two years and twenty-two days [old] when he died. *He told me he was born in Albany, New York*, and he said his name was William *Borney* [*sic*]." (Lewis himself writes the name "Bonner.") "I forget," continues Blevins, "what big college he said he went to back East before he came West, but he landed in New Mexico in 1876 and went to work for the Blank Cattle Company. He was between seventeen and eighteen then, a small fellow and as pleasant a man

257

as you'd ever want to see." Here is a rich imagination.

One old cowman whom Blevins called "Old Charley" offered the Kid $10,000 a year if he would steal 10,000 cattle from Blank's herds and would also give him $200 a month to ride his herds. Later Old Charley was so anxious to break Blank that he offered the kid $1,000 for every Blank cowboy he killed. Money seemed to be plentiful in those days.

Then, while the teller of this yarn was on a roundup, a heavy flood came down, and they saw the body of a man in the river. "We hauled it out," he said, "and when they came floatin' down so fast we just stood on the bank and watched for 'em to drag 'em out. We drug out eleven men, most of 'em shot between the eyes." He said he later heard the Kid demanding money from Old Charley for killing the cowboys.

On and on this character rambles, telling one preposterous tale after another. Pat Garrett had sent word to the fort for help, "and the next morning up came 300 nigger soldiers, and they surrounded the house [McSween's evidently] and their captain come up with a white flag and Billy yelled to him to go back and he didn't and Billy killed him." The soldiers decided to set the house afire, and when they came up to do so, Billy and his partner killed five of them, but they succeeded in setting the fire. Then the Kid kept killing them, but soon found that his efforts were not helping matters.

"The house was burnin' like a house afire by this time," he said, "and Billy went to the piano—he could play the best you ever heard—and he sung 'Home, Sweet Home' as pretty as you please." Perhaps he had studied music in that eastern college!

About five pages later he tells an outlandish tale about the Kid's escape from Lincoln: "Well, there was a black-

smith right by the jail and he kept a good horse. At breakfast time one deputy went after breakfast and left Billy
handcuffed to the other deputy. He throwed Billy a newspaper. Billy was a great reader. Somebody must have given
Billy a sign, for when the deputy bringin' the breakfast was
about sixty yards away, Billy shot from underneath the
newspaper and got the deputy beside him under the right
jaw and then he run to the door and drawed down on the
other deputy and made him kneel. [Where did he get the
gun? And doubtless he failed to make much speed with a
dead man attached to his wrist.]

" 'Let's see you pray,' he said, and, as the deputy kneeled
down, Billy emptied five shots into him and then pulled the
dead man that was handcuffed to him into the blacksmith
shop and laid his hand on the anvil and said, 'Cut me loose
or out comes your brains.' "

Of the Kid's sweetheart, this teller of tall tales said: "Billy
had loved Annie Maxwell for years. He had got to know
her back in Ottaway, Illinois, where his sisters lived. . . .
Annie was a fine-looking girl away up in society back there
in Ottaway, Illinois, and she would come down every summer to visit her old bachelor brother, Pete Maxwell, who
had bought Fort Sumner from the Government. . . .

"Well, Pat Garrett had kept watchin' the Maxwell outfit, waitin' for Billy to come see Annie. Pete Maxwell *didn't
know Garrett,* and so Pat and *three* of his deputies went
there and *stayed and boarded.*"

Billy the Kid decided he was hungry and went to Maxwell's house to get the key to the storeroom, and when he
got to the door, he "knocked." When he got into the room,
Pat shot him, but, believe it or not, after he was shot in the
heart and as he was going down (says Blevins), he asked,
"Who's that in with you Pete?" And "he shot over Pete and

the bullet cut through Pete's shirt into the wall, and Billy went down, but he shot five more times into the floor before he died."

His sweetheart Annie was back in Illinois on a visit at the time, and they telegraphed her, and in "about two months [What was the rush?] they came and *took his body back to Ottaway.*" By actual count the Kid is credited with killing forty-five men in this tale, and Blevins says that "all that interested Pat was the reward, $12,000 from the state and $32,000 from the cow association." Some reward, we might add.

Murder and Mystery in New Mexico, by Erna Fergusson (1948), contains a chapter on Billy the Kid which is fairly dependable except when she follows Upson's account of his birth, the early move to Kansas, and the mother's marriage in Colorado. She also says Billy was a skillful monte player by the time he was eight. Of his first trouble she writes: "He overheard a man make an insulting remark about his mother on the street. Billy, aged twelve, jumped right at the man, twice his size, landed one blow and was picking up a rock when Ed Moulton a prominent citizen, knocked out the bully and won Billy's undying friendship. So it was only natural that Billy, seeing Moulton about to be bested in a fight some time later, should dash into the fray. With his open pocket-knife the boy slashed one of Moulton's assailants who fell bleeding. The man did not die, but Billy thought he had killed him and he ran away." Here is a new version of an old tale.

The author continues to follow Upson in describing the Kid's fights with Indians and his rescue of his friend Segura from jail. Of the murder of Sheriff Brady, she says, "On April 1st, the Kid and *three* others, in Lincoln again, hid behind the adobe wall of McSween's corral. They had dug out the adobe to make loopholes; when Sheriff Brady appeared on the streets they shot him down. Whose shot took effect was never proved. The Kid of course, got the blame."

She admits that "Colonel Fulton, the most impartial student of the period, says the Kid killed only three men alone. Other killings attributed to him were the result of volleys of many guns."

She does not say much about the Kid's escape from the Lincoln jail except that "the Kid slipped his handcuffs, killed his guards, *terrorized the population* and counting as always on his friends, got clean away."

Of his death she writes: "The romantic say that the Kid had hung around Ft. Sumner trying to persuade his sweetheart to go with him to Mexico. Certainly he could have gone alone to Mexico and been safe. But here he was in Ft. Sumner at the home of a friend he trusted. Alone, in stocking feet and armed only with a butcher knife, he was coming to cut a steak off a beef carcass hanging in the entry. In the dark he passed two deputies on the porch.

" '*Quien es?*' he asked, walking into the unlighted room where Pat Garrett sat. 'Who is it?' as though he wished to know which of his enemies was to get him finally.

"Garrett shot, and the Kid fell dead without a word."

In this same year an anthology, *This Is New Mexico*, edited by George Fitzpatrick, was published. One of the selections therein concerns Billy the Kid and was written by Eugene Cunningham, who repeats the legends created by Upson about the Kid's birth, the move to Coffeyville, his mother's marriage in Colorado, his wanderings in Mexico, and his rescue of Segura. Cunningham writes that the Kid was but twelve years old when he had to flee home because "he had driven a knife into a blacksmith."

He describes the killing of Brady thus: "And with Dick

Brewer, Charley Bowdre and others of their side, the Kid concealed himself behind an adobe wall in Lincoln and 'bushwhacked' Sheriff Brady (a Murphy man) and Deputy Hindman."

He does not devote much space to the battle of the Mc-Sween home, but he says that after it was over, "He [the Kid] and the rest of the gang rode like raiding Arabs up and down, stealing horses and cattle, killing a clerk at the Mescalero Reservation when he interfered with a raid, carrying stolen stock to Tascosa on the Canadian River in Texas."

This account is given of the Kid's death: "Pat Garrett sat in Pete Maxwell's house, one of the buildings of the fort's old 'officer's row.' It was the night of July *13* [14], 1881. Pete Maxwell was in bed. He admitted to Garrett that the Kid had been there, but denied knowledge of his whereabouts at that moment. Outside John W. Poe and Tip [sic] McKinney sat waiting for Garrett. And the Kid walked into Maxwell's dark bedroom—

"His pistol rose as he heard or sensed Garrett. The lank sheriff fired and killed the Kid."

Also published in 1948 is a little book by Amy Lathrop entitled *Tales of Western Kansas,* which has some mention of the Kid. The author says he was born William Bonney in New York and his mother moved to Santa Fe, New Mexico, when he was five. The mother remarried and moved to Silver City in 1868, where Billy went to school and at twelve killed a man who had insulted his mother. In this account, the Kid was killed by Garrett in 1880, and the author says that later Brazee [sic] killed Garrett "in self defense." I fail to see the reason for including Billy the Kid in a book on Kansas, but it seems that everyone who writes about the West strives to bring him into the picture.

There was a privately printed book issued in 1949, written by James Marshall, under the title *Elbridge A. Stuart,* which is, of course, a biography of Stuart. Stuart describes the country on his way West, and in touching upon Billy the Kid during some descriptions about New Mexico, he, like almost everybody else, is a bit careless with his facts.

"There was," he writes, "quite a sigh of relief along the Rio Grande and the Cimarron when Billy the Kid was captured, tried, sentenced to die and locked in the jail at *Las Vegas,* New Mexico. From this jail he escaped, killing two men in the process, and lit out for the hills."

Southwest Roundup (1950), by Anne Merriman Peck, is a book seemingly written for young readers and covers many subjects on the Southwest. The author touches upon the Lincoln County War and Billy the Kid, saying, "Sheriff Pat Garrett had the Kid captured and jailed once, but he slipped out of his handcuffs, killed the guard and made off on a horse *someone had waiting for him.* Finally he was trailed to a friend's house in Fort Sumner where he was cornered by Pat Garrett and shot *after a stiff fight.* So ended one of the sagas of the bold bad days in the uncivilized Southwest."

The Texas Border and Some Borderliners, by Robert J. Casey, was published in 1950, and the author devotes a chapter to Billy the Kid under the title "Problem Child." He begins this chapter with, "Down from the hill, as friends were getting ready to bury the murdered Tunstall behind the McSween-Tunstall store, came one of his hands, a stripling cowboy named William Bonney, Billy the Kid. Bonney, who had been out hunting turkey, stood dry-eyed at the grave and, so it is reported, made a public vow to kill everybody who had had anything to do with the murder."

The author proceeds to repeat the old legend about the

Kid's birth, the move to Kansas, where, he says, "the elder Bonney died and the widow, a pretty young woman, went to Denver, married a man named Antrim *whose first name has been forgotten,* and moved on with him to Santa Fe. Mrs. Antrim ran a boarding house in Santa Fe *for six years,* then, in *1868,* the family went to Silver City, where she opened another boarding house while her husband got a job in the mines."

In Silver City the Kid "learned to speak Spanish fluently, to throw a knife, to get the best effects out of crooked dice, to palm a card and to deal from both sides of the deck. . . . In 1872, when he had just turned twelve years, he killed a man who had made some uncouth remarks to Mrs. Bonney. His mother financed his way out of town and thereafter is lost sight of.

"His record for the next four or five years is not very well documented and sounds as if it could have been written by Ned Buntline or a circus press agent." Casey follows Upson's account of the Kid's killing Indians, blacksmiths, and gamblers in Arizona and Old Mexico. He follows the usual account of the killing of Buckshot Roberts, saying his first shot was at Bowdre and his third shot cut off George Coe's trigger finger.

His account of the killing of Brady and Hindman also follows the usual pattern, as does that of the battle at the McSween home and of the killing of Bernstein. Of the last he writes: "He killed Joe Bernstein, a clerk on the Mescalero Reservation, *one night* when he and his gang were running off some horses. There doesn't seem to have been any reason for this killing at all except, maybe, target practice." He also follows the legend of the dropped card when Bell was killed.

Of the Kid's finish, he writes: "On July *13* [14], 1881, he came visiting at the home of Garrett's own brother-in-law, whose wife was a good cook. And when he went out to cut a steak from a quarter of beef that hung on the north porch of the old officers' quarters, now the home of Pete Maxwell, he was careless." When he stepped into Pete's room to ask who the fellows on the porch were, "He never found out, poor little man."

The *Album of Gunfighters*, by J. Marvin Hunter and Noah H. Rose (1950), is a large picture book and a fine collectors' item, but some of the captions are inaccurate. They continue with the legend that the Kid "started his career of crime and murders at the age of twelve years, beginning at Silver City, New Mexico, when he killed a man with a pocket knife. The man is alleged to have insulted his mother." They also repeat the false story of his mother's moving to Colorado after her husband's death in Kansas and marrying Mr. Antrim there. And, of course, they say that the Kid had killed twenty-one men at the age of twenty-one.

Trail Driving Days (1952), by Dee Brown and Martin F. Schmitt, contains a section on Billy the Kid. These authors closely follow Upson's account of the Kid's early life: born in New York as William H. Bonney, moving to Coffeyville, Kansas, in 1862, where his father died; and moving to Colorado, where his mother married Mr. Antrim. They also identify his first victim as the blacksmith who had insulted his mother.

Of the Tunstall killing, they write: "On the chill February morning when Murphy's hired posse swept into Tunstall's ranch and began rounding up the Englishman's cattle, Billy the Kid appears to have been absent from the ranch house. Several versions of the death of Tunstall exist; his men may have deserted him; he may have fired first as

Murphy's deputies claimed; or he may have been shot in the back as Pat Garrett later declared.

"At any rate, Billy learned of his friend's death *before nightfall*. In a cold rage he rode into Lincoln to inform Alexander McSween." They go on to relate that the Kid stood beside Tunstall's grave during the burial and swore he'd shoot down every man who had a hand in his murder.

They credit the Kid with killing Morton and Baker: "On April 1, for a grim Fool's Day trick, Billy got two more of Tunstall's enemies. He hid behind an adobe wall in Lincoln until four of Murphy's men strolled into his gunsights. One of them was Murphy's sheriff, William Brady. The Kid took him with his first shot, and then killed one of the remaining three while they were running for cover." They also repeat the judge's sentence and the Kid's retort, and have the Kid persuade Bell to play a game of monte with him before his escape at Lincoln.

"During the game he *pretended* to drop a card," they write, "leaned forward as if to pick it up from the floor, grabbed Bell's pistol instead, and shot the deputy dead." And after he had killed Olinger, they said, "He had killed his twenty-first and last man on an April evening in 1881." Pat killed him when "he had gone to see the 'only girl he ever loved.'"

In *Frontier Days in the Southwest,* by Jennie Parks Ringgold (1952), the author repeats the legend about the Kid's killing the blacksmith at the age of twelve for insulting his mother. She says that when the blacksmith started for the boy, after the latter had knocked his hat off with a rock, "a bystander knocked him down," and this incident caused hard feelings between the two men. It seems that two men later jumped on the Kid's rescuer in a saloon, and the blacksmith, seeing his chance to get even, joined the other two to beat up the Kid's friend. When the Kid, "who was watching a card game, saw the three attacking his friend, he pulled out his knife and struck at the blacksmith. The knife entered the man's heart and he fell dead. Billy left that night, a fugitive from justice. In the course of his short life of twenty-one years, he killed twenty-one men." This last statement is never omitted!

Glenn Shirley, in his *Toughest of Them All* (1953), devotes a chapter to Hendry Brown and another to Bob Olinger, in which he tells about Billy the Kid. Most of his information is from Siringo, Hough, Hendron, and Burns, none reliable.

"On the evening of April 28, 1881," he writes, "before he was to be hanged on May 13th, he caught Jailer James W. Bell unawares as he was returning the Kid from a privy in the back yard, struck Bell over the head with his shackles and seized his revolver, killing him with it. Ollinger, who had left the Kid alone with Bell while he took the other prisoners to a café across the street, heard the shot and hurried toward the corner of the courthouse. He had left his shotgun in Garrett's office, and he circled the building to come up the stairs at the back. Meanwhile the Kid *had gotten rid of his handcuffs and leg irons.* As he passed through the room he grabbed up the weapon. He saw Ollinger coming at a running walk, and, as the deputy neared the corner of the building, a cigar in his mouth, the Kid stepped to the east window on the balcony.

" 'Hello, old fellow!' he called pleasantly.

"When Ollinger looked up, the outlaw grinned and pulled the trigger. The impact of the blast drove Ollinger's cigar down his throat and tore off the top of his head. He sprawled backward in the dust. The Kid *leaped* outside. Again he raised Ollinger's shotgun and emptied the other barrel into the dead deputy."

The Kid had *not* gotten rid of his leg irons and handcuffs before he killed Olinger. The leg irons were chopped in two later, but he did not get the ankle irons removed until he arrived at the home of a Mexican friend.

F. Stanley (Father Stanley Crocchiola), in his *Desperadoes of New Mexico* (1953), gives a fairly full account of Billy the Kid. His book as a whole, especially in regard to other outlaws of the state, contains much new information, but he repeats too many of the common legends about the Kid.

He says that the Kid was born in Brooklyn, his mother being well known in New York, where her parents had settled when they came from Ireland, and that the Kid's father, William H. Bonney, was an actor who deserted his family when the oldest child was about five years old.

"No doubt," he writes, "the young widow (or abandoned wife) took the two bags of bones she called her children, to Colorado because she heard that high altitudes helped such afflictions as well as that fact that she could make out very well in the mining camps in her line of work as a cook, waitress and general helper in a boarding house. It was while she was manager of a boarding house in Colorado that a prospector named William Antrim courted her and won her hand in marriage."

The Antrims lived in several other places before moving to Santa Fe, where Antrim got a job as teamster along the Santa Fe Trail while his wife ran a boardinghouse. In telling of the Kid's killing of the blacksmith who insulted his mother, Father Crocchiola writes: "This killing is unknown to the public until Garrett's life of the Kid appeared in 1882, about a year after the outlaw's death." In this I am inclined to agree with him; but he continues: "This would place it in the year 1863. Garrett was no where near New Mexico that year and for several years to come." Garrett's being in New Mexico had nothing to do with this killing (if there was a killing at all), and, furthermore, the author has just said that this happened when the Kid was twelve years of age. If he was born in 1859, he would have been only four years old in 1863.

Father Crocchiola follows the Upson account in having the Kid kill Indians and gamblers in Old Mexico, as well as in the ride to San Elizario, Texas, to release his friend Segura from jail. He also says that on the third day of the fire at the McSween home, "Mrs. Julia Mills walked the whole distance to Fort Stanton for Col. Dudley's soldiers."

Of the fire itself he writes: "Mrs. McSween watched the fire lap up her home. Her piano. So much effort it cost to bring it over the Santa Fe Trail for this! She asked the men to move it into the next room in the hopes that the fire would burn itself out before touching it. She sat down. Softly her fingers fondled the keys. Suddenly the opening bars of *Home, Sweet Home* harmonized with the crackling flames. Over and above this she sang the words—the swan song for the home, the piano, but not her courage. . . . She arose from the piano and without a word from her lips, opened the door and *went out to face the bullets.*"

This piano was originally bought in St. Louis by Emil Fritz for his sister and later sold to McSween. Walter Noble Burns also says that Mrs. McSween had brought it from the East.

When she returned from pleading with Colonel Dudley the second time, "of the many rooms in her home three now remained untouched by the hungry flames. Again she sat down to the piano and the *Star Spangled Banner* was the last music to issue from the McSween home." Here we see the influence of Walter Noble Burns again.

Father Crocchiola makes Widenmann a United States marshal and gives a different story of the killing of Tunstall. He also says, "the Kid killed Indian Agency Clerk Joe Bernstein, of the Apache Mescalero Reservation simply because he prevented him from taking some horses."

He declares that the Kid was never tried for the killing of Roberts, though indeed he was tried, at the March 31, 1881, term of the District Court, and pleaded not guilty. On April 5, his attorney, Judge Leonard, withdrew his plea of not guilty and substituted a plea of the jurisdiction. Since Judge Bristol sustained this plea, the defendant went free.

The author also says that Billy had a sweetheart in every town, with so many in Old Mexico "he did not bother to count them." Yet he could never "bring himself to trust any one woman enough to marry her."

He uses the card game and dropped-card version of the killing of Bell, and says that "Bonney claimed later that he tried to keep Bell from running down that flight of stairs, but the guard refused to listen."

Father Crocchiola seems to think Garrett had lain down with Maxwell the night he killed the Kid. "Garrett says he was sitting down when the outlaw came into the room," he writes. "Garrett was tall enough to make a nice center on a modern basketball team. He was six feet six inches. Sitting down, with boots on and a sombrero, with a faint glimmer of moonlight streaking in, the Kid would never have asked '*Quien es?*' It would have been Garrett's funeral. His size would have marked him."

If Garrett was sitting down, I fail to see how high-heeled

boots could have affected his height, and we have no way of knowing whether or not he kept his hat on.

In 1954 there appeared a book on the myths concerning *American Heroes,* by Marshall W. Fishwick, and while he is dealing with the facts and legends about the Kid and the writers who have created and perpetuated these myths, he makes some doubtful statements of his own, such as: "This elusive phantom rider lived a full life before he was old enough to vote, and died just as he should have: *with his boots on and his gun roaring.*" He also repeats as truth the judge's sentence when the Kid was condemned to be hanged and the Kid's impudent answer.

In *Pictorial History of the Wild West,* by James D. Horan and Paul Sann (1954), the old, threadbare legends about the Kid's early years are repeated. He was born William H. Bonney II in New York, and when he was three, his parents moved to Coffeyville, Kansas, where his father died, his mother then moving to Colorado where she married William Antrim. The authors say the Kid got his education in the "mud-caked streets" of Silver City, where he heard men talking of Jesse James and the banks he was robbing. They also continue with the fable of the insulting blacksmith and the Kid's stabbing him to death with a "pen knife."

Although they follow Upson's account closely, they concede that "Upson was an imaginative writer, and Garrett had an understandable reason for investing Billy with all kinds of derring-do. The more garish the youth's skill and the more notches on his gun, the more bold would seem the sheriff's act of killing him. Garrett was sensitive; people were saying he had shot down a mere boy. He made the boy a man of massive stature as outlaws go." They admit that Burns's *The Saga of Billy the Kid* was "a piece of purple prose that made the slumbering legend soar. Burns embellished the boy's more dubious exploits and put some frills on the real ones."

They claim that the Lincoln County War started from an altercation between John Chisum and the small cattlemen, and that the Kid "alternately hired out to each side." They do not devote much space to the battle of the McSween home, but do say that Bernstein was killed "trying to stop the Kid from appropriating some choice steeds when he turned horse-thief after the Three-Day Battle drove him out of Lincoln."

Here again is the judge's sentence and the Kid's answer. Of the Kid's escape and his killing of Bell and Olinger, they write, "On April 28, 1881, while the hulking Ollinger was at La Rue's Bar across the street, Billy got a revolver and killed Bell," and they give three different versions of how it was done. In closing, however, they do argue against the record of twenty-one men on the Kid's death list.

During this same year Paul Wellman's *Glory, God, and Gold* made its appearance, with a number of pages devoted to the Lincoln County War and Billy the Kid. Most of Wellman's information, or misinformation, follows the legends which by now have been used over and over again.

"The Kid," he writes, "was born in New York's Bowery and was taken, as a baby, by his parents to Coffeyville, Kansas, a tough border town where later the Dalton bandit gang was wiped out in a street battle. His father died and his mother took him to Colorado, where she married a man named Antrim. Later they moved to New Mexico and the Kid is said to have killed his first man at the age of twelve— a Silver City blacksmith who spoke slightingly of his mother." After this murder he has the Kid hiding out in the hills and says he never saw his mother again.

Of the Tunstall murder he writes: "On that day Murphy sent a posse to the Rio Felix ranch to take over Tunstall's property, in lieu of a debt the Major alleged was owed him by McSween, the Englishman's partner in the Lincoln store. Tunstall indignantly objected. The possemen were drunk and irresponsible. They shot the Englishman and left him lying dead. Over Tunstall's grave, later, Billy the Kid said with chill solemnity, 'I will kill every one of the men that had a hand in this murder, or die trying. You were the only man who ever treated me like I was freeborn and white.'

"Those two sentences, uttered by a lonely youth to a man in his grave, *constituted the declaration of war in Lincoln County.*"

In describing the deaths of Morton and Baker, he writes that while these two were spurring their horses to get away, "Billy the Kid, sitting in the saddle, fired twice. Morton and Baker spun lifeless out of their saddles. Leaving the three bodies [McClosky had already been killed] to the buzzards, the Brewer deputies rode back to Lincoln." He intimates that no one else fired a shot except the Kid, and thus credits him with many of the killings of that day.

He admits that Charlie Bowdre, Tom O'Folliard, Jim French, Frank McNab, the Kid, and Waite all took part in the ambush of Sheriff Brady, but adds, "The Kid personally accounted for Brady, the man who had sent out the posse that murdered Tunstall."

He says that Brewer's posse went hunting for Buckshot Roberts and found him at Blazer's Mill, although we know that Roberts came in after the posse had arrived. He writes that after the fight, "the posse withdrew its wounded. Roberts quietly bled to death in the mill. Next day he and

Brewer were buried *side by side*—some say in the same grave—near the scene of their battle."

Of the battle at the McSween home, he writes: "Notified of the battle in Lincoln, Colonel N. A. M. Dudley rode into the town with two troops of Negro cavalrymen and a couple of Gatling guns. After he conferred with the leaders on both sides, he withdrew and camped outside the hamlet." This he did not do, for he camped close to the McSween home with threats against the McSween faction if they fired a shot.

"He had concluded, as he later reported," Wellman continues "that the legal sheriff of the county, with a legitimate posse, was in combat with men who were at least technically outside the law. It was a civil affair and Dudley could interfere only if asked to do so by the proper authorities. Peppin, who seemed to be the 'proper authority,' wanted no help, and certainly no interference, from the military."

It is a well-known fact that Dudley was indebted to Murphy and sympathetic to his cause. And although his men did not fire a shot, their presence had a great psychological effect and perhaps turned the tide of battle. Their guns were pointed at the McSween home, and the Colonel's threats had taken some of the fight out of the Kid's followers. Wellman also makes the misstatement that the McSween home was set afire after the cavalry withdrew—they were there at the time, and in fact created the opportunity for the Murphy followers to set the fire.

When the men were no longer able to stay in the burning house, "Suddenly the men in the burning and untenable house came hurtling out in every direction, running for life. So unexpected was the rush, and the fugitives burst forth in such numbers, that it seemed to confuse the Peppin men. A ragged volley roared out, but only two of the fugitives were hit, both wounded. The others, leaping and dodging, threw themselves over the adobe wall at the rear and plunged into the safety of the brush along the Rio Bonita which cut through the town.

"Last to emerge was Billy the Kid. With a revolver blazing in each hand, he sprinted across the McSween patio, bullets singing and thudding about him. Bob Beckwith pitched forward, dead from one of the Kid's leaden slugs. Two other Peppin men were wounded. Then the Kid was gone—diving headlong down into the ravine and lost in the brush. Guts and murderous skill with his six-shooter had saved him."

Of the Kid's capture at Stinking Springs, he writes: "At last Garrett's relentless pursuit cornered him. Surrounded in an abandoned stone house by a posse, the Kid at first fought back, but when his two companions, Bowdre and O'Folliard, were killed, he surrendered." Actually, there was no battle at this time, and only Bowdre was killed, for O'Folliard had been slain earlier at Lincoln.

"Tried at Mesilla and sentenced to hang," he continues, "he was returned to Lincoln for execution. But the Kid wasn't ready to die yet. While Garrett was out of town— making arrangements for the gallows—the young outlaw took advantage of the carelessness of one of the two deputies set to guard him, and managed to get the man's own revolver and kill him. Then he shot the other guard from the window as he came running from where he had been eating lunch. With a *Winchester* in his hands, taken from the jailer's gun rack, the Kid *cowed the crowd of people gathered at the shot,* made someone free him of his manacles and leg irons, and, commandeering a horse, rode away."

He continues with that fable about the Kid's going to

Maxwell's house the night of his death to see a girl. All through his account of the Kid we see the influence of the legends which had been common for years. As yet no one seemed to have had the energy to dig out some truth.

Continuing on to 1955, we find *The American Cowboy: The Myth and the Reality,* by Joe B. Frantz and Julian Ernest Choate, Jr., holding to that legend about the Kid's going to Pete Maxwell's "to be comforted by his *querida*"; and they say further that "the Kid was at Maxwell's in another room," and *"sensing the presence of a stranger in the dark house,* the Kid came quietly into Maxwell's bedroom, where Garrett sat at the edge of the bed." When the Kid asked *"Quién es?"* they say, "Garrett fired twice at the direction from which the sound came, and that was all."

In a chapter on Pat Garrett in the book, *Western Sheriffs and Marshals,* by Thomas Penfield (1955), the author has quite a bit to say about the Kid.

"There are probably more conflicting stories about Billy the Kid," he writes, "than about any western desperado. Today he is almost a folk hero. In the 1880's he was loved by many people and he had loyal friends. There is no doubt that he was a killer of the most deadly type, merciless and fearless and lightning quick on the draw. At the time of his death he claimed to have killed a man for every year of his age—twenty-one men 'not counting Indians and Mexicans.' "

As usual, he follows Upson's account of the Kid's birth and the family's move West, though he does not mention Kansas. He does say, however, that they ended in Santa Fe, and "there Billy lived and played until he was eight years old. Then the family moved to the rough and lawless town of Silver City where Billy went to school but learned far more from the gamblers and outlaws who infested the town. Finally when he was twelve he took the first step on his outlaw career by killing a man who had insulted his mother."

Of the murder of Tunstall, he writes: "One morning in February, 1878, the townspeople saw a posse of twenty men, led by Sheriff Brady, head out of town for Tunstall's ranch. . . . The posse met Tunstall riding cheerfully along the trail into town. Before he could speak they shot him down in cold blood, wheeled their horses, and returned to town. On the hills beyond, too far away to come to their friend's help, were Billy the Kid and Dick Brewer. The next day the Kid stood grimly at Tunstall's grave, vowing to get every one of Tunstall's killers or die in the attempt."

The author passes over many incidents of the war lightly, barely mentioning the fight at McSween's home. In dealing with the Kid's escape from Lincoln, he says Olinger went over to La Rue's saloon to get a drink. He does not mention Bell nor his murder, except to say that after the shooting was all over, the citizens "went into the courthouse to find Bell dead on the stairs and cards scattered on the floor of the room where Billy had been kept."

His account of the Kid's going into Pete Maxwell's room is much the same as many previous accounts. The Kid had questioned the two deputies outside on the porch, and "At the first sound of the voice outside, Pat had frozen. His hand went to his gun. He had recognized Billy's voice as Poe and McKinney had not. Before Billy had time to make out the dark form beside Pete's bed, Pat's gun roared into the midnight stillness, and Billy the Kid lay dead."

Late in 1957 another book with a chapter on Billy the Kid was published—*Badmen of the Frontier Days,* by Carl W. Breihan.

Breihan still has the Kid born William H. Bonney, in

New York, even naming the street as Rivington. He says "the record of his birthplace was obtained in the 1920s from the Kid's uncle, but hitherto has not been published."

He does correct the common error of having the family move to Coffeyville, Kansas, in 1862. But he continues with many of the other legends concerning the Kid's activities in Mexico, killing gamblers, the Indian battles, and the rescue of Segura.

He says that Dolan and Riley were gunmen for Murphy, and on the occasion of the murder of Tunstall, he errs by having only Tunstall, Brewer, and the Kid in his party. He says Murphy's posse "riddled" Tunstall's body with bullets and then tied his body to the carcass of his horse, "which had also fallen under the withering blast of *pistol, rifle and shotgun fire."*

He has the Kid and Brewer watching this murder, with the Kid speaking: " 'Mark them, Dick,' he growled bitterly, 'mark every one of 'em. They're gonna pay—to a man.' "

Details of the killing of Morton and Baker are incorrect, for he says they tried to break away and "Billy calmly drew both pistols and shot both men through the head. *Then he hanged them to a tree as a warning."*

Of the Brady killing, he says that Billy and five of his henchmen "stepped around the corner" and Billy yelled, "Brady!" Then, as the sheriff and his party turned, "they were greeted with a deadly volley." He also says that Buckshot Roberts lived at Blazer's Mill and was its lone occupant when he was killed by the Kid's gang. There were quite a few people at the mill when this battle took place, including Dr. Blazer, Agent Godfrey, David Easton, Andrew Wilson, Blazer's son, Almer, and others. Furthermore, Roberts did not live there.

"Oddly enough," he adds "Roberts and Brewer were

buried in the same coffin the next day." To refute this statement let me quote Mr. Almer Blazer (the doctor's son, who was there) in the *Alamogordo News* of July 18, 1928: "All kinds of stories are told of the burial of these men and I have never seen the facts in print. Brewer lay in the hot sun for several hours, and when we finally got to Roberts, making it safe to go where the body lay, it was in such a state that it was necessary to hurry the burial as much as possible, accordingly every one competent to help were put to making the coffin, digging the grave and other necessary preparations. He was buried that evening with every possible honor under the circumstances, in a home made coffin it is true (there was no other kind for anyone), but it was decently lined with white cloth and covered with black neatly tacked on the boards of which it was made, and as good as could be provided at the time and place.

"Roberts died the next day a little before noon and as it was certain he could not live long the preliminary work on his coffin had been done and was ready by the middle of the afternoon and he was buried about four or five o'clock some twenty hours after Brewer so it is impossible that they were buried in the same coffin, or in the same grave, as some accounts have it."

The Santa Fe *New Mexican* reported: ". . . Brewer's body . . . was buried the next day. Roberts died the following day."

Mr. Breihan's account of the battle of the McSween home is unreliable. He says a young housewife sent a rider to Fort Stanton for help, but after Colonel Dudley brought his Negro troops, he proved to be an ally of Murphy. Indeed, Dudley had always been Murphy's ally and tool, for he was very much in his debt:

After the battle, says Breihan, "the streets and hotels

were littered with the dead and dying." The records show that in this battle the dead were Harvey Morris, Francisco Zamora, Vicente Romero, and Alex McSween of the McSween forces and Robert Beckwith of the Murphy faction. The coroner's jury held an inquest over only five men, according to the records.

Breihan relates that Governor Wallace "invited the Kid to a meeting in the Ellis House. Billy obliged and came face to face with the Governor of New Mexico." If this author had examined Governor Wallace's letter, he would have read: "Come to the house of old Squire Wilson (not the lawyer) at nine (9) o'clock next Monday night alone." And this is where Billy met him.

He also says the Kid's "fixin'" Grant's gun "became the gulf between Pat Garrett and the Kid." This is a ridiculous statement, but then his account of the whole incident is incorrect.

Of the Carlyle killing, he says that when Carlyle entered the room where the Kid's gang was, the Kid saw his own gloves in Carlyle's pocket and became enraged. Then, when Carlyle jumped through a window, "he was not quick enough for the Kid. One shot wounded the officer; a second one killed him as he tried to crawl away."

He writes that after the Kid's capture at Stinking Springs, "Garrett delivered the Kid and his men in *wagons* to the jail in Santa Fe." The prisoners were hauled in a wagon to Las Vegas, and there put on the train next morning and delivered to Santa Fe.

This author also says that Pete Maxwell "lived in a small patio room on the southwest corner of the Bowdre house" —an obvious mistake. According to him, Garrett was calling on Charlie Bowdre's widow when he decided to visit

Maxwell, "so he just stepped across the porch and entered Maxwell's room."

After Garrett shot the Kid, the sheriff "jumped through an open window and flattened himself against the wall," and it was half an hour before anyone got up the courage to go into the room again. And so we go, following the lines of the least resistance, giving added importance to legends already tenacious.

In late 1958, *American Murder Ballads,* by Olive Woolly Burt, was published. The author does not devote much space to the Kid, but she still repeats the same old legends. She says in part: "Billy was a bucktoothed, unkempt, illiterate villain who went about shooting folks for the fun of it. But he is now New Mexico's hero and stands high in the estimation of many good people all over the country."

She says that "according to tradition" that the Kid's first murder was committed "at the ripe age of twelve in defense of his mother's good name," and that "after numerous killings the young outlaw was apprehended and imprisoned," and he "killed two guards." She writes that "Sheriff Pat Garrett finally lay in wait for the Kid and shot him as he came into a dark room. . . . carrying a drawn .41 Colt and a butcher knife. Yet his killing roused the whole countryside against the sheriff, ruined his career as a law man, and, his friends have told him, his disposition." All these events, she writes: "are related in the 'Song of Billy the Kid.'" Perhaps she followed the song instead of history.

Epilogue

Since i have discussed many of the books, pamphlets, and articles whose purpose seems to have been to perpetuate Billy the Kid legends, I think it only fair to mention some that attempt to correct these unreliable accounts. It is pleasing to note that within the past twelve years there have been at least a dozen books, which have taken exception to the false history continually written about Billy the Kid.

One of the first of these is *Pardner of the Wind*, by Jack Thorp and Neil Clark (1945). In a long chapter on Billy, the authors declare that he was greatly overestimated, so much so that eventually he became practically deified. "Actually," they write, "Billy the Kid was just a little, small-sized cow-and-horse-thief who lived grubbily and missed legal hanging by only a few days. He killed, or took part in killing, several people; but his killings were more often on the order of safe butchery than stand-up-and-fight-it-out gun battles. He took part in a range war on the losing side. He died, not in a blaze of glory, but like a butchered yearling, shot down in the dead of night in his stocking feet, when he was armed with a butcher knife and, possibly, though not certainly, with a six-shooter. Yet for all that, romance does cling to his name. Half a dozen books about him have been written and published. The town of Lincoln, New Mexico, thrives on his memory. And many people regard him as a sort of super-Robin Hood of the range, a daredevil of matchless courage, haloed by smoke wreathing upward from fogging guns. He makes a fascinating study in the technique and psychology of literary and national hero creation. Many have told the 'facts' about Bill. Few have agreed about them. The heavy shadow of the 'hero' tradition has made unconscious liars of some; others have lied about him on purpose, loading the public with tall tales to satisfy the appetites of listeners greedy for shudders and blood."

Farther along they say: "The principal peg on which public interest had hung, of course, was the 'fact,' so called, that this beardless youth who died when he was little more than twenty-one, had killed 'twenty-one men, not counting Indians'—a man for every year of his brief life. Armchair appetites demanded good stories about this matchless character, and supply has a tendency to follow demand in the fiction business as well as in the cow business. The stories became better and better, taller and taller, until maybe Old Truthful himself would be ashamed to own an interest in some of them."

In a discussion of various books written about the Kid, the authors conclude: "The final deification came with *The Saga of Billy the Kid,* by Walter Noble Burns, a book in which a cook-up of fact and fiction was served with a literary sauce nicely calculated to please the palates of thousands of readers whose only range-riding was done in pipe smoke. There have been other publications to give 'the facts,' which actually have only enhanced and embroidered the legend. That legend has now grown to such a size that it will not be ignored, even by those who know it to be about nine parts fiction to one part fact."

Like me, these authors believe, and say, "Authentic

knowledge of Billy the Kid, insofar as we have it, is confined to the last four years of his life. He rides out of the shadows of a nomadic boyhood, into the sunlight of intense and recorded action, in the year 1877. What he had done in the eighteen years of his life up to then, is largely conjecture. . . . Many of the killings attributed to him are supposed to have taken place in that unlighted past, beyond proof or investigation. The story of that period is told, allegedly, in the first seven chapters of Garrett's *Authentic Life*, and most later writers have blindly followed his account without recalling all of Garrett's reasons for writing the book."

The authors then analyze the various killings credited to the Kid—some of them doubtful and most of them unheroic. They believe that Garrett and Upson built him up to a super-gunman to enhance the sheriff's reputation and to justify the manner in which he took the Kid's life.

In this same year, 1945, William A. Keleher, an attorney of Albuquerque, New Mexico, and an able historian, had his first book, *Fabulous Frontier*, published. In writing about Garrett's killing of the Kid, he says: "Along with rejoicing in the Territory over the slaying of 'Billy the Kid', there also was a strong undercurrent of criticism of Pat Garrett because of the methods used to do away with the young outlaw. There was much talk that Garrett had not shot it out with the Kid face to face; that he had not beaten him to the draw in accordance with the code of the West, but had killed him when the Kid didn't have a chance. The talk became so widespread that Garrett told his version of the killing in a book entitled, *The Authentic Life of Billy the Kid, the Noted Desperado of the Southwest.*" In this book Mr. Keleher mentions Billy the Kid only in connection with Pat Garrett, but he discusses him at greater length in a subsequent book mentioned later in this chapter.

In the 1949 issue of the Los Angeles Westerners' *Brand Book* (published in 1950) there is an article entitled "N. A. M. Dudley," by Phil J. Rasch. Mr. Rasch has been investigating the history of Lincoln County for some time, and here he provides dependable information on the old soldier who was so prejudiced in his actions during the siege of the McSween home.

He reveals the extent of Colonel Dudley's obligation to the Murphy faction and explains his partiality during the battle of the McSween home in Lincoln. He tells that when Mrs. McSween went to Dudley to plead with him to stop the fighting, "She found him with John Kinney, a notorious desperado and cattle rustler, and George W. Peppin, a tool of The House (Murphy & Co.), who was both the Sheriff and a Deputy United States Marshal. All three were drunk and greeted her with abusive language. To Mrs. McSween's demands for protection, Dudley replied that he was there only to provide assistance in case the civil officers required help, and it appeared to him that Marshal Peppin had the situation well under control. The following morning Kinney and his gang looted the McSween store, while Dudley apparently made no attempt to see that law and order were maintained."

In another place in this article Rasch calls Buckshot Roberts a "head-hunter" because he really was seeking the reward offered for Sheriff Brady's killers when he himself was killed.

In the 1952 issue of the Denver Westerners' *Brand Book* there appeared my own article entitled "With Our Rocking-Chair Historians," in which I take up, in abbreviated fashion, the unreliable books on Billy the Kid and Wild Bill Hickok.

In this same year, also, Jeff C. Dykes' *Billy the Kid, the Bibliography of a Legend,* was published. Note that he calls his book a bibliography of a *legend.* In it he points out errors in the various books listed, without discussion or criticism. In his introduction he declares: "Yet so little is really known of Billy's life and career that what is generally accepted as fact can be easily summarized. His birth in New York on November 23, 1859, is not disputed although no real evidence has ever been offered to support either the time or the place."

In Book V of the Los Angeles Westerners' *Brand Book* (1953), another article by Phil Rasch, entitled "A Note on Henry Newton Brown," appeared. In it he gives us the benefit of his research into matters dealing with the associates of Billy the Kid. Brown was a confederate of the Kid's and was with him when Morton and Baker were killed as well when Sheriff Brady and his deputy Hindman "bit the dust." He was also present when Bernstein was killed. Mr. Rasch relates the high lights of the Kid's activities in which Brown took part—which include most of them—and all of his statements are trustworthy.

In 1954 my own *Six-Guns and Saddle Leather: A Bibliography . . . on Western Outlaws and Gunmen* was published, throughout which I attempted to call attention to the many books containing false accounts, not only of the Kid but of all the western outlaws.

In this same year, too, the University of Oklahoma Press issued a reprint of the Pat Garrett book in the Western Frontier Library. Jeff Dykes wrote a comprehensive introduction to this work, in which he continued the campaign to enlighten the average reader concerning the unreliable stories about the Kid now firmly entrenched in the American mind. Dykes believes that Upson alone wrote the first eight chapters of Garrett's book, for "they drip with florid words in the extravagant style of the frontier writers of the day and are embroidered with poetry from time to time. Upson was a competent reporter with real ability to analyze a situation and to describe it. In preparing these chapters, he was not a reporter but a dime novelist."

"The last eight chapters," writes Mr. Dykes, "are Pat's primary contribution to the book. These chapters are written in the first person for, as Pat explains, 'The reader will perceive how awkward it would appear to speak of myself in the third person.' These chapters cover the events from the time Pat became sheriff of Lincoln County in the fall of 1880 until he killed the Kid on the night of July 14, 1881. In contrast to the rest of the book, they are a rather matter-of-fact account of a man hunt. If Upson wrote them, it seems apparent that Pat permitted Ash few liberties in changing his plain frontier language. It is noted also that not a single line of poetry 'graces' the last eight chapters." Upson claimed to have written every word in the book.

Dykes also holds to the theory that the Kid killed far fewer men than the "one for every year of his life."

In the 1955 issue of the Denver Westerners' *Brand Book* (published in 1956), Mr. Rasch again gives us the benefit of his research. In this issue he has a lengthy article entitled "Five Days of Battle," which is an accurate report of the battle of the McSween home. He is one of the first writers to call the Kid "Henry McCarty" since the old dime novels. Included is a correct account of how Dudley was persuaded to come to Lincoln—not by Mrs. Juanita Mills' going to the fort, but by Sheriff Peppin's writing that one of the Colonel's soldiers, Private Berry Robinson, had been fired upon by the McSween party when he was sent into Lincoln to deliver a letter to the sheriff.

At the end he advances a logical reason for the defeat of the McSween faction, although they could have had in their favor the element of surprise and superiority in numbers: they scattered their forces and went on the defense instead of attacking in one united force. No doubt these tactics lost them the battle, but the psychological effect of the arrival of Dudley and his soldiers could have been a turning point.

Also in 1955 there was published a little book, now already rare, by Ruth R. Ealy, entitled *Water in a Thirsty Land*. It contains the diary and papers of the author's father, Dr. T. F. Ealy, a medical missionary and educator who arrived in Lincoln County in time to bury Mr. Tunstall. His records provide some valuable and interesting eyewitness accounts of the siege of the McSween home, the actions of Colonel Dudley, and other activities. His account of Brady's death I have quoted earlier. Of the fight at McSween's he wrote:

"By July 14, forty armed men stole quietly into town. The next day, Dolan's men of about the same number came into town about dark, whooping and firing shots to the number of about one hundred. The next day there was firing all day. Two of McSween's windows were shot to pieces. On both July 17 and 18 the people remained in their homes, afraid to look out. About noon July 19 Colonel Dudley brought his entire command to Lincoln, as well as a gatlin gun and a cannon which had been repaired for the occasion. He camped a little east of the center of town and said there should be no firing over his camp or he would turn his guns on the house whence the firing came.

"While this order seemed good, it should have been more general and peace should have been ordered all along the line. The result was that those back of Colonel Dudley were frightened away while those in front were allowed to run at large, for it was plain that McSween's house was to be the target."

Like everyone else on the McSween side, the doctor thought that the Colonel exhibited partiality all the way through, as he doubtless did from all existing evidence.

Miss Gates, Mrs. Shields and her family, and Dr. Ealy and his family were taken to Fort Stanton after the battle. "I must say," writes Dr. Ealy, "that while I appreciate the kindness of the military I must not let that kindness affect my honest judgment, viz., that McSween was wantonly murdered and for fear I would tell the story before the officers fixed it up and the public find out the situation, I was ordered *not* to communicate with the outside world unless my communication first went through the adjutant's office for inspection."

In 1955, also, there was an unusual book published entitled *Alias Billy the Kid*, by C. L. Sonnichsen and William V. Morrison. It is rather difficult to comment upon this book. Granted that the old man who claimed he was the Kid seemed to know a great deal about what happened, it was no more than a great many others knew. I still cannot help but believe that the friends who loved Billy and were saddened by his death, the people who prepared him for burial and sat up with his body in the carpenter shop that night, would have known without a doubt whether the corpse was Billy's. The authors themselves seem to have some doubt in their minds about the genuineness of the man's claim. I'm afraid it's another case of the six or seven Jesse Jameses who came to life at various times.

Again, in 1956, Phil Rasch presents some new facts in "A Man Named Antrim," in the Los Angeles Westerners' *Brand Book* of that year. Heretofore no one had taken the trouble to find out anything about Mr. Antrim. He had always been just the stepfather of Billy the Kid, a man who had married his mother in various places.

In this article Mr. Rasch comments on the Upson account of Billy's birth and early years: "None of the statements made by Upson can be substantiated from documentary records. The Clerk of Manhattan reported that a search of the recorded births for the years 1859 and 1860 revealed no mention of a William H. Bonney. The City Clerk of Coffeyville advised that they had no records of deaths as far back as 1862. As a matter of fact, the first non-Indian settler did not arrive until 1868, and the townsite was not laid out until 1871. The County Clerk at Pueblo found that their records of 1862 do not contain any mention of a marriage between William Antrim and Katherine Bonney—and small wonder, for this was neither the time nor the place of Antrim's marriage."

By now serious researchers apparently had begun to dig deeper into the lives of certain frontier characters. Perhaps the few who first complained about the constant repetition of false statements and legends had awakened a desire for the truth.

In this same year there was another article by Rasch, entitled "The Rise of the House of Murphy," in the Denver Westerners' *Brand Book,* in which he relates the true circumstances surrounding the controversy over the will of Emil Fritz, which, I firmly believe, was one of the primary causes of the Lincoln County War.

In 1956 also there appeared *The Tragic Days of Billy the Kid,* by Frazier Hunt. Here, at this late date, more than seventy-five years after the first dime novel, is the first complete biography of Billy the Kid that is worthy of that designation. It had been reported over a number of years that

Epilogue

Maurice Garland Fulton was gathering material for a history of Lincoln County, but, unfortunately, he died before completing his work. It had been said that his material had been gathered with care and that his book was to be the one really authentic history of the Kid. This book of Hunt's is dedicated to Mr. Fulton, with acknowledgment of and thanks for his aid in furnishing him with documents, letters, and other material. Even before reading the book, therefore, I had faith that it would be revealing. I was not disappointed. Here, at last, is an account both reasonable and believable.

I quoted Mr. Hunt earlier, especially with regard to the Kid's mother and the family name. To carry this subject further: "Many people in Silver City learned that his real name was Henry McCarty and they called him that. At times he was also known as Henry Antrim, which was a combination of his own given name and the surname of his stepfather, William H. Antrim. It wasn't long, however, until he was generally referred to as Billy Antrim, and Kid Antrim, then as the Kid—later as Billy Kid, and in the end as Billy the Kid."

And how, one might ask, did he get the name William H. Bonney? "It was a full two years after he had left Silver City and when he was in grave trouble over the killing of the blacksmith," replies Mr. Hunt, "that he began to use the formal name of William H. Bonney; obviously the William H. was borrowed from the given name of his stepfather. No one knows from whence came the surname Bonney. It was an accepted formula of the frontier for a man on the dodge to use an alias, and when he felt he needed one the boy very probably simply hand-picked and adopted William H. Bonney."

Although Upson invented many of the incidents he told

about the Kid's early life, he did not create the name Bonney. The odd thing is, as I have said, that he did not once mention the Kid's real name of McCarty, especially since he had boarded with the Antrims before the Kid assumed another name. It must have been fairly common knowledge that the Kid was born a McCarty. Certainly all the newspapers knew as much.

Now that the ice is broken, perhaps more of the truth will come to light as time passes. In fact, only one year had elapsed after the release of Mr. Hunt's book when another thick volume containing a true history of this place and time appeared: *Violence in Lincoln County, 1869–1881* (1957), by William A. Keleher. It is certainly the most complete and reliable history yet published on Lincoln County and its troubles and on the Kid's life, killings, trial, escapes, and death. Mr. Keleher has long been a thoroughly reliable historian, and to my mind this is his best book to date. It is well annotated, with many excerpts from contemporary newspapers, as well as from letters and court records. Much new evidence is presented relative to the various killings laid to the Kid, his trials, his meeting with Governor Wallace, and the prejudice of the courts, judges, and even the governors before Wallace.

Another book examined, published in 1958, is *George Curry, 1861–1947: An Autobiography,* edited by H. B. Hening. A chapter is devoted to Billy the Kid and the Lincoln County War. Since Mr. Curry was sheriff of Lincoln County after the "war" and later governor of the Territory, he knew the Kid and most of the participants in this feud.

"The story of the Lincoln County War," he writes, "has been told many times and in widely varying versions in numerous books, and in magazines and newspaper articles, as well as in official records of civilian officials and army officers, and in records of court proceedings. The War, as it later became known, was generally attributed in many of these accounts to conflict between big and little cattlemen, or to the struggle for range rights between cattle and sheep growers."

I think Mr. Curry is correct when he says, "The fact is that the War had its origin directly from alleged unethical acts of a lawyer, Alexander A. McSween, who came to Lincoln Town in 1875 with his attractive wife." Mr. McSween was "ambitious and aggressive," and after he had built up a good law practice, bought a ranch, and opened a store and bank in Lincoln, he recognized the possibilities of becoming an influential leader in that section.

One of Murphy's former partners, Colonel Emil Fritz, had returned to his homeland in Germany, where he died. Fritz had left a life insurance policy for $10,000, which his heirs—a brother, Charles, and a sister, Emilie—turned over to McSween for collection.

"When Charles Fritz," writes Mr. Curry, "discovered that McSween had collected the face value of the policy and had obtained the additional allowance of $4,095 for expenses and the claimed 'additional services,' he took his troubles to his friends at the L. G. Murphy & Company store. Murphy, then in Santa Fe, retained attorney Thomas B. Catron, then and for many years after a power in the Territory, and W. L. Rynerson, a prominent attorney at Mesilla in Doña Ana County, to recover the money. Catron and Rynerson obtained a judgment against McSween for the face of the insurance policy, less the $2,500 which the court allowed McSween as his fee."

As time rocked on and McSween refused to pay the judgment, "an execution and writ of attachment were issued against him and also against Tunstall's property. McSween, when he continued to resist payment, was indicted on a charge of embezzlement and warrants were issued for the arrests of both McSween and Tunstall."

This was the most widely discussed subject of the day in that section of New Mexico. Both contestants had many supporters, and as the situation became more acute, people began to take sides actively. Most of the smaller ranchers flocked to the Murphy-Dolan side because the latter, as merchants, had extended credit to them. To protect himself from arrest, McSween began hiring gunmen, among them Billy the Kid. In those days gunmen were plentiful, and seeing what McSween was up to, the Murphy faction also began to recruit hired warriors.

The division of the county into two factions over this issue was the real beginning of the Lincoln County War; and when Sheriff Brady, on the eighteenth of February, 1878, sent a posse of his reckless gunslingers to serve Tunstall with a writ of attachment, that act was destined to be the spark which set the blaze. The cowardly murder of Tunstall by this trigger-happy posse started the shooting war, which before had been only a court fight.

Turning to the Kid's escape after he had killed Bell and Olinger, Mr. Curry writes: "Many stories have been written about the Kid's escape, most of them conflicting in detail. The only witness as to just how The Kid freed his gun hand, was the guard Bell who died when The Kid's gun flamed."

Mr. Curry sums up his theory concerning the Kid's killing of Bell in this fashion: "On April 20, Sheriff Garrett and his chief deputy, Lea, were in White Oaks on official business. At noontime, Deputy Bill [Bob] Ollinger took two prisoners, in jail for minor offenses, across the street to the hotel for food. While Ollinger was gone, Bell took The Kid to the lavatory, just outside the first floor. On their return they had to mount the stairway having a sharp turn about one-fourth of the way up. His guards did not know that it was possible for The Kid to slip his right hand through the handcuff. This he could easily do, as he boasted later. "It is my opinion that as they mounted the stairway The Kid slipped his right hand free. Bell wore his six-shooter loosely in a belt on his left side, as was his habit. The probability is that as the two made the sharp turn on the stairway, The Kid grabbed Bell's gun and shot and killed him."

Everyone has his own version of this killing, but to me the hidden-gun theory that I described in the Prologue seems the most logical.

Near the close of his chapter on Billy the Kid, Mr. Curry writes: "During the time I lived in the old Lincoln County courthouse, in my capacity as State Historian of New Mexico, the interest shown in the bloody career of this little outlaw was a matter of continued wonder to me. The first question asked by most tourists, young and old, and of whatever degree of intelligence, was usually, 'Show me the balcony from which Billy the Kid escaped, manacled hand and foot, onto a bucking horse to make his escape.' Of course, no such spectacular 'movie stunt' ever happened. The Kid mounted a quiet horse held for him in the rear of the building."

All of which gives us some idea of the extent to which the various phases of the falsehoods and legends surrounding the Kid have taken root.

It is encouraging to find that the few new books being written about the Kid today are more truthful and seem to be getting away from the many legends which were standard fare for years. The last book I examined, *The True Story of Billy the Kid*, by William Lee Hamlin (1959), appears to be the result of honest research and is above the average in accuracy. It contains some new material I have not seen in other publications. I am, however, rather skeptical of the many conversations he reports. Who recorded them? Dialog puts more life into writing and makes the story more interesting, but it is a dangerous device to use in a volume that purports to be history.

In speaking of the Kid's early years, he writes: "The facts about these early years are so beclouded by tradition and legend that it is hard to learn what really happened."

He gives a fairly accurate account of most of the happenings of the Lincoln County War, but I think he is mistaken when he claims that the body of Bowdre and the prisoners captured at Stinking Springs were taken to Fort Sumner before their removal to Santa Fe. They were taken to a near-by ranch in order to secure wagons, and thence to Las Vegas to take a train to Santa Fe. He says that the citizens of Las Vegas gathered in the afternoon of Christmas Day to mob Rudabaugh, but were dissuaded by the better and cooler minds. Actually it was Garrett's threat to arm the prisoners which cooled the mob's ardor.

Mr. Hamlin is very sympathetic to the Kid, and, as an attorney, dwells a great deal upon trials and legal matters, but as a whole, I think the book rather reliable, and it is encouraging to see the new trend of the Kid's biographers.

In concluding this account of the literary history of Billy the Kid, I think it would be well to summarize the nature of the misinformation and falsehoods circulated for three-quarters of a century. Most early accounts of the Kid have several elements in common: exaggeration or distortion of fact or outright fabrication; unquestioning acceptance of the wildest tales (indeed, choosing the wildest when several versions were known); abysmal ignorance of cowboy dress and western customs; and misspellings of proper names.

Epilogue

A number of the common errors involve minor details, of little real importance to the over-all story; but repeated and pyramided one upon another, they can assume formidable proportions. As for the names, before the turn of the century, when the country as a whole was less literate than now, many persons spelled by ear, and, indeed, sometimes a man did not know how to spell his own name or spelled it differently at various times himself. However, the most frequently used forms of the names of the people involved with Billy the Kid can be ascertained and should be used by all modern writers on the subject.

More important are the exaggerations and distortions of fact and the outright fabrications foisted on the public with the tag of "authentic" or "true." Historical novels are an accepted form of literature and are read and enjoyed as fiction by people everywhere, but they must be clearly labeled as such. The historical background must be accurate, and the imaginary events related must be plausible and in accordance with the facts. Certainly none of the accounts of Billy the Kid cited in this book fall within this category.

Finally, from this distance in time, it is not likely that every detail of Billy the Kid's life and career can be unearthed or that all the facts can be positively determined, as, for example, how the Kid obtained the gun with which he killed Bell. In such cases it is certainly an author's prerogative to use conjecture or theory—so long as the theory advanced is within the realm of possibility and is identified as theory. Writers need to examine all the evidence critically before drawing a conclusion—it is well known that even eyewitnesses differ in reporting the same happening —and writers must, above all, remember that all is not true that is already in print. The recently published accounts of Billy the Kid are getting closer and closer to the truth, but the truth has been a long time coming. And if in this critical examination of existing works on Billy the Kid I have awakened even one future author to the fact that writing biography or history is more than following his predecessors' footsteps blindly, I shall be amply repaid.

Index

Index

Index

Index

Index

Index